PREFACE

Thank you for your interest in the new and improved *Current Issues*. Based on your feedback and the number of sales, the 35th edition was a huge success. Returning to the classic *Current Issues* format, with extensive background sections and a debate page with each chapter, proved to be very popular with our teachers. So, this year we went back into our history even further and recruited the creator of *Current Issues*, Bruce Jentleson, now a professor of Public Policy and Political Science at Duke University, as an academic consultant for the 36th edition. Bruce's contribution was invaluable to the success of this year's Current Issues.

I also want to thank all of you that sent along your suggestions throughout the year. We will continue to seriously consider every idea you shared with us. Once again, we will offer online updates throughout the school year for all teachers who purchase 10 or more copies of the book. In your response to your feedback, we have simplified the pricing structure. If you order less than 10 copies, *Current Issues* will remain $50 per text. For any order of 10 or more copies, *Current Issues* will be $35 each. All orders should go through our Close Up online store, which can be reached at www.currentissues.org. You may also call 301-374-6651 or you can fax your purchase order to 301-843-0159.

Looking ahead as we continue to improve Close Up's publishing's efforts, we are counting on your feedback to help us create books, videos, and digital materials that will provide you with the teaching tools necessary to inspire and inform your students!

Thank you,

Joe Geraghty
Editor

CLOSE UP PUBLISHING

Editor
Joe Geraghty

Mangaing Editor
Tim Walker

Editorial Consultant
Bruce Jentleson

Art Director
Tisha Finniff

Graphic Designer
Erin Geraghty

Copy Editor
Ann O'Malley

Researcher
Heather Arnold

Writers
Tiffany Farrell
Marcia Friedman
Pherabe Kolb
David Masci
Lyndi Schrecengost
Amy Talbot
David Zack

Close Up is the nation's largest nonprofit, nonpartisan civic educator. Our mission is to help students become informed and engaged citizens. To do this, we work with teachers nationwide, as well as with partners such as the U.S. Congress, the U.S. Department of Education, and the University of Virginia.

Close Up Foundation
1330 Braddock Place
Suite 400
Alexandria, VA 22314
800-Close Up (256-7387)
CurrentIssues.org

BIOGRAPHIES

Tiffany Farrell has contributed to fifteen editions of Current Issues plus several other Close Up publications, including *Perspectives, International Relations,* and *Words of Ages.* She is currently an editor for the Smithsonian Institution. Tiffany earned her M.Ed. from the University of Virginia.

Tisha Finniff is currently the Art Director for the Close Up Foundation. This is her sixteenth edition of designing and producing *Current Issues.* She was also part of the team that produced *Words of Ages, Ordinary Americans,* and the *Bill of Rights* Series. She is the recipient of the following design awards: Apex Award for Excellence; Promo Magazine's Gold Award for Outstanding Phonecard Promotions; as well as an American Graphic Design Award.

Marcia Friedman is an award-winning writer and editor specializing in education. She writes and edits resources for students and teachers and regularly creates performance study guides for the John F. Kennedy Center for the Performing Arts. Besides the current edition, she wrote for *Current Issues* from 1991 to 1994 and 2003 to 2008. She holds a M.Ed. in curriculum and instruction from George Mason University and a B.A. in foreign affairs from the University of Virginia.

Joe Geraghty has been with Close Up for 27 years, starting as a program instructor in 1984. For 23 years he worked on Close Up's weekly public affairs television program on *C-SPAN* and produced award-winning educational documentaries. His award highlights include a Gavel Award from the American Bar Association for his work on *Profiles of Freedom: A Living Bill of Rights* and a Grand Award for Best Documentary from the New York Festivals for Fight for Freedom. Joe has recently been named Close Up's Senior Director of Academic Outreach and Publishing.

Bruce Jentleson is Professor of Public Policy and Political Science at Duke University, where he served from 2000 to 2005 as Director of the Terry Sanford Institute of Public Policy. In 2006-07, he was a Visiting Senior Research Fellow at Oxford University and the International Institute for Strategic Studies in London, as well as a Fulbright Senior Research Scholar in Spain. Mr. Jentleson also served as a senior foreign policy adviser to Vice President Al Gore and the Gore-Lieberman presidential campaign from 1999 to 2000. He is currently a member of Close Up's Board of Directors.

Pherabe Kolb worked for Close Up from 1995-1997, serving first as an instructor on Close Up's high school programs and then as a writer on *Current Issues* and other publications. Following her time at Close Up, Pherabe was a journalist for *Congressional Quarterly,* graduated from Northwestern University School of Law, and practiced legislative and federal affairs law in Washington, D.C. She now manages strategic planning and communications projects for an educational and cultural nonprofit organization.

David Masci has been a senior researcher at the Pew Research Center in Washington, D.C., where he works on legal issues and serves as an in-house writer and editor. Before that, he spent 14 years working as a staff writer at Congressional Quarterly. In addition to his work at Pew, David also is a principal at FLUENT Communications, LLC, a small writing and communications firm in Washington, D.C. David holds a J.D. from the George Washington University Law School and a B.A. in Medieval History from the Maxwell School of Citizenship at Syracuse University.

Lyndi Schrecengost has worked as a freelance writer and marketing consultant since 2000. She specializes in education, health, and advocacy, and has co-written several nonfiction books in the area of on nutrition, fitness and anti-aging. Lyndi is also a principal at FLUENT Communications, LLC, a writing and communications firm in Washington DC. Lyndi holds an M.A. in Literature from American University, a B.A. in Communication Arts from Grove City College, and certification from the University of Denver's Publishing Institute, a professional program in book publishing.

Amy Talbot has worked for the Close Up Foundation, on staff and as a freelance writer, since the 1990s. She has contributed to many editions of *Current Issues,* both as a writer and as managing editor. As Managing Editor of Academic Publications for Close Up, she worked on several other publications, most notably *Words of Ages: Witnessing U.S. History Through Literature.*

Tim Walker was a writer/editor at the Close Up Foundation from 1990–1999. He then spent five years at the Southern Poverty Law Center, a civil rights organization in Montgomery, Alabama, before returning to the Washington, D.C., area to work at the Public Broadcasting Service. Tim is now a multimedia producer for a national education association.

David Zack is a National Board Certified Teacher who currently teaches social studies at the Thomas Jefferson High School for Science and Technology in Fairfax, Virginia. He is a thirty-year civic education veteran having served as a teacher, teacher trainer, adjunct professor, and as a writer and managing editor for numerous publications. David was the senior writer for *Current Issues* in the mid-1980s and the Managing Editor of Close Up Publications from 1987–1992.

TABLE OF CONTENTS

THE FEDERAL GOVERNMENT

INTRODUCTION

"We the People": the U.S. Constitution begins with these famous words. They emphasize a guiding principle in the founding and functioning of the United States—that of a nation run by the will of its citizens. The United States is a republic, governed by democratically elected representatives who deal with complex national issues on behalf of the American people. The Constitution outlines the rights and responsibilities of citizens and the structure of government. Within that framework, government officials formulate public policy—the plans that address the nation's goals and that govern relations with other countries.

The federal government consists of three branches: the executive, the legislative, and the judicial. Each plays a different role in creating and implementing public policy. In short, the legislative branch makes the laws, the executive branch implements the laws, and the judicial branch interprets the laws. Although these three mandates are distinct, by constitutional design the branches must work together. The framers of the Constitution wanted to prevent any one branch from gaining too much power, so they created a system of "checks and balances" wherein each branch has the authority to overrule the others in certain circumstances. These complex interactions among the branches ensure that the nation's policies reflect the will of the majority of citizens while respecting the rights of those in the minority.

The American people also play an important role in policymaking. By voicing an opinion, joining or supporting a special interest group, donating money to an election campaign, and voting, citizens influence the direction of the country. With the advent of the Internet, citizens have found new ways to make their voices heard. Contacting senators and representatives to support or oppose legislation is now easier than ever with email. Voters can contribute money to special interests and election campaigns online, and they can organize demonstrations and promote candidates through social media like Twitter and Facebook. These tools and others allow individuals to become immediate, active participants in the democratic process.

In 2011 and 2012, Congress and President Barack Obama fought a series of intensely partisan battles over budgetary issues, ranging from raising the nation's debt ceiling to extending existing tax cuts. At the same time, the Supreme Court issued one of the most significant rulings in decades when it upheld President Obama's health care law.

The Executive Branch

The executive branch, often called "the administration" or "the White House," includes the president, the cabinet departments, and federal agencies. Examples of cabinet departments include the Department of Defense and the Department of Education; the Securities and Exchange Commission and the Social Security Administration are examples of agencies. Despite the framers' intention to limit the power of the executive branch, in terms of size and scope, it is by far the largest of the three.

The president appoints many of his senior officials—such as cabinet secretaries, undersecretaries, and agency directors—and they must be confirmed by the Senate (the "advice and consent" provision in the checks and balances system). But the vast majority of executive branch employees are career civil servants whose jobs do not depend on which president occupies the White House. In this way, the work of the federal government can continue even when the presidency changes hands.

According to the Constitution, the executive branch carries out Congress's laws by issuing regulations or administering programs. Indeed, many laws grant the executive branch broad regulatory authority, giving the president and his team the opportunity to determine how legal requirements are actually implemented. But

Every year, the president of the United States delivers a State of the Union address to a joint session of Congress. In the speech, the president reports on the general condition of the nation and outlines the legislative agenda of the administration.

the president also relies on his staff to take an active role in advancing policies that may or may not be priorities for, or even agreeable to, members of Congress. For example, each year the president's Office of Management and Budget sends Congress a proposal outlining government spending for the coming year, but Congress has the "power of the purse," so it ultimately decides how much money each program receives.

The administration also proposes to Congress new laws and other policy changes. In complex political maneuvering, presidential staff and congressional leaders can compromise so that laws and budgets agreeable to both sides can be enacted. In other instances, laws get bogged down in committee or the president can veto legislation—an important example of checks and balances at work. When no consensus can be reached, "Washington gridlock," or a stalemate, results. This situation often arises when the president and the majority in Congress represent opposing political parties.

As commander-in-chief of the armed forces, the president is responsible for the conduct of declared wars and other military actions. Here, President Obama participates in a ceremony to mark the end of the Iraq war at Andrews Air Force Base in December 2011.

Finally, the Constitution names the president head of both foreign and military policy. As the official head of state, he leads U.S. relations with the rest of the world (foreign policy). As part of these duties, the president appoints and receives ambassadors, negotiates treaties, and meets with foreign leaders and dignitaries. As commander-in-

KRISTOFFER TRIPPLAAR/POOL/CORBIS

chief of the armed forces, the president is responsible for the conduct of declared wars and other military actions. Although the administration has substantial leeway in foreign and military affairs, legislators check some of these powers. The Senate confirms ambassadors and ratifies treaties, and Congress ultimately declares war and funds military operations.

The Legislative Branch

The legislative branch, Congress, is made up of two bodies. The Senate provides equal representation for the states with two senators each for a total of one hundred members. The House of Representatives has 435 voting members, but the number of representatives for each state is determined by the state's population—the more people residing in the state, the more members it is allotted. The framers envisioned Congress as the workhorse of the federal government.

The Work of Congress. According to the Constitution, Congress has the power to raise, print, spend, and borrow money; regulate interstate and foreign commerce; declare war and raise an army; ratify treaties and confirm presidential appointments; and make all laws necessary to execute these powers. This last power—making laws—has become the main focus of Congress's work. Proposed legislation becomes law when the majorities of both the House of Representatives and Senate agree to its passage and the president signs it.

Making Laws. A member of Congress must introduce every piece of legislation. If outside interest groups, individual constituents, or the president want to propose legislation, they must first persuade a senator or representative to sponsor their proposal, called a bill. The road to passage is often long and difficult; few bills ever become law.

Committees. After a bill is introduced, it is assigned a number and referred to the appropriate committee. If the committee chair thinks a bill is worthy of consideration, a subcommittee may hold public hearings in which witnesses testify for and against the proposed legislation. If the subcommittee approves the bill, it then gives the bill to the full committee. The full committee may or may not approve the bill. If approved, the bill may be sent to the House or Senate for debate.

The Debate and Vote. The powerful Rules Committee sets guidelines for debate in the House of Representatives. There is no equivalent committee in the Senate. Generally, House members are held to a strict time limit for debating a bill, while senators usually have unlimited time for debate. Bills are often amended in committee and during floor debates, and at some point a final vote is called or a bill is sent back to committee.

If the House and Senate pass different versions of the same bill, a conference committee of representatives and senators works out the differences. The conference compromise bill is then returned to each chamber for final debate and a vote. If both the House and Senate pass the same version of the bill, it goes to the president. The president can sign the bill into law or veto it. If he vetoes the bill, Congress may override the veto by securing a two-thirds majority vote in both houses.

Hazards Along the Way. It is easier to kill bills in Congress than to pass them. Powerful committee chairs can decline to consider bills, committees can completely change a bill's intent by adding amendments, or individual senators can delay votes indefinitely. Filibusters, wherein senators speak as long as they want on any topic, are used to extend debate and obstruct voting on a bill. Filibusters continue until three-fifths of those senators present (usually 60) vote for "cloture," or the close of argument.

PRESIDENT OBAMA, CONGRESS, AND FREE TRADE

Free trade treaties have always been a politically divisive issue, but in 2011 many observers hoped it might be the one issue upon which the President and Congress could find common ground. Democrats, as well as many congressional Republicans, wanted to ratify treaties with Colombia, Panama, and South Korea at the same time, as this would give a much-needed boost to the U.S. economy. Obama wanted Congress to begin work on an agreement with South Korea that had been reached in December 2010, but lawmakers refused to move forward unless the president gave them treaties with Colombia and Panama as well. The Obama administration had balked at this ultimatum, feeling that Colombia and Panama had not done enough to protect labor rights and the lives of labor leaders. Meanwhile, Republicans accused the administration of simply trying to appease union allies who feared the loss of jobs to foreign competition. By October of 2011 the standoff had finally come to an end, with all three treaties being ratified—a rare moment of bipartisan accord at a time generally characterized by intense partisanship.

Influencing Legislation. When considering so many complex bills, how do individual members of Congress make decisions? First, these officials have access to the world's best library as well as a research staff to help them learn about important policy issues. In addition, constituents call, write letters, and send email expressing their views. And during hearings, committees seek the advice of outside experts. But there are other forces that affect legislation as well.

Comprised of individuals and corporate members, special interest groups—such as the oil industry and environmental conservation groups—often hire lobbyists to argue their case. Lobbyists try to persuade senators and representatives to vote a particular way on upcoming legislation and often direct their clients' money to political campaigns to gain access to elected officials. In 2007, in response to several scandals, congressional leaders adopted changes to ethics rules in an attempt to diminish the influence of these groups.

Congress and President Barack Obama

The historic election of 2008 resulted in the nation's first black president, Barack Obama, who took office in January 2009. Democrats running for Congress that year rode the wave of support for Obama, and the new 111th Congress saw Democratic gains in both chambers.

The 111th Congress. With Democrats solidly in the majority of both the House and Senate, the 111th Congress passed and President Obama signed a number of major laws, many of them aimed at addressing the causes of or easing the effects of the economic recession. The cornerstone of these efforts was a $787 billion economic stimulus package that included provisions to create jobs, aid state and local governments, extend unemployment compensation, and spur consumer spending. Another major new law overhauled the rules governing the banking and finance system with the aim of preventing future crashes and protecting consumers. The most controversial legislation passed was the sweeping overhaul of the U.S. health care system, which established new rules for employers and health insurers and mandated that all Americans buy or acquire health insurance by 2014.

2010 Election and the 112th Congress. In the 2010 midterm election, government spending, continued high unemployment, and disapproval of health care reform helped sweep Republican candidates to a majority in the House of Representatives. Although the Democrats also lost seats in the Senate, they managed to hold onto a slim majority in that chamber.

With a greater number of Republicans, most of them opposed to government spending, the 112th Congress presented immediate challenges for the Obama administration. In 2011, for instance, GOP leaders in Congress and the administration engaged in a number of tough, acrimonious battles, first over the fiscal 2012 budget and then over whether to extend the nation's debt ceiling (the government's legal authorization to continue borrowing money). In both cases, a government shutdown was narrowly averted by last minute negotiations.

Early in 2012, Republicans in Congress and the White House were at it again, this time fighting over a proposed extension of a 2 percent cut in the payroll tax. Both sides wanted to extend the cut until the end of the year, but GOP leaders refused to agree to the proposal until negotiators came up with enough savings to offset the loss in revenue from extending the tax cut. Eventually, the Republicans gave ground and, in February 2012, agreed to extend the tax cut without

In 2011, President Obama and Republicans in Congress clashed over how best to re-invigorate the U.S. economy. Surrounded by his GOP colleagues, House Speaker John Boehner of Ohio speaks during a news conference on Capitol Hill about a payroll tax cut bill.

conditions. Weeks later, GOP leaders and the White House also managed to work out differences and enact legislation aimed at making it easier for businesses to create jobs. Still, both sides predict more difficult negotiations ahead, as the budget and other issues loom and the November 2012 election approaches.

Congress and the White House also have fought over foreign policy, notably the administration's timetable for withdrawal of American forces from Afghanistan. Some in Congress (many of them Democrats) have called for a faster withdrawal, while others have urged caution and have even argued against setting any timetable. Obama, citing his decision as "one of the most difficult I've made as President," has argued that withdrawal from Afghanistan, along with the earlier winding down of the war in Iraq, is critical as the nation begins to refocus attention and resources on resolving economic and other domestic problems.

The Judicial Branch

The judicial branch—made up of the federal court system—settles legal disputes between individuals and federal, state, and local governments. The federal judiciary's primary authority is to interpret the U.S. Constitution, as well as other federal laws and treaties; that is, to say what a specific law actually means and how it should be applied to a particular set of facts. In an important example of checks and balances, the Supreme Court, as well as lower courts, may determine that a federal law is unconstitutional. If a law is deemed to violate the Constitution and is struck down, it can only be resurrected if Congress passes a new law that does not run afoul of the court's decision or if the Constitution is amended (a very difficult process) to accommodate the old law.

The federal court system consists of the Supreme Court, thirteen regional circuit courts of appeals, and ninety-four federal district courts. Deciding which kinds of cases can be brought in federal court versus state court is often a complicated legal matter. Essentially, federal courts hear disputes involving federal law, between the citizens of two different states, or involving a local or state government, or the federal government. The district courts serve as trial courts, where disputes are initially heard. If litigants are unhappy with the outcome of their case there, they may be able to appeal to one of the thirteen circuit courts to review the decision.

The Supreme Court justices: Top row (left to right): Sonia Sotomayor, Stephen Breyer, Samuel Alito Jr., and Elena Kagan. Bottom row (left to right): Clarence Thomas, Antonin Scalia, John Roberts, Anthony Kennedy, and Ruth Bader Ginsburg.

The Supreme Court. Cases that come before the Supreme Court are mostly on appeal from lower federal or state courts and are chosen by the justices. Each year, the Court receives roughly 10,000 petitions from which the justices select fewer than 100 cases to hear, usually involving matters of great public importance or issues on which lower courts have offered differing decisions. The Supreme Court term typically runs from October through May, with many decisions being announced during the summer recess.

A Job for Life. In an example of how the Constitution's system of checks and balances works, the president nominates Supreme Court justices, but the Senate must approve the appointees. These justices serve for life, unless they resign or are impeached.

Court Trends. Decisions of the nation's highest court have greatly affected U.S. political and social life. During the 1950s and 1960s, the Supreme Court, led by Chief Justice Earl Warren, made sweeping changes regarding laws affecting civil and individual rights. The Warren Court struck down racial segregation and government-sponsored prayer in public schools. During the 1980s and 1990s, the Court led by Chief Justice William Rehnquist scaled back some of these rulings in an attempt to reduce the size and scope of the federal government.

New Faces on the Court. Within the first year and a half of his term, President Obama appointed two new associate justices: Sonia Sotomayor, who replaced David Souter in 2009 and Elena Kagan, who replaced John Paul Stevens in 2010. With the new members joining Associate Justice Ruth Bader Ginsburg, the Supreme Court now includes three women, comprising one-third of the nine justices—a historical first. In addition, for the first time in its history, the Supreme Court has no Protestant members and instead includes six Roman Catholics and three Jewish members.

The ideologies of each justice profoundly influence the Supreme Court's rulings and therefore have a lasting impact on the nation's laws and policies. Conservative justices generally favor a strict interpretation of the Constitution, while liberal justices often prefer a broader interpretation of the Constitution that suits changing circumstances. Justices Alito, Roberts, Scalia, and Thomas, are generally thought of as conservative in their views, while Justices Breyer, Kagan, Ginsburg, and Sotomayor are seen as more liberal. Justice Kennedy is considered a "swing vote" because his views vary by issue and are sometimes unpredictable. It was Chief Justice Roberts, however, who sided with the liberal wing when he voted to uphold the Affordable Care Act in June 2012.

How the Federal Government Works

Case Study: The Keystone XL Pipeline

Because of the system of checks and balances established in the Constitution, much of the work of the federal government is collaborative. That does not mean that the three branches always work together or in tandem. But often, all three are intimately involved in the making of public policy. The debate over the Keystone XL oil pipeline extension project is a good example of this convergence of the roles and responsibilities of the three branches around a complex set of policy challenges and constituent demands.

Proposed in 2008, the Keystone XL extension project is part of a broader pipeline system created to convey synthetic crude oil from the Athabasca Oil Sands in northeastern Alberta, Canada, to multiple destinations in the United States, including refineries in Illinois, Oklahoma, and along the Gulf Coast of Texas. The proposed 1,179-mile Keystone XL pipeline is projected to move about 700,000 barrels of oil each day down through the middle of the United States to Texas refineries. Hoping to move forward on the project, TransCanada sought a building permit from the federal government (called a Presidential Permit), which is required because the pipeline will cross the Canada/U.S. border. But the project has stalled due to environmental and other concerns.

Proponents of the pipeline argue that Keystone XL will allow the United States to increase its energy security, reduce its dependence on foreign oil, and stimulate the economy by creating tens of thousands of new jobs. Opponents have countered that the pipeline crosses sensitive wilderness areas, could produce an environmentally disastrous oil spill, and is meant to transport crude oil that will go to Asia rather than the United States and thus will not contribute in the least to the country's national security or energy independence.

The Obama Administration Decides ... Sort of. Almost from the moment its application was filed at the beginning of 2009, Keystone XL was attacked from a number of quarters, with lawsuits, protests from citizens, and criticism from environmental lobbyists and many Democratic members of Congress. As the process moved forward, a number of agencies involved in the review weighed in. For example, in July 2010, the Environmental

Protection Agency issued a statement criticizing the environmental impact study that had been conducted for Keystone XL because it failed to adequately examine contingencies for oil spills and other safety issues. Finally, in November 2011, President Obama, responding to fears that the Keystone XL pipeline could cause a BP-style oil spill in America's heartland, decided to postpone a decision until 2013 in order to give policy-makers more time to make a thorough environmental review.

In Congress and the Courts. But Republicans in Congress argued the president was putting off the decision for political reasons. Specifically, they said, the president was unwilling to anger allies in the environmental movement (especially before the 2012 election), but also did not want to outright reject a project that could create thousands of new jobs. In December 2011, GOP leaders in Congress succeeded in attaching a provision— requiring the administration to make a decision on the pipeline within 60 days—to legislation extending an existing payroll tax cut for two months. Republicans gambled because the president had a strong desire to extend the tax. But one month later, Obama seemed to circumvent the mandate when he rejected the pipeline, arguing that the 60-day deadline had not given his administration enough time to properly assess the pros and cons of the project. He then urged TransCanada to reapply, saying that he would be happy to reconsider their application. Indeed, a few months later, the president applauded a decision by TransCanada to begin building the southern-most section of the XL pipeline (which does not require federal approval) from Cushing, Oklahoma, to Port Arthur, Texas.

In March 2012, Congress entered the fray again when Senate Republicans introduced legislation that would have overridden the normal permit process and forced the administration to approve the construction of the pipeline. The measure did not win Senate approval.

Meanwhile the project has been the subject of countless lawsuits, ranging from action taken by oil refiners who oppose the delays in approving the project to environmental groups suing the federal government to release documents pertaining to meetings between government officials and energy industry lobbyists. In addition, the president's Republican opponent in the 2012 presidential election promised to make the Keystone XL a campaign issue to showcase what he believes is the administration's weak record on energy and job creation.

THE FEDERAL BUDGET

INTRODUCTION

The U.S. federal budget is the single most important piece of legislation passed each year. Typically, the battle over the budget is a silent war, fought inside the beltway by lobbyists, the White House, and Congress. Recently, however, as the nation's debt has become a hot campaign topic and Congress is deeply divided between the two parties, the budget battle has been more public—and more partisan—than it has been in over a decade.

KEY QUESTIONS

- Should Congress pass a balanced budget amendment?

- Should Congress ban earmarks?

- Should Medicare be changed to a voucher system?

The budget is often said to represent the nation's values. How much money should be spent on education? Defense? Anti-poverty programs? Health care? Border security? But even before legislators can begin slicing the pie, they must agree on its size. Democrats in Congress tend to favor using government programs to invest in infrastructure and innovation and address economic and social problems, which sometimes requires higher taxes, usually on the wealthiest individuals and corporations. Republicans generally prefer a smaller government role and lower taxes, believing that wealth created at the top of the economic chain will "trickle down" and that the private sector is better suited to address many issues. The current Republican leadership is deeply opposed to any new or increased taxes.

Some economists argue that a balanced budget is the only way to ensure the United States's future economic stability, while many others say that borrowing money is a necessary and safe way of paying for the things government needs to do and that providing tax cuts for the very wealthy while banning any increases in taxes across the board is both selfish and dangerous. Most Americans agree that the ballooning U.S. debt—which stood at about $15 trillion in 2012—is cause for concern. Debate over the nation's finances and the proper role of government has dominated the political campaigns of 2012.

BACKGROUND

The Federal Budget Process

Setting Priorities. The federal budget, created and debated each year, is a plan for how the U.S. government will take in money, as well as how it will spend it. Developed by both the president and Congress, the budget outlines the nation's priorities for the coming year and describes how the government will reach those goals. For instance, if elected officials decide increasing border security is a priority, they may allocate more federal funds to build fences and increase monitoring. Working together, and sometimes against each other, the president and Congress decide how much money the government will spend on defense and homeland security, health care, education, "safety net" programs, foreign aid, science, preservation and conservation of national parks, and hundreds of other programs. In addition, lawmakers must estimate how much revenue the U.S. Treasury can expect to take in from taxpayers.

The President Develops a Budget. In the executive branch, the Office of Management and Budget (OMB) is responsible for drawing up the president's budget for the coming fiscal year, which always begins on

Spending a Tax Dollar

20¢	17¢	20¢	13¢	7¢	17¢	7¢
Defense	Non-defense discretionary spending[1]	Social Security	Medicare	Medicaid	Other entitlements[2]	Interest on the debt

[1] Such as education and foreign aid.
[2] Such as food stamps and farm aid.

Source: Office of Management and Budget

October 1 and ends the following September 30. The president relies on the OMB to produce a budget that reflects the administration's priorities. After compiling requests from the various agencies in the executive branch, the OMB submits a budget to the White House for approval. The president then sends the administration's budget to Congress no later than the first Monday in February.

Congress Takes Over. No federal agency or program can operate without receiving both approval and funding from Congress. Congress grants approval for each program by passing an authorization bill, which states the program's goals, Congress's rules and regulations, and the agency's spending limits. Then lawmakers must approve a separate appropriations bill, which actually gives the designated agency the money to run its program. This dual system — authorization, then appropriation — is designed to create a fiscal check by having programs discussed first on their merits and then on their costs.

Congress is also responsible for raising money, or revenue, for the federal government. Lawmakers raise money by collecting taxes and authorizing the U.S. Treasury to borrow more, if necessary, to make up for any difference in the amount of revenue collected and spent. The House and Senate are supposed to approve a joint budget resolution by April of each year. The resolution sets guidelines for how much the government can spend and predicts how much revenue it will collect. Later in the year, the legislators pass a second budget resolution, which reflects any recent changes in the economy and in expected revenue. If appropriations bills already passed by Congress exceed the new limits, members draw up a reconciliation bill to bring spending within the limits set by the second budget resolution.

The Basics of the Budget

The Whole Pie. Government spending is divided into four main categories for budgeting purposes: defense, non-defense discretionary, mandatory, and interest on the national debt. Revenue comes from individual income taxes (about 45 percent of the annual revenue in 2012), payroll taxes to fund Social Security (34 percent), corporate income taxes (14 percent), and various other sources.

Defense spending, including veterans benefits, is the largest outlay for the federal government each year.

Government Printing Office employees ready copies of President Obama's FY2013 budget in February 2012.

Non-defense discretionary spending pays for all of the budgetary programs for which funding is adjusted by the president and Congress every year. This includes such items as environmental protection, education, highway construction, food safety inspections, flu vaccines, and much more.

Mandatory, or entitlement, spending covers programs such as Social Security, Medicare, and Medicaid, which the government is obligated by law to fund. These programs are called entitlements because anyone who qualifies is entitled to receive benefits. Within the next ten years, entitlement spending could consume nearly half of the federal budget. The proportion of retirees will continue to grow so that by 2040, at least one in four Americans will be eligible for Social Security and Medicare benefits. That demographic shift will cause first Medicare and then Social Security to face shortfalls.

The fourth main category of the budget is annual interest on the national debt. Every year, the government must set aside money to pay down the debt owed to creditors. As the debt grows, so does this obligation. Failure to pay would diminish the credit rating of the United States, raising interest rates on the debt that already exists and making it more difficult for the United States to get loans.

Entitlement Spending. Social Security is the largest and most expensive federal program. Established in 1935, the program serves more than 56 million men, women, and children and is the main source of income for many older Americans. Social Security receives much of the credit for reducing the poverty rate among senior citizens from 50 percent in the 1930s to about 10 percent in recent years. Two-thirds of the program's beneficiaries are retirees; the rest are disabled workers, spouses and families of deceased workers, and children.

According to an April 2012 government report, Social Security reserves will be exhausted in 2033 (several years earlier than predicted last year). Without changes, Social Security will continue to function, but will only be able to pay benefits from the revenues it collects from payroll taxes, amounting to roughly three-quarters of currently scheduled benefits. Proposals include raising the cap on how much income can be taxed for Social Security, raising the retirement age, reducing benefits, or diverting contributions to private investment accounts. Despite the projected shortfall, reform has proved politically difficult because Social Security is a hugely popular program.

President Lyndon B. Johnson signs the Medicare bill into law on July 30, 1965. Enacted to aid the sizeable number of elderly Americans who were poor and suffering from ill health, today Medicare serves more than 45 million Americans of all income levels. Combined, Medicare and Medicaid—its twin program for the poor and disabled—consume one-fifth of the U.S budget.

Medicare. Americans over age 65 and people with disabilities are automatically eligible to receive government Medicare benefits. Medicare helps pay for nursing care and other routine medical services for more than

47 million people today and federal estimates suggest that the number of eligible seniors will be closer to 80 million by 2030. Like Social Security, Medicare operates with a trust fund, but unlike Social Security, the Medicare program is already spending more than it takes in. Medicare's trustees estimate that the trust fund will be exhausted by 2019.

Medicaid. Similar to Medicare, Medicaid is a government program aimed at providing health care to those who are not able to afford it. Unlike Medicare, it provides funding for low-income individuals and families regardless of age. The program works in concert with the states and is the largest single source of money for health services for poor people in the United States.

Taxes. The main source of government revenue is tax payments. Currently, individuals pay taxes on the income they receive, including salaries from employers, interest payments on investments, and profits on the sale of assets. The current income tax system is progressive, meaning higher earners pay a larger share of their earnings to the federal government. There are also many caveats in the U.S. tax code that specify which types of income—such as interest earned on investments—are taxed at which rates. Corporations also pay taxes to the U.S. government, amounting to about 9 percent of total federal tax revenue in 2010, with individual income tax and payroll tax revenue making up more than 80 percent of the total. Nonprofit organizations and academic institutions do not pay federal taxes. Overall, Americans paid about $2.2 trillion in federal income taxes in 2011.

A Government Beyond Its Means

Budget Deficits. Deficits occur when the government spends more than it takes in. To make up the difference, the U.S. Treasury must borrow money by selling government bonds to investors. Some economists worry about the effects of heavy government borrowing. Competition between the government and other borrowers can drive up interest rates, making it more expensive for individuals and businesses to borrow for private investment. Government borrowing also increases the national debt.

The National Debt. The national debt, currently more than $15 trillion (roughly $49,000 per citizen), is the total sum of money borrowed by the government from the U.S. population, lending institutions, foreign banks, and the government's own holdings, most notably the Social Security trust fund. The debt—along with the amount of interest the government owes on it—is predicted to rise for the foreseeable future. Some economists fear that growing debt could dampen long-term investment and lead to an economic depression.

Competing Budget Visions

The stage for the recent budget battles was set more than a decade ago. In 2000, the United States was enjoying its largest budget surplus in history. Immediately after taking office in January 2001, President George W. Bush and a Republican Congress enacted sweeping, across-the-board tax cuts. Those tax cuts, along with two largely unfunded wars in Iraq and Afghanistan and the expansion of entitlement programs created massive annual deficits throughout the decade. The 2007-09 economic recession made the nation's fiscal health even worse.

When President Obama took office in 2009, he and the Democratic-controlled Congress passed an economic stimulus package of spending increases and tax cuts that cost another $790 billion. Many Americans reacted angrily to the ballooning national debt. In the 2010 election, the Republicans reclaimed the House of Representatives on a ground swell of public support for budget cutting.

Several major confrontations between 2011 and 2012 brought the federal government to the brink of a shutdown with most of the conflict being resolved only temporarily. The Bush tax cuts, set to expire several times, repeatedly have been extended with strong support from Republicans and reluctant support from President Obama, who believes that middle-class tax cuts should remain in effect but that significant tax cuts for the very wealthiest Americans should not stand. The past year also brought a high-stakes debate over the debt ceiling, which is the limit on how much money the U.S. Treasury can borrow to carry out government mandated functions. House Republicans campaigned vigorously in opposition to raising the ceiling, insisting that the government needed to stop taking on debt. Ultimately, a deal was reached to raise the ceiling temporarily, effectively kicking the can down the road.

The 2013 budget process promises to be a bruising fight. Several contentious battles of the past few years resulted in the creation of automatic and deep future cuts in important government budgets such as defense if compromise is not reached. Another challenge will be the budget cap—

or how much money Congress should be divvying up. The two Houses of Congress—controlled by different parties as of Spring 2012—will be working with two different budget caps, which is certain to cause major headaches as Congress works to draft spending bills. Many analysts believe that much of the work on the 2013 budget will be done after the November elections but before a number of end-of-year budget deadlines.

The President's Proposal. In February 2012, President Barack Obama proposed his 2013 budget, incorporating many of his election year priorities and commitments. The proposal includes $3.8 trillion in spending and $2.9 trillion in revenue, leaving a budget deficit of approximately $900 million. The budget reflects the president's stated goals of growing the economy through investment and education, lowering the national debt, decreasing the inequality gap between high-and lower-income Americans, and cutting costs. These goals would be achieved through a combination of tax increases on the very wealthy; closing tax loopholes for some corporations and industries, particularly energy; and enacting funding cuts across the board including significant reductions to defense.

President Obama sent the administration's budget to Congress in February 2012. House Republicans responded with an updated version of their previous year's budget, called "The Path to Prosperity: A Blueprint for American Renewal." Here, Rep. Paul Ryan (R-WI), the plan's architect, holds up a copy of the proposal at a Washington, D.C., news conference.

AP PHOTO/JACQUELYN MARTIN

The House Republicans' Budget. In March 2012, the Republicans in the House responded to the president's budget with a very different proposal of their own. Presented by Rep. Paul Ryan (R-WI), the chair of the House Budget Committee and the chief budget architect for the Republicans in Congress, the proposal included dramatic changes to the tax code, deep spending cuts, and no new revenue streams.

A highly controversial point in Ryan's plan is his idea, first introduced in 2011, to transition Medicare from a government-run insurance plan to a system in which senior citizens would receive money to subsidize their purchasing of private insurance. Ryan also proposed restructuring Medicaid as a system of grants directly to the states, so that state lawmakers would have more control and negotiating power over funding and prices.

Supporters praise Ryan's proposal for being one of the first serious attempts by Congress to rein in entitlement spending. Critics denounce it as an attempt to place the burden of debt reduction squarely on the shoulders of the elderly and economically vulnerable. A version of the Ryan plan passed the House in March 2012 without a single Democratic vote.

The Simpson-Bowles Plan. Several alternative budget proposals have gained attention in recent years, most notably the Simpson-Bowles plan, introduced in December 2010 and named for Erskine Bowles, a university president and former adviser to President Bill Clinton, and Alan Simpson, a former Republican U.S. senator from Wyoming. The plan—which combines cuts in entitlement and defense spending with tax increases—emerged from a bipartisan commission established by President Obama to seek long-term solutions to the government's debt problems, though the president has not adopted many of its proposals. In April 2012, the plan was voted on in the House and received only 38 votes, but aspects of it continue to be popular with lawmakers from both parties.

CURRENT ISSUES

Balancing the Budget. The idea of amending the Constitution to require a balanced budget each year in which receipts (in the form of taxes) exceed outlays (what the government spends) has been around for years, with almost all Republicans supporting the measure. The Tea Party—the anti-tax, populist conservative movement that rose to prominence in 2010—has made a balanced budget amendment (BBA) a hallmark of its platform. In 2011, Republicans in both Houses of Congress proposed BBA bills, though neither passed.

This high-speed rail track in Illinois was funded by the 2009 American Recovery and Reinvestment Act. Supporters of the government's economic stimulus efforts believe such projects create jobs and provide critical investments in the nation's infrastructure. Opponents argue that it did little to increase employment or lower debt.

Proponents of a balanced budget amendment to the Constitution argue that the same rules that apply to a family's budget at home should apply to the budget of the federal government: don't spend more than you make. The huge debt that America is accruing will be passed on to the next generation and the one after that, crippling the chances for our children and grandchildren to achieve the "American Dream." Amending the Constitution to require that Congress pass a balanced budget is the best possible remedy to spur job creation, say supporters of a BBA. If businesses are freed up from worrying about a debt crisis—and its attendant concerns of inflation, increasing taxes, and higher costs to borrow money—then they can invest in growth and hire more workers. After all, point out BBA proponents, 49 states have some type of a balanced budget requirement, and the federal government should too.

Balanced budget amendment opponents argue that the BBA would make it very difficult for the federal government to take the kinds of emergency measures needed during a recession or international crisis—such as economy-saving deficit spending or expensive military action. They also point out that comparing the federal government's budget to that of an average family must also include the family that sensibly and carefully uses credit to take out a mortgage, or a car loan, or funds to finance their children's education. Debt is not inherently a bad thing, many experts argue, and investors have always valued American debt because the American government is a trustworthy borrower. Critics of the BBA effort acknowledge that a careful and reasonable debt reduction package is important as the nation moves further out of recession, but say a balanced budget amendment should not be a part of such a plan.

To Earmark or Not? A legislative earmark is federal funding for a specific entity or project, usually requested by a member of Congress for his or her district. While members of Congress are barred from supporting earmarks that directly result in financial benefit to themselves or their family members, it is common practice for them to advocate for specific entities within their districts or states to receive government funding. "Special interest" groups and their lobbyists—groups of citizens or corporations who have particular policy goals—are part of a multi-billion dollar industry to sway Congress to send money their way. The earmarking practice has both critics and supporters and is often a contentious issue during political campaigns and legislative budget seasons. Over the past few years, members in both house of Congress have tried to pass legislation banning the practice. In 2011, the House effectively enacted a moratorium on earmarks though the Senate voted down a similar measure in 2012.

Earmarks for legislators' "pet projects" frequently reward campaign donors and local constituents at the expense of the larger needs of the

Budget Cutlery

©2010 Clay Bennett
Bennett Chattanooga Times Free Press

nation, and sometimes directly enrich the pockets of the legislators themselves. The worst part, say proponents of a ban, is that these actions are currently legal and undisclosed according to the rules Congress sets for itself. Furthermore, the practice of earmarking is a direct contributor to the American public's extremely low approval rating of Congress. Banning earmarks permanently will put an end to this unpopular and unethical practice, critics argue, and rein in wasteful spending at the same time.

Earmark supporters respond that this so-called "wasteful spending" regularly includes funding for such items as transportation infrastructure in cities with clogged roads; research dollars to university hospitals that are finding cures for diseases like cancer; and community programs that serve children, the poor, and the ill. Despite efforts by the opposition to make such expenditures seem malfeasant and unethical, they are, in fact, simply government doing what it is supposed to do: generate revenue and then spend that revenue for the good of the people. Such critics argue that eliminating the ability of the legislature to direct funds leaves too much power in the hands of the executive branch and its agencies, regardless of which party is in power.

Medicare Reform. Paying out health care benefits to eligible Americans represents about one-fifth of the U.S. budget—a share that, as the U.S. population ages and baby boomers begin to retire, is likely to increase. The impact of this expense on the fiscal health of the country could be devastating and almost all experts agree that as is, the system is unsustainable. Policymakers have responded with major reform proposals for the Medicare program, including a Republican plan to change the current "pay-as-you-go" mechanism to a private voucher system, in which the elderly are given funds to purchase insurance in the private marketplace.

Proponents of such a plan argue that the costs of entitlement programs are becoming ruinous to the American economy, and that if left unchanged will pass on a bankrupt country to future generations. The current Medicare system leaves consumers in the dark about the real costs and quality of health care practices, according to critics, and keeps ownership of health care in the hands of the government in Washington rather than with patients. Supporters of the overhaul believe that empowering the elderly through providing subsidies to purchase private insurance—plans in which quality and premium controls are in effect—will create better market competition, forcing insurers and providers to keep costs down and quality up for all patients.

HOW HIGH ARE TAXES?

The U.S. income tax system is a progressive one, meaning that there are different tax rates that increase as income levels increase. Currently, the lowest tax rate, applied to income between 0 and $17,400 is 10 percent; the highest rate, applied to income above $388,350, is 35 percent. Americans are taxed on their "next earned dollar," a complicated system by which different parts of a person's income are taxed at different rates. Essentially, you pay less in taxes on your first dollar than on your last. The easiest way to calculate the average rate a particular person is paying is to determine his or her "effective tax rate" by dividing the tax paid by the adjusted gross income, which is gross income minus deductions, adjustments, and credits. Despite a common perception that the American people are currently over-taxed compared to previous decades, current rates are some of the lowest in modern history. In 1981, the highest tax rate was 70 percent; in 1944, it was 94 percent. In addition, the United States (including both the federal government and the states) collects less in taxes as a share of the economy than nearly any other developed country.

Opponents of such large-scale changes to the Medicare program acknowledge that entitlement reform is needed to ensure the fiscal health of the nation. But they say that the private voucher proposal will essentially gut Medicare, a system that millions of American seniors depend on and which is a hallmark of the American "safety net." Furthermore, they contend, a voucher plan has been proven more costly to administer, based on past attempts. Most worrisome, critics point out, is that budget analyses of such proposals find that they will leave low- and middle-income seniors short of the cash needed to buy health care, essentially forcing the most vulnerable of the elderly to bear the brunt of the cuts.

OUTLOOK

As always, the federal government faces tough choices in setting its budget. These decisions become more consequential as deficits add up, debt grows, and the needs of the American people and economy become more prominent. Debates over raising revenue and spending money are highly charged, exacerbated by the lingering effects of the global recession and the deep partisan divisions on Capitol Hill. The two parties offer significantly different goals and visions for the nation, and nowhere are these more apparent than in their competing proposals on what services the federal government should provide and how it should collect the money to do so.

THE DEBATE: THE FEDERAL BUDGET

Congress should pass a balanced budget amendment.

PRO: American families cannot spend more than they make so why should the government be allowed to do so? America's future generations are going to be saddled with massive debt if the country continues to spend more than it takes in. Reining in government spending is the way to grow and protect the economy moving forward, which can only be done with a balanced budget amendment. Forty-nine states have such a requirement and so should Congress.

CON: Just as American families borrow to pay for such important investments as a car, a home, and an education, so does the federal government borrow to pay for the things the nation needs. Constraining future Congresses from being able to enact important economic policy in the face of a crisis by requiring a balanced budget is dangerous and must be avoided. Instead, the parties should work together to find compromise and reduce the deficit while still allowing Congress to create the programs that Americans need and count on.

Congress should ban earmarks.

PRO: Earmarks are a dishonest and wasteful practice that must be ended. Allowing legislators and their campaign contributors to profit from taxpayer money they have directed toward their districts gives all elected officials a bad name and causes Americans to lose faith in their government. Ending this unethical practice will restore integrity and save money.

CON: Earmarks are not just a series of cash cows; instead, they fund research, education, construction, and development all intended to create jobs, enrich communities, and help American citizens prosper. Removing the ability for Congress to decide where and how tax dollars are spent gives far too much power to the executive branch, regardless of who is in the White House.

Medicare should be changed to a voucher system.

PRO: Protecting the health of American seniors is important but the current system is broken and threatens to bankrupt the country. Changing the implementation of Medicare to subsidies to help seniors buy private coverage gets government out of the business of practicing medicine and empowers consumers, which in turn will increase quality and effectiveness in the system.

CON: It will be a disaster for Americans who are in their golden years or at the end of their lives. While the Medicare system does need changes to make it more effective, eliminating the pay-as-you-go system in favor of vouchers is dangerous and has proven more costly to implement. And it is likely to leave poorer seniors without the money they need to purchase adequate coverage and care at the time when they most need it.

CONSTITUTIONAL ISSUES

INTRODUCTION

The first ten amendments to the U.S. Constitution are known as the Bill of Rights. Added to the Constitution in 1791, these amendments were designed to protect individual freedoms and to limit the power of the federal government. The Bill of Rights guarantees Americans the freedoms of expression, religion, and association. It also establishes a fair process for people accused of crimes and shields them from "cruel and unusual punishment." Although the Bill of Rights lists many liberties, other sections of the Constitution also grant rights to the American people.

KEY QUESTIONS

- Are airport screenings an unreasonable violation of privacy?

- Should the Supreme Court's Citizens United decision be overturned?

- Does limiting the constitutional rights of suspected terrorists protect national security?

Today, many controversial debates— such as airport security screenings, campaign fundraising restrictions, and the legal rights of suspected terrorists—stem from conflicting interpretations over what rights are guaranteed under the Constitution. Much of the wording in the Constitution and its amendments is general; therefore, Americans often disagree on how this language applies to certain situations. Such conflicts often have to be resolved in court.

The nine justices of the U.S. Supreme Court decide which cases they will review each term based on a number of considerations, including whether lower courts have handed down conflicting opinions on the issues in the case, and whether there are issues of significant interest to the American people. Based on these narrow criteria, the Court hears only a small fraction of the cases filed each term. The Court's decisions ultimately determine whether laws are constitutional. Some people believe that the Court should interpret the Constitution strictly according to the literal intentions of its authors. Others think that the Supreme Court should apply the spirit of the framers' ideas to modern-day situations. Such conflicts keep alive the debate over the meaning of the Constitution and its impact on Americans' daily lives.

BACKGROUND

Guaranteeing Individual Rights

Written in 1787, the Constitution needed to be ratified by nine of the existing thirteen states to become law. Many states approved the document with the provision that Congress would add amendments listing individual rights. James Madison of Virginia, a member of the first Congress, wrote the proposal that formed the basis of these amendments. In December 1791, ten amendments collectively known as the Bill of Rights were ratified by the states and became part of the Constitution.

Although they are now more than 220 years old, many of the ideas expressed in the Constitution and in the Bill of Rights still provoke public debate today, including those described below.

Freedom of Religion. Part of the First Amendment reads, "Congress shall make no law respecting an establishment of religion, or prohibiting the free exercise thereof." The courts have interpreted this to mean that government and religion should be separate. However, Americans often disagree on how to maintain this separation without interfering with a person's right to practice religion. Some Americans, called "separationists," believe

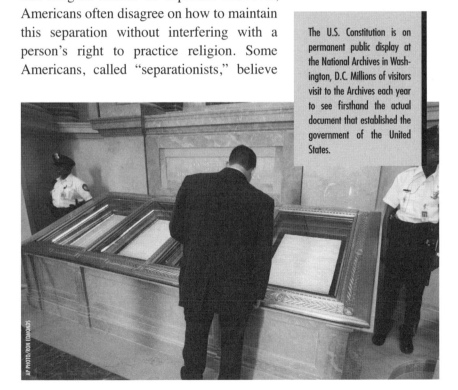

The U.S. Constitution is on permanent public display at the National Archives in Washington, D.C. Millions of visitors visit to the Archives each year to see firsthand the actual document that established the government of the United States.

that to protect religious liberty, the line between religion and government should not be crossed. Others are "accommodationists" and think that the government should make allowances for the long religious tradition in U.S. society. Many Americans fall somewhere in between these two views.

Historically, the Supreme Court has ruled on both sides of this issue: holding, for example, that public schools cannot require students to say prayers at the opening of the school day, but allowing some religious displays (such as nativity scenes, Christmas trees, and menorahs) near government buildings if their placement and context does not imply government endorsement of religion.

Freedom of Expression. The First Amendment also forbids Congress from making laws that prevent Americans from speaking or writing freely. The courts have ruled, however, that the right of free expression can be limited. For example, the First Amendment does not allow speech or writing that: (a) makes false statements about a private person's character, (b) specifically plans the violent overthrow of the government, or (c) incites a riot. However, the amendment does allow citizens to hold peaceful meetings and public protests asking the government to correct a perceived wrong.

The Supreme Court is sometimes asked to decide whether unpopular speech should be protected in the same manner as popular speech. The Court has ruled that burning the American flag is a form of free speech protected by the First Amendment and that local governments cannot outlaw the display of racist symbols, such as a Nazi swastika. People who support such rulings say that even offensive speech should be protected to ensure that the government does not censor citizens' views. Others argue that outlawing certain types of inflammatory or hurtful speech does not violate the First Amendment.

The Right to Bear Arms. The Second Amendment protects "the right of the people to keep and bear arms." After the American Revolution, the first Congress wanted to ensure that people could, if needed, form armed militias, such as the National Guard. The wording of this amendment has caused much debate about whether it gives individuals the right to own any gun for any reason. Individuals who collect guns, use them for sport, or keep them for self-defense often cite the Second Amendment when criticizing gun control laws. Lawmakers who support restrictions on the ownership of firearms say gun control laws are needed to stop gun violence and that the right to bear arms refers to state militias, not private

AP PHOTO/EVAN VUCCI

The U.S. Supreme Court decides whether laws are constitutional or not. Given their power to interpret the law and define the government's relationship to the people, the building where the Court meets is often the center of public protest.

individuals. In 2010, the Supreme Court ruled in *McDonald v. City of Chicago* that state and local governments cannot curtail Americans' Second Amendment right to bear arms.

Protecting Suspected Criminals. The Bill of Rights requires the government to treat fairly any persons accused of crimes. Several amendments address the rights of suspected criminals.

- The Fourth Amendment protects persons from "unreasonable searches and seizures."
- The Fifth Amendment forbids forcing suspects to testify against themselves; protects defendants from double jeopardy (being retried for crimes for which they were previously found not guilty); and prevents the government from taking a person's life, property, or freedom except in ways specified by law.
- The Sixth Amendment guarantees the right to a "speedy and public trial" by jury, the right to an attorney, and the right to confront opposing witnesses.

Cruel and Unusual Punishment. The Eighth Amendment forbids "cruel and unusual punishment" but does not specify what "cruel and unusual" means. In a 1958 ruling, the Supreme Court held that the amendment must "draw its meaning from evolving standards of decency that mark the progress of a

CAMERAS IN THE COURT?

Visitors to Washington, D.C., who are willing to stand in line—sometimes for days—can watch cases being heard before the U.S. Supreme Court. The ability to see and hear the nine justices as they listen to and question arguments for and against important constitutional issues gives everyday citizens the chance to see their government in action. However, this opportunity is only available to the few who are able to attend in person. That is because the Supreme Court does not allow cameras in its courtroom, although audio recordings are available. News media organizations eager to offer coverage of high profile cases continue to pressure the Court to reconsider its position, pointing to the fact that many state and international courts now televise their proceedings. Proponents of allowing cameras in the Supreme Court say it would increase interest and understanding of the important issues the Court weighs each term. Opponents, including a majority of the Court's justices, worry that the presence of cameras could change how lawyers and justices behave, potentially undermining the judicial process.

maturing society." As social values have evolved, Americans' tolerance for certain types of punishment has changed. For example, punishments such as whipping and branding were once considered the norm, but today those practices are considered barbaric and have been outlawed.

Capital punishment—the "death penalty"—has been used in America since colonial days but has been the subject of significant public debate in the last 50 years. In 2012, 33 states and the federal government allowed capital punishment. Supporters of capital punishment believe it is an important deterrent to serious crime and is justified in the most serious cases. Recent debates have focused on whether the defendants facing the death penalty have access to adequate legal representation. Opponents of capital punishment point to statistics that show poor and minority defendants are more likely to be sentenced to death or wrongfully convicted; since 1973, more than 130 people have been released from death row after new evidence revealed they were innocent. New technology that allows the genetic fingerprints found in a person's DNA to be matched against evidence gathered at a crime scene has helped to exonerate many of these defendants.

Unspecified Rights. The Ninth Amendment acknowledges that no listing of rights can be truly complete. It states that rights not specifically mentioned are "retained by the people." In other words, the government must honor rights that are defined in the future. For example, the Supreme Court has recognized the right to privacy, the right to vote, and the right to travel, even though they are not specifically mentioned in the Constitution. However, the Court has most often based such rights on the Fourteenth Amendment, rather than the Ninth Amendment.

The Fourteenth Amendment. Originally, the Bill of Rights applied only to the federal government, but the Fourteenth Amendment extended most of those protections to the actions of state and local governments as well. Section one of the Fourteenth Amendment reads in part, "No state shall make or enforce any law which shall abridge the privileges or immunities of citizens of the United States; nor shall any state deprive any person of life, liberty, or property, without due process of law; nor deny to any person within its jurisdiction the equal protection of the laws."

Federalism. In a federalist system, national and state governments share power. The Tenth Amendment says that powers not given to the federal government, nor prohibited to the states by the Constitution, are reserved for the states or the people.

This monument depicting the Ten Commandments was placed in front of the Dixie County Courthouse in Cross City, Florida, until a federal court ordered its removal because it violated the Constitution's separation of church and state.

An airline passenger is checked by an advanced imaging technology scanner while going through the Transportation Security Administration checkpoint at Hartsfield-Jackson Atlanta International Airport.

CURRENT ISSUES

Airport Security Screenings. The Fourth Amendment to the U.S. Constitution protects people from "unreasonable searches and seizures" by the government. The Supreme Court has generally required that for a search to be "reasonable," it must be supported by "probable cause" that an individual may have participated in illegal activity. Usually the question of whether probable cause exists is decided by a judge and confirmed in a written warrant. In these instances, the government's responsibility to protect public security and safety outweighs the individual's right to privacy. This balancing act between the need to keep the public safe from harmful activity, while ensuring that innocent individuals are not subjected to unreasonable searches, is at the heart of the debate surrounding airport security screenings.

Following a number of hijacking incidents in the 1970s, the Federal Aviation Administration began the practice of screening passengers and their luggage before they were allowed to board commercial air flights. In *U.S. v. Davis* (1973), the Supreme Court upheld this practice of warrantless "administrative searches," as long as they were "no more intrusive or intensive than necessary, in light of current technology, to detect weapons or explosives," were "confined in good faith to that purpose," and that passengers could avoid the search by electing not to fly.

On September 11, 2001, hijackers boarded commercial air flights in the United States and crashed them into the World Trade Center buildings and the Pentagon, killing thousands on the ground and hundreds in the air. Later that year, Congress established the Transportation Security Administration (TSA) and charged it with improving the efforts to keep dangerous passengers and objects from ending up onboard all types of transportation, but in particular, commercial airliners. TSA now has 43,000 officers in more than 450 airports across the country. TSA screens more than two million passengers daily using a variety of techniques, including x-ray machines, metal detectors, and hand searches of bags and people.

Following several high profile incidents in the late 2000s, in which suspected terrorists were able to smuggle dangerous materials and weapons onboard flights, TSA stepped up security efforts. In 2010, TSA installed "full-body scanners" in select airports to see through passengers' clothing to reveal concealed weapons or objects, and instituted a more thorough form of body "pat-down" for randomly selected passengers, including children and the elderly. These new techniques raised concerns among constitutional rights advocates and passengers that perhaps the government was going too far in attempting to keep airplanes safe.

Supporters of increased airport security say that the government's need to protect the public from terrorism warrants these enhanced security precautions. Since the high volume of airline passengers prevents screening individual people based on the "probable cause" that they might be planning an attack, instead all passengers must undergo a minimum level of screening, and a randomly selected few get an enhanced screening such as a pat-down. Many passengers believe these security measures are a small price to pay for ensuring they are boarding a safe flight.

Opponents of these enhanced security measures say the possibility of one dangerous person boarding a flight is not sufficient justification to invade the privacy of all passengers. Subjecting all passengers to these increased measures is "unreasonable," and therefore unconstitutional,

AMENDING THE CONSTITUTION

Ratified in 1788, the U.S. Constitution has withstood the test of time—but not without revision. The Constitution has been amended 27 times, via a long process that has proved difficult to repeat in the modern era (it has been amended only five times in the last 50 years). A proposed change to the Constitution must be approved by a two-thirds vote in both houses of Congress and then ratified by three-fourths of the states. This process can take years and many amendments lose momentum before ever reaching the end. Despite these odds, in 2012 members of Congress proposed dozens of constitutional amendments, including ones to require a balanced budget, prohibit spending on political campaigns, abolish the electoral college, and ban burning of the American flag. Though none are likely to be approved this session, they are a reminder of the power to change this important historical governing document.

because it assumes that everyone is a possible threat. These advocates believe that it would be more efficient and effective to focus enhanced security screening only on individuals whose background or behavior indicates that they may be a threat to public safety, as is the norm in other countries with a history of terrorist threats, such as Israel.

Furor over Citizens United. When George Washington was elected president of the United States in 1789, campaigns consisted primarily of public speeches and written discourse published in the few newspapers and pamphlets that existed at the time. By the late 20th century, political campaigns had become big business, with candidates for federal office spending millions of dollars on multimedia advertising, sophisticated marketing, and extravagant public events staged across the nation.

In the 1970s, following the political scandals of the Watergate era, Congress passed the Federal Election Campaign Act to rein in the influence of money on electoral politics. The restrictions imposed by this law were soon challenged in court, with opponents claiming that, in politics, "money talks," and therefore any restrictions on money in politics amounted to a violation of the First Amendment freedom of speech. The Supreme Court partially agreed with this sentiment, holding in *Buckley v. Valeo* (1976) that most limits on how much a candidate could spend were unconstitutional, but that government could limit how much money an individual or group could give to a candidate or campaign. In 2002, Congress passed the Bipartisan Campaign Reform Act (BCRA) to ban "soft money" contributions (large sums of unregulated funds given to political parties). In 2003, the Supreme Court upheld its major provisions in *McConnell v. Federal Election Commission*. But in 2010, the Supreme Court reversed its position on part of this opinion in a way that would have major implications for the 2012 presidential election cycle.

In *Citizens United v. United States* (2010), the Court held that the government could not prohibit spending by corporations in candidate elections because this activity is protected by the First Amendment, effectively establishing that corporations are guaranteed some of the same rights as individuals under the Constitution. The lifting of these restrictions paved the way for the development of "SuperPACs," a term used to describe political action committees that can raise and spend unlimited sums of money from corporations, unions, associations, and individuals to advocate for or against political candidates, but cannot give directly to candidates themselves. By mid-2012, there were 538 SuperPACs that had raised more than $200 million and spent more than $100 million on the 2012 federal election cycle alone.

Proponents of SuperPACs and the Citizens United decision say that it has led to an increase in the amount and diversity of political speech. Opponents claim that it has only increased the influence of money on election outcomes and could lead to corruption. These critics are urging the Supreme Court to reconsider its decision in Citizens United by choosing to review a number of state cases that hinge on this ruling. At the core of all these cases is the fundamental question of whether the government's interest in preventing corruption in politics is outweighed by the First Amendment right to freedom of speech as expressed through financial contributions.

Supporters of campaign contribution and spending restrictions, like those struck down in the Citizens United case, believe that the government has a compelling interest in safeguarding the political process from corruption. They argue that campaign contributions should be restricted to help allow all viewpoints, regardless of their financial strength, to be heard and that corporations are not people who are guaranteed rights. These advocates contend that rich citizens and corporations should not have more say on election outcomes than those with less money do. By regulating

political contributions and spending, the government can create a level playing field on which all voices, not just those of well-funded special interests, can be heard. They believe the Supreme Court should take up this issue again, and rule differently this time, or that the Constitution should be amended to prohibit this type of activity.

Opponents of campaign finance laws applaud the Citizens United decision and claim that individuals should be allowed to participate freely in the political process without interference from government. Allowing individuals and corporations to give unlimited money to causes and candidates they support is consistent with the First Amendment and is not an inherently corrupt practice, they say. Freedom of speech is a fundamental right, which protects individuals and the corporations they create from laws that infringe on their ability to express their political opinions. Although the government has an interest in keeping politics free of corruption, this interest is not compelling enough to override a constitutional right, so these advocates believe the Supreme Court decision in Citizens United should stand.

Indefinite Detention. The attacks of September 11, 2001, caused the United States to completely overhaul its approach to dealing with suspected terrorists, sparking discussions about constitutional rights that are still being debated today. As national security, intelligence, and law enforcement officials began scouring the globe for al-Qaeda leaders and other terrorist suspects, the federal government struggled with how best to adhere to its constitutional principles while at the same time responding to a dangerous and fast-moving threat.

In 2002, the United States began moving captured suspected terrorists to a new detention and interrogation facility at the American naval base in Guantanamo Bay, Cuba. The severe methods used to question, detain, and try the individuals being held there soon became a controversial symbol of the war on terror and U.S. policies toward suspected terrorists. These suspects, labeled "enemy combatants," were subject to enhanced interrogation techniques that some called torture, and would eventually lead to an international outcry and calls for reform. In 2006, the Supreme Court ruled that these detainees were protected by international laws designed to protect prisoners of war, prompting Congress and the president to propose new laws to govern the treatment of these suspects.

Human rights activists in Los Angeles protest the treatment of suspected terrorists being held at the U.S. naval base in Guantanamo Bay, Cuba.

Later that year, Congress passed a law that specified how these suspects could be prosecuted and said that they should appear before military commissions, rather than courts of law, if they were accused of terrorist-like activities. In the name of national security, this law prevents individuals suspected of terrorism from exercising many of the constitutional rights afforded to criminal suspects in the United States. As a result, these suspects may be held indefinitely, without opportunity to challenge their detention, and may not be protected by certain procedural rights that traditional defendants are guaranteed. Initially President Obama, first as a candidate and later as president, said he would close the facility at Guantanamo and that he would move these cases to the U.S. criminal justice system. But in 2011 after a series of court rulings and political setbacks thwarted this approach, he announced that the military commissions would continue but with additional legal safeguards for the suspects. In 2012, the al-Qaeda leaders suspected of planning and executing the 9/11 hijackings were finally brought to trial before a long awaited and highly publicized military tribunal proceeding, highlighting the divide over whether these methods of prosecuting suspected terrorists are legal and fair.

Opponents of military tribunals and indefinite detention say both practices run afoul of the spirit of the Constitution and the rule of law. Even though it may turn out that many of these individuals committed heinous acts of war against American citizens, these critics believe that curtailing their rights only damages the United States and its reputation for being a country that treats all human beings with fairness. The argument that national security would be undermined if these suspects were tried in a traditional court has not been fully proven, they say, and regardless, the risk of undermining American values in the process is not worth it.

Proponents of the military tribunal system say that it is basically fair and that prosecuting suspects accused of terrorism requires different procedures tailored to the sensitive and dangerous nature of these situations. For example, they say, the transparency of criminal justice proceedings could allow intelligence secrets to be revealed, endangering military and law enforcement efforts. In addition, the ongoing nature of the terrorist threat, and the number of lives at stake, requires limitations on the rights of these suspects and in some cases warrants indefinite detention. These advocates believe that the procedures governing military tribunals and the treatment of enemy combatants are fair and appropriate to this serious situation.

OUTLOOK

The Constitution is a living document, amendable by the American people and interpreted by the courts. However, the modern era has posed challenges to defining Americans' rights that the framers could never have anticipated. The current debates over security at airports, campaign finance laws, and the treatment of suspected terrorists are rooted in Americans' differing interpretations of what rights the Constitution does and does not protect and to whom they should be applied.

THE DEBATE: CONSTITUTIONAL ISSUES

Airport security screening measures are an unreasonable violation of privacy.

PRO: Forcing all airline passengers to endure invasive body scans or embarrassing pat-downs by TSA officers is unreasonable and a violation of the Fourth Amendment. Individuals have a right to privacy and should only be screened in this way if there is some specific suspicion that they may be carrying dangerous materials onboard a flight.

CON: The government has an obligation to protect all airline passengers from the threat of a terrorist incident in the sky. It is not feasible to identify specific individuals for enhanced security screenings, so everyone should be subjected to the same techniques. The need to protect the flying public from terrorist activity outweighs any one person's right to privacy.

Corporations and individuals should not be allowed to spend unlimited amounts of money on political campaigns.

PRO: Money in politics is out of control. The First Amendment was not intended to protect corporations' ability to spend unlimited funds to influence elections, drowning out the voices of everyday people. The Supreme Court should reverse its decision in the Citizens United case and allow restrictions on corporate campaign spending, or else the Constitution should be amended to outlaw it.

CON: In politics, money equals speech. Since the First Amendment protects freedom of speech it also protects the rights of individuals and corporations to spend as much as they want to participate in the political process. The government's interest in preventing political corruption is outweighed by the free speech rights of individuals and corporations, therefore the Supreme Court ruling in the Citizens United case was rightly decided and should stand.

Limiting the legal rights of suspected terrorists is necessary to protect national security.

PRO: Individuals suspected of planning or committing terrorist acts against the United States should be treated as dangerous threats to national security. The U.S. criminal justice system is not the appropriate place to try these suspects nor should they be afforded the same rights as suspects of ordinary crimes. As long as military tribunals are conducted in a fair and impartial manner, then the rule of law will be upheld.

CON: Ensuring that suspects of the most egregious crimes are guaranteed certain rights is the hallmark of the U.S. Constitution and the American way of life. To limit these rights, even in the name of national security, is to subvert the principles upon which this nation was founded. Using military tribunals, limiting suspects' procedural rights, and detaining them indefinitely is not what justice should look like in the United States.

CRIME AND DRUGS

INTRODUCTION

One of government's primary responsibilities is to provide for public safety and protect citizens from crimes. Because the Constitution divides authority between the federal and state governments, some crimes fall under federal jurisdiction whereas others are handled by states, counties, and cities.

KEY QUESTIONS

- Should marijuana be legalized?

- Should strict sentencing laws be maintained?

- Should the death penalty be abolished?

Fighting crime presents an enormous challenge to authorities because many people believe multiple economic and social factors contribute to crime. Consequently, policymakers disagree on where to focus crime-fighting resources. Some argue for more law enforcement and tougher punishments. Others call for combating underlying problems like poverty, unemployment, and splintered families.

Facing pervasive illegal drug use and a spike in violent crime in the 1980s, governments passed laws stiffening fines, mandating minimum jail sentences, and increasing funding for law enforcement and prisons. After peaking in 1992, violent crime rates have been steadily dropping, but illicit drug use, particularly of marijuana, has continued to rise. Furthermore, increased law enforcement efforts have led to increased incarceration. Today, one in 100 adults in the United States are in jail, the highest incarceration rate of any nation in the world.

Citizens and policymakers continue to debate crime-fighting strategies. Is it best for America to have so many of its people in jail—and to pay the costs for doing so? Are sentences, including the death penalty, fair and effective? What more can be done to reduce illegal drugs and problems surrounding their sale and use? Now that states and the federal government face tight budgets, many lawmakers are taking a renewed look at the costs and benefits of crime-fighting efforts.

BACKGROUND

Crime in America

Experts disagree on the causes of crime, but many cite poverty, drug abuse, lack of employment and education opportunities, weak or ineffectual law enforcement, and judicial practices that fail to rehabilitate convicted offenders or keep such criminals off the streets. Some experts blame easy access to firearms. Others contend that violent and explicit entertainment—like movies, music, and video games—lowers people's moral standards and fosters a more crime-prone culture.

The crime rate's continued decline has proven equally hard to explain. Between 2001 and 2010, the murder rate dropped 15 percent and the property crime rate fell nearly 20 percent. Many analysts were surprised because they normally expect crime to increase during hard economic times. Some experts attribute the ongoing drop in crime to improved law enforcement practices and stricter prison sentences. Others cite improved domestic violence protection or the aging population (because older people are less likely to commit homicide). Another factor is improved DNA testing procedures, which not only free the wrongly convicted, but also now increase the likelihood that law enforcement prosecutes the right person to begin with.

Despite progress, citizens and policymakers remain concerned about the crime rate, which is still high. In 2010, a violent crime was committed every 25 seconds. Mass shootings in schools and other public places in recent years have shocked and alarmed Americans. Gangs continue to become entrenched perpetrators of violence and property crimes. And Internet fraud like financial scams and identity theft—stealing personal information and using it to access bank accounts or make fraudulent purchases—is on the rise.

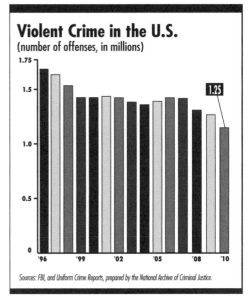

Violent Crime in the U.S.
(number of offenses, in millions)

Sources: FBI, and Uniform Crime Reports, prepared by the National Archive of Criminal Justice.

Illegal drug sales and use also remain a problem. In 2010, 22 million Americans aged 12 or older—nearly 9 percent of the population—reported using illegal drugs. Such drugs include marijuana, cocaine (including crack), heroin, methamphetamine, hallucinogens, inhalants, or prescription drugs used for illicit purposes. Although methamphetamine and cocaine use have dropped, marijuana and nonmedical prescription drug use have increased. According to U.S. government estimates, in 2007, the economic impact of illegal drug use on American society totaled more than $193 billion.

Combating Illegal Drugs. Drugs have long been considered a public safety problem in the United States. Beginning in the early 20th century, the federal government began efforts to criminalize the use of certain drugs that were found to be harmful or addictive. In 1914, the Harrison Narcotics Act outlawed certain narcotics and made it a crime to possess or sell them. In 1956, the Narcotics Control Act established fines and criminal sentences for possession of marijuana.

During the 1960s, social upheaval led to increased use of illegal drugs and widespread problems of addiction and drug-related crime. The federal government responded in 1973 by creating the Drug Enforcement Administration and launching "the War on Drugs," a coordinated effort to eliminate activity surrounding illegal controlled substances.

The problem of illegal drugs extends well beyond America's borders. Most of the illegal drugs sold and consumed in the United States are grown and produced elsewhere, and then smuggled into the country by land, sea, and air. The Mexican land border and the coastal border along the southern part of the United States are the most common entry points for illegal drugs. Drug organizations in Mexico and Central America are engaging in increasingly violent tactics that are claiming tens of thousands of lives south of the border. The United States has given billions in aid to countries in the region to help them fight drug cartels.

Back in the United States, although the illegal drug trade is often thought of as an urban, inner-city problem, high demand for drugs in the suburbs and rural areas have brought drug crimes to every part of America. In 2012, the federal government spent about $25 billion on this fight.

Crowded Prisons. Many people credit stricter prison sentencing and law enforcement efforts begun in the 1980s with reducing the crime rate. However, the approach created other problems. The United States now

imprisons 1 out of every 100 adults—that is 2.3 million people—and has the highest rate of incarceration of any nation in the world. In the last two decades, state spending on corrections has skyrocketed, making it the fastest growing budget item after Medicaid. The bill for federal, state, and local corrections comes to about $68 billion annually.

Between 1985 and 2005, the prison population in Texas, known for strict sentencing and law enforcement, jumped 300 percent. In 2005, the state started experimenting with sentencing reforms. It strengthened its probation system and enhanced community corrections approaches to keep low-level offenders out of prison. Crime rates have dropped and the reforms could save $2 billion.

Critics also point out that African American men are disproportionately repre-sented in prison, and some accuse the criminal justice system of racial bias. Pointing to the fact that more than half of all prisoners released are expected to be back in prison within three years, other critics contend that more must be done to rehabilitate prisoners.

Guns. Firearms—handguns, rifles, and shotguns—are the tools used in a majority of murders nationwide. That has made them a focal point in efforts to fight crime. In 2010, the U.S. Supreme Court ruled that the Second Amendment to the U.S. Constitution grants citizens the right to keep and bear arms. However, some Americans question whether the amendment was intended to protect Americans' rights to own any gun for any reason and whether in the interest of security, government is allowed to curtail this freedom.

Federal and state governments have made many attempts over the years to limit who can buy guns and how and where they can be purchased. The Gun Control Act of 1968 prohibited certain individuals, such as convicted felons, from possessing firearms. In 1993, the Brady Handgun Violence Prevention Act required the federal government to establish a background check system and mandated a five-day waiting period for anyone buying a handgun from a licensed dealer. In 1994, Congress banned the sale of certain types of assault weapons (for example, handguns that can automatically reload every time the trigger is pulled), but the law expired in 2004 and was not renewed. States have also attempted to limit the sale and use of guns but in 2010, the Supreme Court ruled in *McDonald v. City of Chicago* that state and local governments cannot curtail Americans' Second Amendment right to bear arms.

"STAND YOUR GROUND" LAWS

Gun rights supporters argue that firearms deter crime by serving as an essential tool for self-defense. Supporting that view, twenty-one states have passed "Stand Your Ground" legislation. These laws allow an individual to use deadly force in any public space without first trying to retreat if he or she believes force is necessary to prevent bodily harm or death. Under such statutes, individuals are typically  immune from criminal prosecution and civil lawsuits. "Stand Your Ground" laws came under national scrutiny after the March 2012 shooting death of Trayvon Martin in Sanford, Florida. The unarmed 17-year-old was shot by George Zimmerman, a neighborhood watch volunteer, who police did not immediately arrest because he claimed self-defense. The Martin shooting sparked nationwide protests, like the one pictured here, calling for Zimmerman to be charged. Critics argue that "Stand Your Ground" laws create a vigilante culture that encourages citizens to take the law into their own hands and allows them to commit violence without being held accountable. Supporters, however, say these laws prevent violent crime and allow victims to protect themselves from harm.

The American public is divided about the issue of gun control. Gun ownership and use have long played a prominent role in American history and culture, and Americans own hundreds of millions of handguns, rifles, and shotguns. According to a 2011 Gallup poll, forty-three percent of Americans favored making gun laws more strict whereas forty-four percent favored keeping them as they are now and eleven percent preferred less strict laws. Recent shootings, like the January 2011 rampage in Arizona, in which six people were killed and Congresswoman Gabrielle Giffords and thirteen others were injured, do not appear to have swayed more Americans or legislators to favor stricter gun laws.

Juvenile Crime. Increases in the number and severity of crimes committed by minors in the 1990s led many jurisdictions to adopt laws that enabled their justice system to treat young defendants (normally dealt with in a separate juvenile court system) as adults. A majority of states allow judges to transfer a juvenile to adult court if they believe the alleged crime or the juvenile's past history warrants it. However, as the juvenile crime rate began a steady decline along with rates of other types of crime, advocates for children began questioning whether treating young people as adults was the right thing to do. Their concerns were bolstered in part by two landmark Supreme Court decisions. In *Roper v. Simmons* (2005), the Supreme Court banned the death penalty for juveniles finding it an unconstitutional violation of the Eighth Amendment prohibition on "cruel and unusual punishment." In *Graham v. Florida* (2010), the Supreme Court expanded that idea and prohibited minors from being sentenced to life in prison without the possibility of parole for crimes that did not involve homicide.

CURRENT ISSUES

Legalizing Marijuana. Marijuana is the most widely used illegal drug, and nearly half of all nonviolent drug arrests are marijuana-related. According to the 2010 National Survey on Drug Use and Health, 17.4 million Americans aged 12 or older used marijuana at least once in the month prior to being surveyed, an increase over previous years. Many people perceive the drug as less harmful than other illegal drugs or even alcohol, and that may account for its continuing rise in usage among adults and teenagers.

Complicating matters is the fact that sixteen states and the District of Columbia allow the sale and use of small amounts of "medical marijuana"

AP PHOTO/ERIC RISBERG

In California, medical marijuana dispensaries like this one can sell small amounts of marijuana to adults with a doctor's prescription. Critics point to abuse of the system, noting that people without medical conditions can still easily obtain or purchase prescriptions. Legalization of marijuana would eliminate that problem, proponents say.

to adults with a doctor's prescription. Cancer patients and others suffering from chronic pain report quick and effective relief from marijuana without the side effects of more potent prescription painkillers. However, under federal law, the drug remains illegal. Federal authorities can still prosecute anyone who grows, sells, or possesses it, even if it is legal in his or her state.

In a 2011 Gallup poll, 50 percent of Americans said they believed the use of marijuana by adults should be made legal. In the 2012 elections, citizens in Washington state and Colorado will vote on resolutions making recreational use of marijuana legal in their states, which, if approved, would set up a further conflict with federal law. The growing perception of marijuana's safety and the disparities between state and federal law have added new impetus to the debate about whether marijuana should be legal nationwide for adult use.

The war on drugs simply is not working, particularly with regard to marijuana, say legalization proponents. Drug laws send too many people to jail for nonviolent offenses and have created a black market run by ruthlessly violent drug cartels based in Mexico and Central America. Law enforcement resources would be better spent arresting violent criminals and breaking up gangs than rounding up people for having an ounce of marijuana. Furthermore, proponents of legalization argue that marijuana is less harmful than alcohol and should be regulated and sold like alcohol. Legalization would make individuals safer by enabling government regulation of the quality and strength of the substance and by not forcing users to turn to the black market for purchases. Furthermore, legalization makes communities safer by reducing a driver of crime, eliminating the incentive to abuse medical marijuana privileges, keeping marijuana out of the hands of youth, and creating a new lucrative source of legal tax revenues.

The government must protect individuals and society from harmful, toxic substances, and that is why marijuana was outlawed in the first place, say opponents to legalization. Prevention and law enforcement work by reducing the amount of marijuana available and strongly discouraging its use. Marijuana use—and abuse and addiction problems—would skyrocket if it were legal, and young people would likely be harmed the most. People who use marijuana show reduced alertness as well as learning and memory problems. Easy access to marijuana would result in more accidents on roads and in workplaces, missed education opportunities, and lost productivity. Removing marijuana from the black market would not reduce gang crime because gangs would simply shift to other illegal drugs. The costs to

SHOULD ALL BULLYING BE CRIMINALIZED?

Bullying refers to repeated and aggressive physical or verbal behavior meant to threaten, harass, hurt, or embarrass a person. When this occurs using email, social media, or the Internet, it is often called cyberbullying. And the consequences can be deadly. In the last decade, several high-profile cases of teenage bullying have ended in young people committing suicide. Teenagers have been charged with bullying-related crimes, including invasion of privacy, stalking, criminal harassment, hate crimes (crimes motivated by racial, sexual, or other prejudice), and civil rights violations. In response to these crimes, forty-eight states and the District of Columbia now have bullying laws. Most of these laws direct schools to develop policies to prevent and protect students from bully-ing. In nine states, however, bullying now can result in criminal penalties of fines and jail time. One proposal before Congress would also make bullying a federal crime. Critics of criminalizing bullying argue that harassment, hate crimes, and other laws already exist to prosecute the worst offenders. Some also worry that determining where free speech crosses the line to bullying will rarely be clear-cut.

society for treatment and rehabilitation would far outweigh any savings in law enforcement or increased revenue from taxing sales.

Sentencing Reform. The number of Americans in prison has reached an all-time high. Federal prisons are 60 percent over capacity and more than half of these inmates are drug offenders. Many states also face prison overcrowding, in part to a major increase in the number of nonviolent drug offenders being thrown behind bars since the mid-1980s. Many current laws do not give options for sentencing someone to probation or rehabilitation instead of prison. Some require minimum sentences. Given the burden to the corrections system, as well as the social costs of having so many citizens locked up and saddled with prison records for life, more state and national policymakers are considering making prison sentencing more flexible. Proposals for sentencing reform include removing mandatory minimum sentences for nonviolent offenders; making more nonviolent offenders eligible for probation, rehabilitation, or early release; and encouraging compassionate releases of severely ill or elderly prisoners. Such proposals have led to debates over whether they will harm public safety.

The strict sentencing of criminals has worked, say proponents of tougher sentencing. The American people demanded a solution to rampant crime in the 1980s, and now they are safer than they have been in decades. Mandatory tough sentences ensure that people who break the law will be punished equally and severely. Locking up offenders prevents them from committing more crimes for a long period of time and deters other criminals. Furthermore, with stronger sentencing, victims of crime and people in formerly crime-ridden neighborhoods can rest assured that justice has been served. Locking up criminals also benefits the economy, because businesses can operate with less worry and lower costs for security.

Mass incarceration is a financial and social disaster, say advocates of large-scale sentencing reform. The states and the federal government are wasting taxpayer money jailing nonviolent offenders who pose no threat to society. Furthermore, this practice needlessly ruins lives and creates cycles of poverty. People with prison records often are discriminated against in hiring decisions, and they find themselves unable to vote or get help like food stamps. Spending resources on rehabilitation, work programs, and counseling better serves public safety by helping minor offenders become productive law-abiding members of society. Reform also allows corrections programs to focus resources where they are truly needed—keeping violent criminals locked up.

Reviewing Capital Punishment. The death penalty has been a legal form of punishment (mostly for crimes of murder) throughout most of U.S. history. However, in the case of *Furman v Georgia* (1972), the U.S. Supreme Court ruled that the death penalty was unconstitutional because its random and unguided administration represented "cruel and unusual punishment," which is prohibited under the Eighth Amendment. The Court later set guidelines for a constitutional implementation of the death penalty, and in 1976, reinstated capital punishment, saying that states had sufficiently revised their death penalty laws to uphold the Court's guidelines. Currently, thirty-four states and the federal government allow it, and a majority of Americans support its use.

However, in recent decades, the fairness of the death penalty has come under increased scrutiny, which has caused some states to prohibit it. In 2011, Illinois became the sixteenth state to ban capital punishment. In signing the bill passed by the legislature, Governor Pat Quinn—who previously supported the death penalty—said that it was impossible to create a capital punishment system free of mistakes. Illinois had been under a moratorium since 2000, when evidence emerged of improper trials with at least a dozen death row inmates wrongly condemned. Concerns about inaccuracies and the human and financial costs of the death penalty have

caused some former supporters to reconsider capital punishment—but has not lessened the fierceness of the debate.

Critics argue that imperfections in the U.S. legal system make it impossible for states and the federal government to administer the death penalty fairly, consistently, and accurately. The release of death row inmates exonerated by DNA test results or by findings of improper legal procedures raises serious concerns that innocent people have been put to death. That's something no moral and just society should ever tolerate, say anti-capital-punishment advocates. Opponents worry that the death penalty discriminates by race and geography, disproportionately falling on African Americans and people from the south. Furthermore, they point to evidence that suggests the death penalty fails to deter violent crime and costs more than twice as much as giving a criminal a life sentence.

Supporters of capital punishment argue that the Constitution clearly permits its use and states and the federal government should be able to impose the death penalty for the worst crimes. Capital punishment deters crime by sending a clear message that murder and serious federal crimes like espionage and treason will not be tolerated—and preserving this important tool is worth any increased costs of trying and convicting capital offenses. Advocates also believe that society owes family and friends of crime victims a sense of justice and closure and the death penalty achieves that restitution. Proponents contend that worries about uneven use of the death penalty are exaggerated, saying that as long as the punishment fits the individual crime, it is not unjust to give a death sentence. Finally, they argue that with today's DNA testing and all the appeals and protections available to death row inmates, the chances are remote that an innocent person would be executed.

OUTLOOK

Wary of changes that might jeopardize public safety or make them appear "soft on crime," many lawmakers have so far shied away from comprehensive reforms of the nation's criminal justice system. For the near future, changes will likely continue to be incremental and mostly at the state level as lawmakers address budget concerns as well as the opinions of their constituents on topics such as sentencing, guns, and marijuana use. Many experts believe that the gradual decline in the use of capital punishment is likely to continue. Despite popular support, more states are finding its application too costly and fraught with risks.

THE DEBATE: CRIME AND DRUGS

It should be legal for adults to possess and sell marijuana.

PRO: The war on marijuana is misguided. Marijuana is safer than alcohol and medically useful. Jailing people for possessing small quantities makes no sense, ruins lives, and wastes law enforcement resources that should be targeting violent criminals instead. Legalizing—and regulating and taxing—marijuana would make individuals and communities safer.

CON: Marijuana is a harmful, toxic substance that should remain illegal. The drug reduces alertness and causes learning and memory problems. Legalizing it would increase use as well as treatment and rehabilitation needs. Users would be more prone to traffic accidents and less productive at work and school. Legalization would do too great a harm to society.

Strict sentencing laws must be maintained.

PRO: Falling crime rates show that America's get-tough-on-crime approach works. Strict sentencing ensures equal and severe punishment, prevents lawbreakers from committing more crimes, and deters others. Strict sentencing also guarantees justice will be served. Going "soft" on crime makes society less safe and raises security costs on citizens and businesses.

CON: Mass incarceration comes with unsustainable financial and social costs. Long sentences for nonviolent offenders waste money and destroy lives. Flexible sentencing that allows for probation and rehabilitation reduces recidivism and overall crime rates. Reforms would enable corrections systems to focus on keeping violent, dangerous criminals locked up.

The death penalty should be abolished.

PRO: Capital punishment cannot be administered fairly and accurately. Therefore, as a just society, the United States must abolish it to avoid any risk of an innocent person being put to death. Furthermore, ending the death penalty—and the expensive process of trying, convicting, and executing death row prisoners—will save millions of dollars.

CON: The death penalty works. Even when it is not administered consistently across race, geography, and other factors, it remains a just punishment and vital deterrent for the worst crimes committed against law-abiding American men, women, and children. Today's DNA testing and appeals process make it almost impossible to execute an innocent person.

THE ECONOMY

INTRODUCTION

The state of the economy affects everyone. It governs how much money people earn, how much money they save, and what they can afford to buy. Consequently, the economy is an important issue to most Americans—and the one most likely to influence the way they vote. Economists measure growth in terms of wages, productivity, job creation, and the cost of living. These indicators show policymakers, investors, and the public the latest trends.

KEY QUESTIONS

- Should the government work to close the gap between the rich and poor?

- What is the best way to spur job creation?

- Should the government provide aid to ailing businesses?

In the fall of 2008, the world was hit by the worst economic recession since the Great Depression of the 1930s. Beginning in 2006, many areas of the United States saw a rapid decline in the once booming housing market. As interest rates—or the cost of borrowing money—rose, home values stagnated or decreased. Buyers who took on adjustable rate mortgages defaulted when their payments increased, many lost their homes to foreclosure, and loan companies nationwide declared bankruptcy.

By 2008, those losses hit investment banks that had bought the risky loans and soon some of the nation's oldest investment firms declared bankruptcy. As more banks went under, the shockwaves hit every part of the economy both here and abroad. The U.S. stock market lost more than 8,000 points in a two-year span. Businesses large and small cut back production and hiring and U.S. unemployment reached levels not seen in the last quarter century.

The fallout from the 2008 financial crisis continues. Policymakers disagree about what the federal government should do to ensure recovery. Some argue that tax cuts offer the best prospect of long-term economic growth and job creation. Others insist that the United States must do more to generate jobs and address rising income inequality. Finally, some say the government must take serious and painful steps to cut the deficit including eliminating aid to companies facing financial difficulties.

BACKGROUND

The Tools of Economic Policy

Government's Role. The American economy encompasses the production, distribution, and consumption of goods and services. U.S. lawmakers and economists often struggle to determine the best way to regulate the economy. When officials need to influence the economy, they use three major tools—fiscal policy, monetary policy, and trade policy.

Fiscal Policy. Congress and the president aim to promote steady economic growth, full employment, and stable prices through fiscal policy—the use of the federal government's taxing and spending powers. In addition to raising or lowering taxes, the government bolsters the economy by spending taxpayer dollars on specific programs—such as those that provide additional jobs—and on subsidies for important industries, like agriculture.

Monetary Policy. The federal government tries to promote steady growth without high levels of inflation or unemployment. It does so by controlling the amount of money in circulation. This function, called monetary policy, is entrusted to the Federal Reserve, the central bank of the United States. In 1913, Congress created the Federal Reserve, commonly called the Fed, to provide the nation with a safe, flexible, and stable financial system. The Fed issues U.S. currency and regulates short-term interest rates to banks.

Trade Policy. Trade—the exchange of goods and services among nations—typically increases a country's overall standard of living. Trade policy includes promoting exports, restricting imports when necessary, and pursuing agreements that boost trade benefits.

When Should the Federal Government Intervene?

The Framers of the Constitution devoted few words to the role of the government in the economy of the young nation. As the decades went by, some policymakers found it necessary to expand the federal government's role in the nation's economy, often in response to events such as wars, economic downturns, or concerns over poverty, health care, or jobs. Others, however, believed that the government should stay out of the economy and allow the market to determine prices, wages, and who wins and who loses in a capitalistic system.

Chairman Ben Bernanke and the Board of Governors of the Federal Reserve Board are charged with making U.S. monetary policy and regulating the flow of currency in the economy.

AP PHOTO/MANUEL BALCE CENETA, FILE

One side of the debate, popularized by British economist John Maynard Keynes in the 1930s, maintains that only the federal government has the resources to deal with big national problems like poverty or recessions. Keynesians believe that the federal government should increase demand for goods and services in an economy by cutting middle class taxes and raising government spending to create jobs and bolster ailing businesses. Pumping more money into a slumping economy will spur economic growth as people spend their newfound dollars, creating more demand for products and thus increasing production and jobs.

The other side of the debate professes that a large federal government role in the economy actually stifles growth by preventing the market from functioning naturally. This free market theory, popularized by Friedrich von Hayek, an Austrian economist writing at the same time as Keynes, states that the government should stay out of the economy and instead reduce regulation, cut taxes (especially to investors and businesses), and decrease federal spending on social programs. Businesses, with the help of new investors, will produce more goods, thus increasing demand and furthering production and the need for more jobs. According to this "supply side" theory, the proper role for the government during the current recession is to allow the economy to operate free from interference.

The Obama administration and the Republican leadership in Congress have sparred over competing ideas on how to strengthen the weak economic recovery from the 2007-09 recession. President Obama favors a certain level of government spending to boost hiring and support ailing industries —as evidenced by the government's role in the bailout of the auto industry and the 2009 economic stimulus package. Republican lawmakers have consistently opposed Obama's economic policies, arguing that the best way to foster economic growth is through limited government spending and tax cuts.

Measuring the Economy

Statistics form the heart of economics, providing a snapshot of the relative health of the economy. Consumers often make decisions about big purchases, such as homes and cars, when they feel secure about their jobs and the economy overall. Bankers use statistics to monitor the performance of American companies and other indicators to help them decide where and when to invest. This data also enables policymakers to steer the economy toward growth.

Inflation. Inflation is the continuing rise in prices for goods and services. The higher the rate of inflation, the faster prices go up. Unless accompanied by a comparable increase in wages, inflation lowers the standard of living. In other words, people can afford to buy less. Inflation particularly hurts people living on fixed incomes, such as retired Americans. A high rate of inflation also induces people to buy on credit and to forgo saving money. The economy suffers when individuals do not save because banks then have less money to lend for investments. Inflation has been low in recent years—between one and four percent since the early 1990s, and most recently, 2.7 percent in 2012.

The government can control inflation in a variety of ways, but the most common method is through monetary policy. The Federal Reserve Board can reduce, or tighten, the money supply by raising interest rates. When interest rates go up, consumer spending decreases, and prices level off or go down, thus reducing inflation. When the Fed reduces interest rates, it increases the money supply, and consumer spending increases.

Unemployment. The rate of unemployment refers to the percentage of men and women who want to work but cannot find jobs. Because there are always people between jobs, the unemployment rate is never zero. Many economists consider the economy to be at full employment when 4 percent or less of the employable population is looking for work. Traditionally, unemployment hits groups such as minorities, women, white males with limited education, and out-of-school teens harder than others.

Unemployment also affects federal, state, and local government treasuries. When men and women are out of work, they pay less or no taxes. As a result, the government acquires less revenue but has to pay out more in unemployment compensation and other social support services.

The average unemployment rate stayed steady for 2006 and 2007 at around 4.6 percent. The financial crisis of 2008, however, forced many businesses to lay off workers to avoid bankruptcy, and state and local governments have slashed more than half a million public sector jobs to close deficits. In October 2009, the unemployment rate hit 10.1 percent, the highest in 25 years, and gradually decreased to around 8 percent in mid-2012.

Recession. A recession is a period of economic decline marked by rising unemployment and reduced production, spending, and consumer demand. To stimulate economic growth and pull the economy out of a recession, the Fed can make more money available to banks for lending by lowering the interest rate it charges them. The government can combat recession through fiscal policies, such as funding programs to create jobs or reducing taxes to leave consumers and businesses with more cash to spend.

Historically, the U.S. economy has gone through cycles of recession and recovery. The most dramatic downturn began in 1929 when the stock market collapse led to the Great Depression of the 1930s. The financial crisis of 2008 has been described by some economists as the "Great Recession" because of its global reach and huge impact on so many facets of the economy.

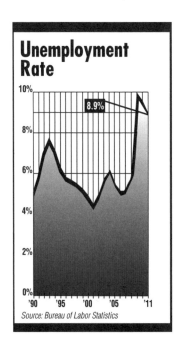

Unemployment Rate

Source: Bureau of Labor Statistics

Productivity. The rate of labor productivity refers to the amount of goods and services produced per person per hour. A rising rate of productivity usually leads to higher wages and profits and lower prices. Although high productivity and modernization are generally considered good for the economy, they can change the nature of the workforce and sometimes increase unemployment. For example, new machines and computers can reduce the need for workers, as does relocating a factory to another country with cheaper labor. U.S. business productivity remained flat for 2011, leading some policymakers to raise concerns about U.S. businesses losing ground to foreign competitors who can produce goods and services of higher quality for less cost to consumers.

International Interdependence. Increasing levels of trade among the world's nations has made them more interdependent than ever before. For example, as the world's largest importer, the United States creates jobs overseas. Similarly, the strength of the U.S. economy depends significantly on how well American products sell in foreign markets. Furthermore, the U.S. economy can be adversely affected by rising costs of certain imports, such as oil, a necessity to fuel transportation and industry.

The world's leading industrial nations meet annually at the Group of Eight (G-8) summit. The G-8 countries—Canada, France, Germany, Italy, Japan, Russia, the United Kingdom, and the United States—discuss trade agreements, unemployment problems, exchange rates, and economic difficulties, and try to develop cooperative solutions. As more nations became key players in the global economy, a larger Group of 20 (G-20) was formed in the late 1990s.

The Stock Market. People invest in the stock market by buying shares of ownership, called stocks, in companies. If businesses make profits, their stocks generally go up in value. In recent years, millions of working citizens began buying stocks through mutual investment funds and employer retirement plans—enabling more Americans to profit from the market's highs, but also making them more vulnerable to its lows. The Dow Jones Industrial Average (a measure of stock market activity and the performance of the 30 top companies in the United States) went from a record high of 14,000 in 2007 to 6,500 in 2009 due to the 2008 financial crisis. This huge loss of economic value prevented many companies from expanding, which in turn hurt production output and increased unemployment.

Recent Economic Developments

From Boom to Bust. From 1992 to 2000, the U.S. economy went through the largest expansion in postwar American history, fueled by technological innovation and the rising stock market. Many of the stocks that increased most in value in the 1990s were in the telecommunications and technology sectors—Internet, telephone, computer, and fiber-optics companies. However, many of these stock prices were based on projected rather than previously reported profits. By 2001, many projected profits failed to materialize, which caused the values of many technology stocks to plummet. Meanwhile, recession set in as retail sales and manufacturing decreased, and unemployment and bankruptcies increased.

THE OCCUPY MOVEMENT

Occupy Wall Street was a protest that began on September 17, 2011, in Zuccotti Park in New York's financial district. Activists gathered there to show their displeasure with the current state of the U.S. economy where 1 percent of the people control more than 30 percent of the wealth. Chanting "We are the 99 percent!" the protesters vowed to stay until their demands were met; among them: banking and financial institution reform, more jobs, a more equal distribution of income in the United States, and forgiveness of student loans. News of the protest spread via the media but also through social networks, YouTube, and the movement's own websites. Soon similar Occupy encampments sprang up in cities across the United States—from Washington, D.C., to Oakland, California, to Biloxi, Mississippi. The protest also spurred protest movements around the world in countries experiencing the same economic upheavals due to the global recession. Eventually, however, police and other authorities dispersed the protesters for health and safety reasons.

Throughout this period, the Fed tried to stimulate consumer and business spending by lowering interest rates thirteen consecutive times starting in 2001. The resulting low mortgage rates helped spur demand for housing and led to skyrocketing home prices in and around many cities. Between June 2004 and June 2006, the Fed raised the interest rate 16 times to discourage inflation. The increase in rates led to the bust of the housing "bubble" beginning in 2006, ushering in a period of devaluing home prices, mortgage foreclosures, and lender bankruptcies. By early 2008, many U.S. investment banks that had bought risky mortgages took billions of dollars in losses and made thousands of job cuts. These losses also meant banks had less money to lend, resulting in a "credit crunch" that made it hard for borrowers of all kinds to obtain loans for everything from new cars to factory expansion.

By the fall of 2008 some economists described the U.S. economy as in a "death spiral" and the government had to act quickly to prevent a disaster. Congress approved a $700 billion rescue package for ailing industries and the Fed freed up more than $900 billion for banks to lend to investors, as well as another $1.3 trillion in loans for businesses other than banks and investment firms. One month into his term as president, Barack Obama signed into law a $787 billion stimulus bill aimed at giving certain sectors of the U.S. economy, such as health care and energy, a financial shot in the arm. All of these programs dramatically increased U.S. budget deficits and led some to question the extent of government intervention in the economy. Others, however, believe that without these efforts the U.S. economy would have suffered even greater losses.

Tax Cuts. In 2001 and 2003, Congress passed $1.7 trillion in tax cuts at the urging of President George W. Bush. The 2001 legislation reduced income taxes, expanded retirement and savings programs, and repealed the estate tax. Those cuts were based on projected surpluses; however, the government began running deficits in 2002. Policymakers blamed the recession, the wars in Iraq and Afghanistan, increases in entitlement spending such as Medicare prescription drug benefits, and reduced tax revenues. The 2003 tax cuts — intended to help spur economic growth — further reduced income taxes and cut rates on capital gains and dividends. Most of these tax cuts were set to expire in 2011 but President Obama and Congress reached a deal in 2010 to extend the cuts until January 1, 2013. Although the president opposed reducing taxes for the wealthiest Americans, he agreed to the compromise to preserve middle class tax relief. Supporters argue that the tax cuts have contributed to increased consumer spending and business growth. However, detractors say that they overwhelmingly favor the richest Americans who have failed to invest their savings from the cuts back into the economy.

Traders on the floor of the New York Stock Exchange get ready for another day. Many people from all walks of life invest their savings in stocks through mutual funds and retirement accounts with their employers.

CURRENT ISSUES

Income Inequality. The United States has always been a country of rich and poor. But what has traditionally separated America from other nations is that in between the rich and poor lies a strong middle class whose values and hard work helped build this nation. Today, however, the middle class is disappearing as the gap between rich and poor widens. It is estimated that one percent of Americans own more than one-third of the nation's wealth while the remaining 99 percent controls the rest. And of that 99 percent, the bottom 50 percent possesses only 2.5 percent of the nation's wealth. Some say that this unequal distribution of wealth and income in the United States creates "two Americas" where those with the financial means can live in the best neighborhoods, send their children to the best schools, and maintain a comfortable lifestyle while the majority of Americans are shut out of any chance to move up the economic ladder due to their low starting point.

Many say that income inequality needs to be addressed by the government. These advocates point out that since 1980 more than 80 percent of the increases in income in the United States have gone to the top 1 percent. The main reason for this, they claim, are economic policies that favor the rich. These advocates want to see more government regulation of business to close corporate tax

According to current estimates, about one percent of Americans own about 33 percent of the nation's wealth. Many people took to the streets in the fall of 2011 to protest what they saw as an unequal distribution of income in the United States.

loopholes and stop unfair labor practices that shut out unions and collective bargaining agreements. They also want to see income redistributed through increased taxes on the wealthiest of Americans coupled with tax relief for the struggling middle class. Finally, those who advocate for increased government action believe that the poorest Americans suffer the most and call for not just an increase in the minimum wage but its replacement with a living wage, one that is high enough for an individual or a family to live on without further assistance from the government in the way of food stamps or other subsidies.

Others believe that free markets, and not the government, should determine income levels in a capitalist economy. Those supporting a free market approach point out that historically the gap between the rich and the poor widens and then compresses over time. On the contrary, they say, fewer government regulations are needed to encourage long-term economic growth over short-term gains in income equality. Further, supporters of the free market say that the real reason for income inequality in the United States is the loss of low-skilled, middle class jobs. As the U.S. economy has moved from one based on manufacturing to one based on information services and technology, a greater emphasis has been placed on a highly-educated, highly-skilled workforce. According to these individuals, the way to close the income gap is not by taxing the rich but through increased educational opportunities for all so that more Americans have marketable skills to offer to potential employers.

Job Creation. More than 13 million people are out of work and about an equal number are considered to be "underemployed"—working at jobs whose pay is below what their experience or skill level would bring in a healthier economy. During the Great Depression of the 1930s, when faced with even larger numbers of unemployed, the federal government created jobs through the Works Progress Administration, or WPA. Men and women built hospitals, paved roads, cleared trails in national parks, and even constructed monuments to past presidents in the nation's capital all in an effort to give workers a paycheck that they could use to pump more money back into the economy. Today, job creation by the government can be done more indirectly through tax cuts and other incentives.

One group believes that by cutting payroll taxes—the tax every employer pays for its workers that goes directly into the Social Security —trust fund—employers will have extra funds to hire more workers, thus reducing unemployment. This group believes that small businesses are the best target for this kind of incentive as they are more likely to use the funds to hire rather than absorb the tax savings as profit. In addition to tax cuts, this group also calls for further government spending in certain industries to stimulate economic growth and encourage more hiring. This group points to emerging industries such as bio-fuels, "green" energy (wind and solar power), and technology firms as places where government grants and loans can be used to spur job creation and provide future benefits for all citizens.

Others disagree. This group points out that payroll tax cuts and stimulus packages have a shelf life and eventually the money runs out. Without further government assistance, businesses will be forced to cut back and the jobs created under these programs will be lost again. These critics say that permanent tax cuts aimed at wealthier Americans is a better way for the government to create jobs. They point out that with more money to invest in businesses through stock purchases or by providing funds for start-up firms, the "1 percent" are not hurting the American economy but actually helping it. Companies can now expand—and hire more workers—with this new injection of cash. The way for the government to stimulate job growth, this group maintains, is not through a direct grant from the government to a few select firms but to let the market determine who will best benefit from the government's tax policies.

Government Aid to Ailing Industries. At the height of the recent financial crisis many businesses, some long established companies, went out of business. The investment firm Lehman Brothers declared bankruptcy in 2008 and Merrill Lynch and Bear Stearns, two other investment banks, were bought out by rivals. When AIG, the nation's largest insurance company, appeared to be teetering on the brink, the Fed stepped in and loaned it $85 billion to stay afloat. Soon the term "too big to fail" began to be heard in business and government circles—a company may be too large and employ too many people to be allowed to go out of business.

Some say that the government should provide aid to companies or entire industries that are experiencing hardships in these tough economic times. These individuals say that these firms truly are too big to fail in that they employ, in some cases, tens of thousands of people. If the government does not provide financial assistance to these firms, many people will lose their jobs and be forced to seek government aid in the form of unemployment insurance and subsidized public health and nutritional programs. In the end, individual assistance such as this may end up costing the government more than a bailout. In addition, the failure of large companies has a

Construction workers demanding more jobs in Minnesota stage a protest at the state capitol. Some question if it is the government's responsibility to create jobs or if the demands of the marketplace should determine who works and who does not.

ripple effect across the rest of the economy, affecting others businesses such as suppliers and customers. Supporters of these efforts point to the recent $25 billion government bailout of U.S. automakers General Motors and Chrysler as successful examples. As part of the bailout package both companies agreed to restructure their management organization and production systems. According to experts, nearly 1.5 million jobs were saved and both companies now report increased profits and have begun to hire more workers at their plants. In addition, both companies are paying back their government loans.

Others say that government loans to ailing companies ignore a basic economic principle in a capitalist system—in a competitive marketplace, some businesses are destined to succeed while others fail. There are probably good reasons why those companies are failing as well. These critics say that government loans to help prop up failing businesses actually promote bad business practices in that it was the mismanagement of the company that got it into trouble in the first place. They contend it is up to the company's mangers to correct their mistakes to survive and not the government's responsibility to save inefficient industries. These critics also question the entire too big to fail concept. How big is too big they question—100 employees? 500 employees? How does the government decide who gets

An assemble a van at a General Motors plant in Missouri. GM was able to stay alive through the recent recession only because of government loans totaling nearly $7 billion.

AP PHOTO/JEFF ROBERSON

a bailout and who does not? These critics point out the Lehman Brothers, a 150-year-old firm with thousands of employees around the globe, was allowed to go bankrupt but AIG, an equally large company, got billions of dollars in government assistance. Some fear that bailout decisions could be based on political factors (campaign contributions and high-pressured lobbying efforts, for example) rather than on real economic need.

OUTLOOK

The economic well-being of every American depends on robust economic growth, job opportunities for all, and a cadre of risk takers willing to invest in new businesses and technologies. As economic pain has spread since the 2008 financial crisis, the health of the U.S. economy is a major concern for every voter, politician, investor, and entrepreneur. With high unemployment still an issue, recovery from the recession has been slow. Policymakers are left with several choices to provide relief—extend tax cuts, provide aid to businesses that need help, or create jobs. But another choice is to allow the boom to bust to boom cycle of the economy play itself out.

THE DEBATE: THE ECONOMY

The government should work to close the gap between rich and poor in the United States.

PRO: Middle class wages have been flat for more than 20 years while the incomes of those in upper reaches of the economy have soared. It is time for the government to force businesses to recognize unions and give workers a greater share of profits, transform the minimum wage to a decent living wage, and increase taxes on the wealthiest Americans so that they pay their fair share.

CON: American capitalism is based on the concepts of competition and self-reliance. It is up to free market capitalism, not the government, to determine where opportunities will arise. The United States economy today is technology based and demands a highly-educated, highly-motivated workforce. The opportunities to get ahead are there for all who are willing to get an education and work hard and, in that way, close the income gap.

Tax cuts for small businesses help spur job creation in the U.S. economy.

PRO: Small businesses are the backbone of the American economy. The government can encourage job creation among small businesses through cuts in payroll taxes and loans and grants for new product research and development. Small businesses, unlike large corporations, have a greater desire to grow and one way they can do this is by having more cash on hand to hire more workers.

CON: Payroll tax incentives for small businesses eventually have to be repealed, which means business owners will still have to lay off people. Instead, make permanent tax cuts for investors and entrepreneurs who will use the savings to start new businesses and support the expansion of established companies. Jobs will be created where they are needed most without direct government interference.

The government should aid ailing businesses.

PRO: Without government bailouts thousands, perhaps millions, of people would lose their jobs. By keeping people employed, the government spurs overall economic growth since workers in these companies can continue to pump money into the economy. Some firms are simply too big to fail and need government assistance to prevent further joblessness.

CON: A company in need of government assistance is in trouble for a reason—bad management, risky investments, or a lack of innovation. Government bailouts of troubled companies encourage—even reward—bad business practices. The government should stay out of the investment business and let the market determine who wins and loses.

EDUCATION

INTRODUCTION

Today, American citizens tend to take for granted the idea of a free, government provided, public education system for all students from kindergarten through the twelfth grade. But that was not always the case.

Early on, Americans and their leaders believed parents should be responsible for teaching their children. The concept of universal public education evolved slowly, from religious elementary schools for boys only to today's large and comprehensive systems. Although states are primarily responsible for public education, federal involvement has steadily increased since the mid-twentieth century.

Today, Americans believe that a strong national education system is vital to U.S. competitiveness in a global economy. The Obama Administration's Race to the Top program provides grants to states that implement innovative programs to keep American schools competitive with those of other nations.

KEY QUESTIONS

- Should Congress reauthorize No Child Left Behind?

- Should the government work to make college more affordable for more students?

- Does standards-based education prepare U.S. students for the modern world?

Currently, nearly 50 million students attend public schools, including about 1.5 million students who attend charter schools, publicly funded schools that operate independently. More than 6 million students pay tuition to attend private schools, of which many are run by religious groups. More than 1.5 million students are schooled at home.

Despite many individual success stories, the state of U.S. public education is a controversial issue. Some believe schools provide students with an inferior education as reflected in international test scores where the United States ranks lower than many other nations. Others believe that schools are not failing and that the nation must continue to work toward guaranteeing that all students regardless of where they live or how they learn receive the best education possible. Amid these and other controversies the central question still remains—what is the best way to educate U.S. children for the challenges that await them?

BACKGROUND

Public Education in the United States

Public education in America started, ironically, in the home. The early colonists believed that individual families, churches, or peers were responsible for schooling young people. Once youngsters (usually only boys) learned a few Bible passages and basic arithmetic, however, it was back to the fields where they were most needed. It was not until the early 19th century that the idea of public schools took hold in the United States.

Horace Mann was made secretary of the newly created Massachusetts State Board of Education. In this position, Mann advocated for basic elementary schools (or common schools) for boys and girls. These schools would teach a common core curriculum and would be supported by taxes on property raised from the local community. Mann believed that all citizens had an obligation to pay for children to be educated, even if the children were not their own. As the editor of *The Common School Journal*, Mann spread his ideas from state to state. Soon, common schools could be found across the nation. For this reason, Horace Mann is sometimes referred to as "the father of American education."

Movement and Change. As the nation moved west, so did the idea of tax-supported public education. Surveyors in the Midwest designated sections of townships for public schools. Teachers' Colleges sprang up around the country specializing in the education and training of school teachers. Furthering ones education after elementary school soon became a necessity as the country grew and the economy expanded. Junior and senior high schools were soon commonplace in the United States. At the turn of the 20th century with a new wave of immigrants reaching America's shores, schools were seen as a way to "Americanize" the newcomers. The public school

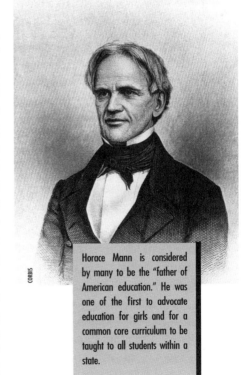

CORBIS

Horace Mann is considered by many to be the "father of American education." He was one of the first to advocate education for girls and for a common core curriculum to be taught to all students within a state.

system helped millions of immigrant children learn English and the skills necessary to succeed in their new country.

During this time, states and local communities took responsibility for running the schools, with local school districts determining programs of study, selecting books, and hiring teachers, while a state board of education distributed funds to local schools, set accreditation standards, and certified teachers. Thus, the concept of local control led to the establishment of a highly decentralized national public school system that remains today.

Public Education Evolves

School Desegregation. Funding for public schools has traditionally come from local property taxes. But local real estate taxes vary widely. Wealthy districts, in which land, homes, and buildings have a higher market value, take in more taxes and thus can afford more modern schools and higher teacher salaries than can districts with lower property values. Usually these economic differences followed racial lines with wealthier white districts having better schools than poorer black districts. A system of "separate but equal" schools developed over time, with the lines of separation drawn along the racial divide in the United States. Black students were often prevented from attending superior white schools even when those students lived in white districts.

In the landmark case of *Brown v. Board of Education of Topeka, Kansas* (1954), the U.S. Supreme Court ruled that "separate but equal was inherently unequal" and that racially segregated public schools were unconstitutional. Later court decisions ordered schools to desegregate. To comply, many school districts began busing students to schools outside their neighborhoods to bring together children of different races and ethnic backgrounds. But not all districts agreed with the Court's decision, resulting in protests, riots, and even some communities shutting down their schools rather than submit to court ordered busing. In some cases, federal troops were needed to ensure compliance and some state governments took control of local schools to make integration a reality.

The Great Society. In the 1960s, President Lyndon Johnson tried to address the problem of poverty through his Great Society programs. Among them, he proposed three new federal education programs, which became law with the Economic Opportunity Act (1964), the Elementary and Secondary Education Act (1965), and the Higher Education Act (1965). Included in these laws were provisions funding Project Head Start for disadvantaged preschool-aged children and establishing college loan programs.

IDEA. In 1975, Congress passed the Education for All Handicapped Children Act, landmark legislation that extended civil rights protections to children with disabilities. Renamed the Individuals with Disabilities Act (IDEA) in 1990, the law calls for free and equal access to education through age 21 for students with disabilities (ranging from mild learning impairments to multiple physical handicaps). The law requires instruction to be in the "least restrictive environment" possible, preferably in classrooms alongside students without disabilities. Today the law governs how state and public agencies provide education services to more than 6.5 million infants, toddlers, and school-aged children with disabilities.

Many school districts across the United States used busing as the major means of desegregating schools after the 1954 Supreme Court decision in *Brown v. Board of Education of Topeka, Kansas*, ordered schools to integrate with "all deliberate speed."

Bilingual Education. In 1968, Congress passed what became known as the Bilingual Education Act. That law encouraged states to create programs to teach English to nonnative speakers, sparking an expansion of bilingual education in which students receive native language instruction in their main subjects while also learning English.

School Reform

A Nation at Risk. In 1980, Ronald Reagan ran for president vowing to shut down the U.S. Department of Education, which had been in existence in one form or another since 1867 to provide support for states and local communities as they built their fledging school systems and later to act as a clearinghouse for research in teaching and learning. Reagan believed that the federal government should stay out of education and leave schools and schooling to the states.

After the election, Reagan's Secretary of Education, Terrel Bell, was given the task of shutting down the cabinet department. Bell decided first to study the condition of America's schools before he pulled the federal government out of the education business. He established a blue ribbon panel to travel the country to see firsthand how schools were faring. In 1983, the National Commission on Excellence in Education issued its report titled *A Nation At Risk*. In a blistering attack on U.S. public education the report spoke of a "rising tide of mediocrity" in the nation's schools and stated that if an "unfriendly foreign power had attempted to impose on America the mediocre educational performance that exists today, we might well have viewed it as an act of war." The report called for increased high school graduation requirements, longer school days and school years, greater teacher accountability, and an increased (not decreased) role for the federal government in education.

A Nation At Risk was a watershed document, sending shockwaves across the nation and starting what has become known as the school reform movement. In the nearly 30 years since *A Nation At Risk*, presidents, governors, mayors, and countless education experts have implemented hundreds of reform efforts.

Currently, nearly 50 million students attend public schools, including about 1.5 million students who attend charter schools.

School Choice. Traditionally, public school students could only attend a public school in their neighborhood. Arguing that such a system

confined some students to failing schools, policymakers and advocates began proposing school choice programs. In these programs, parents receive a state or federal government grant to help them pay for their children's education at private schools of their choosing. Despite some public misgivings and occasional court challenges, major voucher programs exist in jurisdictions such as Arizona, Maine, and Washington, D.C.

Charter Schools. Since the 1990s, charter schools have been favored by some reformers despite the protests of public school advocates and others. Nonprofit groups or for-profit companies run the schools, which are free from school board regulation and other rules governing traditional public schools. Currently, about 5,600 charter schools exist in forty states and Washington, D.C., and serve about 2 million students.

No Child Left Behind. Despite some successes of the school reform movement, in the years since *A Nation At Risk* U.S. student test scores have remained relatively flat. In 2001, President George W. Bush proposed, and Congress passed with bipartisan support, the No Child Left Behind Act (NCLB), a sweeping reauthorization of the 1965 Elementary and Secondary Education Act.

NCLB aims to close achievement gaps among students from different ethnic and socioeconomic backgrounds, as well as among those with special needs or learning disabilities. Among its requirements, NCLB mandates that states test students annually in reading and mathematics from third grade through eighth grade and at least once in high school. States are required to create and administer tests, revise teaching strategies, offer tutoring programs, and more. Federal funding is tied to the results and states that do not adhere to the law's requirements risk losing those federal dollars.

NCLB also requires all states to have a highly qualified teacher in every classroom. In most states, to be highly qualified, a teacher must have a college degree, a state license, and competency in subjects taught. According to the U.S. Department of Education, about 97 percent of core academic classes were taught by highly qualified teachers in 2010. As most states, however, have instituted different versions of what constitutes a "qualified" teacher, some question the validity of such statistics.

While lauding the law's goals, increasing numbers of people are criticizing aspects of NCLB and its implementation. Congress must weigh

AP PHOTO/TED ANDRESKI

Secretary of Education Arne Duncan has said that No Child Left Behind "is broken." One of the fixes he and the Obama Administration have suggested is to give states the option of being released from having to meet yearly gains in test scores in exchange for additional reform programs.

these and other concerns as it continues to debate reauthorizing NCLB in the coming year.

CURRENT ISSUES

The Future of NCLB. Under NCLB requirements, each state develops its own curriculum and annual tests in mathematics and reading. NCLB holds states and schools accountable for their students' scores on those annual tests. Schools that do not show adequate yearly progress for all groups of students risk being labeled as failing. NCLB requires all public schools in all fifty states to have a 100 percent passing rate by 2014. The rigid accountability requirements and harsh punishments for not meeting those requirements, from the loss of federal education funds to the closing of failing schools, have been unpopular with many parents, educators, school administrators, and legislators.

Some say that after more than 10 years it is time to scrap NCLB and declare it a failure. These opponents argue that the current law forces schools and teachers to overemphasize test preparation and rote learning at the expense of critical thinking and problem solving skills and the study of other subjects like history, geography, and the arts. They point out that the law's strict testing requirements leads to mislabeling schools as failing or at-risk, when, in fact, they offer strong overall programs that are suited to the needs and abilities of their students, not a national standard. In addition, critics see NCLB as an unwanted federal intrusion into a policy area that has, for hundreds of years, been solely a local concern—the education of children within a state. Opponents believe that local citizens elected to local school boards are in the best position to decide what their children should learn.

Those who support NCLB point out that in the nearly 30 years since *A Nation at Risk,* reform efforts led by the states failed to improve education in the United States. Although proponents say there is still much work to be done, they point out that due to NCLB, test scores for most states have risen, competent teachers are in the classrooms, and all 50 states have developed and implemented standards of instruction for all core subjects taught in public schools. Also, supporters of NCLB claim it is a valuable tool for state education evaluators and parents because test scores clearly show how schools are performing on the two most fundamental subject areas for students' future success—mathematics and reading. Reading and math tests offer a uniform and objective measuring stick, they assert, that allows valid comparisons from school to school. Furthermore, the law's supporters contend that using the current strict measures prevents schools from falling back on past practices of hiding the lagging progress of low-performing students.

Increasing Federal Student Loans. For many years, college was only an option for the privileged few. Most people who graduated from high school immediately entered the work force or received special training for a particular job or career. But today, in a highly competitive economy, a college degree is seen as an essential way to "get ahead." For many people the cost of a college education is soaring out of reach. The average yearly cost to attend a public university in the United States is about $20,000 and for a private university it jumps to over $35,000. While most Americans would agree that making college affordable and accessible for everyone is worthy, the way to reach that goal is highly debatable.

President Obama has set a goal of America having the highest proportion of college graduates in the world by 2020. The United States currently ranks twelfth out of 36 developed nations. One way to achieve this goal is to make college more affordable to a greater number of people

Standardized testing has increased significantly in the last 10 years.

by investing more money in federal student loan and grant programs. Supporters of this plan say that it will give help where assistance is needed the most by providing the financial means most individuals need to attend college. In addition, career switchers in their middle years will also have the opportunity to explore new avenues for training and future employment at institutions of higher learning without such a career move financially hurting them to a great degree. Supporters say that in a time when there is a demand for highly trained, highly skilled workers, a college-educated workforce here at home means fewer jobs will be shipped overseas. Increasing student loans now, they say, will aid America's economic growth in the future.

Those who oppose increasing federal student loans are not averse to lowering college education costs. They believe, however, this goes about it the wrong way. Some say that increasing student loans and federal grants actually *increases* tuition costs for everyone. They point out that most universities know that many of their students receive federally backed financial aid. According to these critics, every time the government increases student loans, universities inevitably raise tuition rates to match the hikes in federal funding. What is needed, these opponents claim, is not more federal dollars but fewer. With decreased student loans available, fewer students will be able to attend college and as universities see a decline in their enrollment levels they will be forced to reduce tuition.

Standards-Based Education. Some say that NCLB, with its emphasis on a standards-based curriculum that varies from state to state and students taking high-stakes tests based on those standards, forces many teachers to "teach to the test." Critics argue that this approach robs educators of their creativity, preventing them from trying new teaching methods that incorporate the kind of technology that students will face once they graduate. If a surgeon from 100 years ago was brought forward to the present day he would be lost in a modern operating room filled with light, assistants, and the latest medical equipment. A teacher from the same time period would find a current classroom very familiar. Once she got used to seeing a diverse student body and a few other modern conveniences she would find that schools have changed very little—students sitting at desks, a single teacher at the front of the room, textbooks, and tests would not be strange to her.

Many experts say that the way to reform education is to change what teachers teach. Educators should allow students more freedom to explore real world issues outside of the classroom, using technology to join forces with their peers around the country and the world to find common solutions to common problems. Furthermore, many experts believe schools should foster creative and constructive thinking rather than simple memorization of facts for a multiple-choice test that determines the success or failure of a teacher and a school.

Proponents of curriculum standards claim that an unfocused curriculum is what got the United States into the educational mess it finds itself in today. These people say that education in the United States during the 1960s and '70s was a time of experimentation such as open classrooms, experiential education, and wide ranging course choices at the high school

DAVE GRANLUND © www.davegranlund.com

IN SCHOOL AND IN DEBT—FOR A LIFETIME?

A senior in high school today has seen the cost of going to a four-year college double in his or her lifetime. It is estimated that 2 out of 3 college students today will have on average $19,000 in debt once they graduate. Currently, more than $1 trillion is owed for student loans, exceeding national credit card debt for the first time in history. And most college graduates have a hard time paying off their loans due to a tight job market that force many of them to take lower-paying jobs than their degree might otherwise guarantee. For many Americans, college debts follows them throughout their lives. A recent study showed that Americans 60 years old and older owed more than $36 billion in unpaid student loans.

level. Without a standard curriculum and benchmarks for students and teachers to follow, teachers could teach what they wanted with little or no consequences. These critics believe that a high school diploma did not guarantee a true K-12 education during this time.

By holding teachers accountable, these proponents say, school systems are better able to not only ensure that a well-designed curriculum is being taught but that the students are learning it. Standards supporters state that teachers are still able to be creative in the classroom as long as what they teach are the standards themselves. They also claim that students armed with the basic skills and knowledge base found in state standards are better equipped to face the future than were their nonstandards-taught counterparts.

OUTLOOK

Education policy involves many complex issues. A major concern continues to be fairness and equity and how education might be a tool for giving everyone, regardless of background, a chance to succeed. Policymakers are also looking beyond America's borders, thinking about how to prepare American students to compete with highly educated peers abroad for the best jobs in the global economy.

THE DEBATE: EDUCATION

No Child Left Behind should be reauthorized.

PRO: NCLB is closing the achievement gap because for the first time, it offers parents and policymakers a uniform measuring stick for assessing students' progress. Eliminating the program now would throw out a decade of steady improvement in the nation's schools. On the contrary, instead of abolishing or softening the law a better change would be to strengthen the measuring sticks by developing national standards and tests.

CON: NCLB has failed. In the race to get 100 percent of students passing standardized tests we have forgotten what education is all about. The joy of learning and the excitement of discovery have been replaced by the daily grind of rote memorization and countless practice tests. It is time to abolish NCLB and return the control of schools and curriculum to local communities.

The government should make college more affordable.

PRO: A college education ensures success for the individual and the nation. But the cost of a college education is out of reach for many potential students. Increasing the amount of money the government provides for student loans and grants will reduce these costs and college will become affordable for all who wish to attend. While the investment may be high today, the pay off will be in higher paying jobs for U.S. workers and robust economic growth for years to come.

CON: A college education should not be subsidized by the federal government. There are other ways to bring down costs than spending taxpayer dollars on student loans and grants. It is a fact that universities will increase tuition rates if they know the federal government is going to "foot the bill." The way to decrease tuition is to help only those students in true financial need and not everyone who wants to go to college. Tuition will fall when student enrollments drop.

Standards-based education helps students succeed in the modern world.

PRO: Standards-based education models give teachers the necessary tools and benchmarks they need to meet each year to help their students succeed and prepare them for the 21st century. The basic knowledge and skills in reading and math that students gain from this curricular model gives them a solid foundation from which to pursue further and deeper study that will allow them to stay competitive with the rest of the world.

CON: "Teaching to the test" is undermining U.S. education. A system based on a strict set of standards is usurping the creativity and innovation out of teaching and learning. The world has moved on and K-12 education must do the same. Preparing students for the 21st century requires courses and content anchored in today's world and a focus on constructive and creative thinking.

ENERGY

INTRODUCTION

Without energy, everything would literally come to a halt, from cars to factories to the lights that shine in millions of homes and businesses. For the United States, access to affordable sources of energy is a constant source of concern. Americans make up only five percent of the world's population, yet consume 20 percent of its energy. And while the United States produces a disproportionate amount of the world's goods and services, much of its energy comes from overseas, making the country vulnerable to outside powers. In addition, more than 80 percent of our power needs are met by burning fossil fuels—oil, coal, and natural gas— which emit carbon and contribute to global climate change.

KEY QUESTIONS

- Should fracking be greatly expanded?

- Should the United States invest more in renewable energy?

- Should the United States again begin building nuclear power plants?

Until the late 1950s, the United States was largely self-sufficient, producing almost all of the energy it needed. In the last 50 years, however, the gap between domestic production and consumption has widened. But new trends and practices may be moving the country in a different direction. New technologies, like hydraulic fracturing ("fracking") are dramatically increasing domestic output of oil and natural gas, which means that the United States is now supplying more of its own energy needs. At the same time, the country is looking to renewable sources of energy, like wind and solar, to help provide more power in the future. Nuclear energy also is making a comeback because it does not emit carbon and thus does not contribute to climate change.

But these new trends all raise important questions. For instance, while fracking has increased energy production and made the United States more energy self-sufficient, the practice also has contaminated drinking water and raised other environmental concerns. And although nuclear power does not produce carbon and thus does not contribute to climate change, it is not without its own unique risks. Finally, many believe renewable energy will never be affordable and reliable enough to provide more than a small fraction of the nation's energy needs.

BACKGROUND

The Pre-Petroleum World

During the 18th century, most Americans lived on farms and largely used firewood for heat and other energy needs. But by the early decades of the 19th century, the United States was becoming more urban and industrialized. Migration to the cities and the rise of factories brought with it a new source of energy: coal.

Coal ushered in the Industrial Age. In addition to heating homes and powering factories, coal helped to create a transportation revolution—both at sea (steamships) and on land (railroads). Firewood remained an important source of fuel, particularly in rural areas. Other sources of power—wind and water, whale and other animal oils, and even kerosene derived from petroleum—also played a role in providing energy to 19th-century Americans. As the century progressed, however, coal became the nation's dominant source of power, a position it would hold well into the 20th century.

But by the beginning of the 20th century, a new energy industry, one built around oil, was already taking shape. And within decades, oil would supplant coal as the most important source of energy in the United States and around the world.

The Emergence of the Oil Economy. Long before the modern oil industry was born, nations were using petroleum and petroleum products in everything from war to construction. The first modern oil wells and refineries were not built until the middle of the 19th century. At this time, oil was being refined into kerosene, which is largely burned to provide light and heat. The modern oil economy did not take off until the introduction of the automobile just before the turn of the 20th century. Unlike trains and steamships, cars needed oil to power their internal combustion engines. And with the growing popularity of automobiles came a growing need for refined petroleum.

While the extraction and refining of petroleum started in the 19th century, many historians contend that the modern oil industry came into being with the discovery in 1901 of an oil gusher at a field called "Spindletop," just outside the southeast Texas town of Beaumont. Soon Spindletop was producing 100,000 barrels of oil a day, much more than any field before it. The find led to the rapid development of many more oil

Oil gushes from a derrick at Spindletop Oil Field in 1901. The first major oil strike in Texas, Spindletop produced 800,000 barrels of oil in its first nine days.

fields, not just in Texas, but also in other states, including California, Colorado, and Oklahoma.

Within a decade of the Spindletop find, the United States was the world's largest oil producer. Around the same time (1913), Henry Ford began using the modern assembly line to mass-produce cars, making the automobile affordable for many, and eventually, most Americans. In addition to powering a growing number of cars, oil was increasingly being used to fuel ships, airplanes, and power plants. It also became an integral material in the production of plastics, fertilizers, and many other important materials and products. By 1940, oil had replaced coal as the world's primary source of power. During World War II, access to abundant oil supplies helped the allies (particularly the United States and the Soviet Union) produce and power the tanks, planes, and ships used to defeat the Axis powers (Germany, Italy, and Japan).

The End of American Dominance. After World War II, the United States and its western allies continued to dominate the oil industry. Seven major oil companies (five of which were American) called the "Seven Sisters" controlled over 80 percent of the world's oil production. But by the 1960s, the dynamic in the world's oil markets was shifting. Many countries in the developing world—such as Egypt, Nigeria and Saudi Arabia—were finding and developing large oil fields. Meanwhile, in the United States, oil production was peaking and oil imports were growing from roughly 10 percent of consumption in 1955 to 20 percent in 1965.

In 1968, Kuwait, Libya, and Saudi Arabia formed the Organization of Arab Petroleum Exporting Countries (OAPEC), with the aim of using its collective clout to better control the oil market. By 1973, OAPEC had grown to include 10 Arab countries and all but one of the biggest oil producers in the Middle East. That same year, the organization flexed its muscles—imposing an oil embargo on the United States in response to its support for Israel during the October 1973 "Yom Kippur" war between the Jewish state and the Arab countries of Egypt and Syria. While the embargo did not isolate Israel from the United States, it did prove to be a disaster for the U.S. economy. In a matter of months, the price of a barrel of oil quadrupled (from $3 to nearly $12), leading to huge price increases, rationing of gas, and shortages at the pump. Long lines of cars waiting hours at filling stations soon became the norm in American towns and cities and economic growth gave way to recession.

Although the OAPEC embargo ended six months after it began, it showed the United States how vulnerable it had become to overseas oil suppliers. That vulnerability would only grow as the United States imported an ever-larger share of its oil—from 25 percent in the early 1970s to 50 percent by the late 1990s.

At the same time, OAPEC—which soon spawned the Organization of Petroleum Exporting Countries (OPEC) in order to include non-Arab oil exporting states—would never again be unified enough to establish a major oil embargo. As a result, prices eventually began to fall. By the 1990s, American motorists were paying roughly the same price for gas (adjusted for inflation) as they had been before the 1973 embargo. However, in the last decade, oil prices have risen again—this time driven by increased demand, not from the United States and other Western countries, but from fast-growing developing nations, like Brazil, China, and India.

Energy Sources

The United States gets its energy from a diversity of sources, including hydroelectric, nuclear, and solar. However, its three primary sources of energy are petroleum (37 percent), natural gas (25 percent), and coal (21 percent). These three are called "fossil fuels" because they have been formed from the organic remains of prehistoric plants and animals. The burning of fossil fuels by humans is the largest source of emissions of carbon dioxide, which is one of the greenhouse gases that contribute to global warming.

Petroleum (Oil). In 2010, the United States imported less than 50 percent of the oil the country consumed—the first time that had happened in 13 years. Imports were highest from Canada, Mexico, Saudi Arabia, Venezuela, and Nigeria. In fact, the United States is the world's third largest producer of crude oil, with the biggest area of production around the Gulf of Mexico.

Long lines gather at the pumps during the Arab oil embargo of the 1970s.

After the oil embargo crisis of 1973–1974, the United States took steps to ensure it would always have oil reserves on hand. To address this issue, the federal government created the Strategic Petroleum Reserve—a series of underground facilities that hold up to a 160-day supply of oil.

Natural Gas. Natural gas, like the other two fossil fuels, is a nonrenewable resource. It takes thousands, possibly millions of years to create it, and it cannot be replaced. The estimated amount of natural gas has grown due to the success of new technologies in extracting natural gas from shale rock, found in more than 20 states. The shale gas boom in recent years is due largely to advances in technology related to hydraulic fracturing (fracking), which creates artificial fractures around well holes or bores.

Coal. Of the three fossil fuels, coal is the largest domestically-produced source of energy in the United States, generating about half of the country's electricity. U.S. coal reserves contain 12 times as much energy as all of the oil in Saudi Arabia. Coal is mined in 27 states, but can be found in other states as well.

Nuclear Energy (Fission). According to the U.S. Energy Information Administration, nuclear power supplies only 8.5 percent of America's total energy needs. However, many look to it as the answer to the country's greenhouse emissions problem because it produces no carbon emissions. Nuclear energy is the only noncarbon source that can supply what is known as base load energy—the constant minimum needed to run a household's most basic functions, such as refrigeration and lighting.

Renewable Energy Sources

Renewable energy sources in the United States account for eight percent of its energy supplies. These sources include hydroelectric, wind, geothermal (such as geysers and hot springs), solar, and biomass (biological material from living or recently living organisms; this would include forest waste or certain types of plants such as corn or sugar cane). These energy sources are called "renewable" because they are self-generating and cannot be depleted. One of the issues with renewable energy sources, such as wind and solar, is that they cannot meet baseload energy requirements because they only produce power when certain conditions are present (when it is windy) and thus do not offer a consistent supply of energy.

Nuclear Fusion. While nuclear fusion is still being developed, it could eventually produce enormous amounts of carbon-neutral energy and replace fossil fuels. Not to be confused with nuclear fission, which powers existing nuclear plants and does not occur in nature, nuclear fusion mimics the process by which the sun or other high-energy stars create heat and light. The raw materials needed for nuclear fusion—water and silicon—are plentiful and, unlike nuclear fission, fusion reactors do not produce any dangerous, long-lasting radioactive waste.

Changing Environmental Costs

Decline in Coal Use. The Energy Information Administration projects that U.S. coal consumption will fall in 2012 to its lowest level in more than 15 years. New tougher pollution regulations, aging coal-burning power plants, and the plentiful availability of cheap natural gas have lowered the demand for domestic coal, of which the United States has vast reserves, particularly in the Powder River Basin in Montana and Wyoming. Some speculate that U.S. coal producers will find other markets abroad, particularly China, which is a huge consumer of fossil fuels. Environmentalists point out that even as coal use in the United States continues to decline, American coal exports—which climbed from 60 million tons in 2009 to 100 million tons in 2011—will continue to contribute to global warming.

Carbon Emissions Rules. Another factor in the decline of coal use in the United States was the release of the Environmental Protection Agency's (EPA's) new carbon rules in 2012. Under the Clean Air Act, the EPA has the power to regulate greenhouse emissions if it decides that climate change poses a threat to public health. In March 2012 the agency did just that, unveiling the first federal standards to limit carbon gas emissions from electric power plants, the biggest source of climate pollution. Any new plant built in the United States can emit no more than 1,000 pounds of carbon dioxide per megawatt-hour. The rule only applies to new power plants, however, which means that hundreds of existing coal-fired power stations will be exempt.

New Fuel Efficiency Standards. International tensions and escalating oil prices have taken a toll at the gas pump, and at a time when Americans are still struggling in the aftermath of the 2007-09 recession. In 2012, Americans were paying upward of $4 for a gallon of gas at the pump.

In December 2007, Congress passed the first changes to U.S. fuel economy standards in nearly 20 years, raising standards for cars, SUVs, and pickups by about 40 percent—to 35 mpg by 2020. In April 2009, President Obama introduced even more aggressive U.S. fuel efficiency standards, requiring an average of 39 mpg for cars and 30 mpg for trucks by 2016.

And in July 2011, the administration announced its intentions to pursue the next phase in its national vehicle program, increasing fuel economy to 54.5 miles per gallon for cars and light-duty trucks by model year 2025.

But while environmentalists and even the 13 major automakers applaud the new standards, car dealers do not. Dealers believe that the new fuel economy rules would add $3,000 to the price of a new car by 2025 and would "price out millions of buyers from the new-car market," thereby endangering the auto industry's recent comeback. The National Automobile Dealers Association argues that fuel economy standards must be based on consumer demand, and not be an arbitrary number pulled out of the air.

But while coal is the focus of much recent regulation, natural gas has not entirely escaped scrutiny. In April 2012 the EPA issued its long-awaited fracking rules—regulations designed to curb air pollution caused by hydraulic fracturing. The new rules, which officials say could reduce harmful emissions from drilling by 95 percent, cover the period after drilling when natural gas is still venting but before it begins actual production. For now, drillers can flare or burn off the gas, but starting in 2015 they will lose that option and will have to begin collecting it.

CURRENT ISSUES

Fracking and Other New Technologies. Until recently, drilling went in one direction: straight down. Now, drills can snake in virtually any direction, opening areas that were previously impossible to reach with vertical drilling. Hydraulic fracturing or fracking, involves injecting water into rock formations, particularly shale, which releases oil and natural gas trapped in the rock. Largely as a result of these two new technologies, the production of oil in the United States has increased—from 7.6 million barrels a day in 2008 to almost 9 million barrels this year. Energy experts expect production to continue to climb—to 10.2 million barrels or more by 2020. These technologies have had an even greater impact on natural gas production. In the last few years, the amount of proven natural gas reserves has doubled, from one trillion to two trillion cubic meters. Meanwhile, the price of natural gas is only one-sixth of what it was at its 2009 peak.

Many in the oil and natural gas industries and others contend that fracking is turning the United States into an energy superpower. Not only is this new technology making energy cheaper for everyone, it is also ensuring that, in the future, the United States will not have to rely so heavily on foreign countries to supply its energy needs. New drilling also has brought tens of thousands of construction and engineering jobs to many areas, particularly in the industrial Midwest, hard hit by the 2008 recession. In addition, American manufacturers (particularly in energy intensive industries, such as steel and chemical production) have been bringing factories back from overseas to take advantage of cheap and plentiful natural gas.

But environmentalists say that fracking is already causing environmental damage in many of the areas where the practice is common. More specifically, they point out that lubricants and other chemicals used in the hydraulic fracturing process have seeped into, and in some cases, contaminated drinking water supplies. Meanwhile, above ground, fracking vents chemicals, like sulfur oxide and methane, which can cause respiratory and other health problems. And in some states, like Ohio and Oklahoma, scientists now think that fracking may have caused small earthquakes. Rather than further damaging the earth to extract more fossil fuels, they say, the United States should be investing more in renewable energy sources.

Renewable Energy. Creating a more viable renewable energy sector in the United States has been a cornerstone of President Obama's energy policy. Under his administration, the federal government has allocated tens of billions of dollars in loans and tax breaks to promote everything from the manufacture of wind turbines to the creation of solar power plants.

A hydraulic fracturing (fracking) operation in eastern Colorado. Fracking is dramatically increasing American oil and natural gas production, but is also prompting environmental concerns.

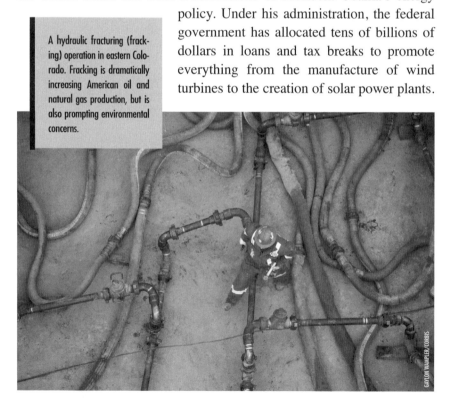

Part of the White House strategy is to nurture a vibrant "green" industrial sector in order to make the United States a leader in all of the major renewable energy technologies—be it the manufacture of electric cars that use no gasoline to new kinds of solar panels that capture more of the sun's energy than traditional photovoltaic cells.

The White House also has looked to protect fledgling industries from what they see as unfair foreign competition. In May, for example, the government slapped a 31 percent tariff on solar panels imported from China after U.S. solar manufacturers complained that the Chinese were dumping their panels on the American market at below cost in order to drive U.S. manufacturers out of business. Many environmentalists also propose a new national tax on oil, coal, and other carbon-based fossil fuels. This proposed carbon tax aims to encourage Americans to better conserve energy and to prompt them to consider renewable options, such as installing solar panels in their homes or purchasing an electric vehicle.

Promoters of renewable energy sources argue that government help for the nascent green energy industry is justified, because renewable sources are relatively new and tend to be more expensive than traditional energy products, such as oil and natural gas. That being said, it is just a matter of time before renewables become more affordable and can compete on price with oil and other fossil fuels without government support, they say. Still, advocates say if it takes another few years or even a decade of government help, it is in the nation's interest to promote green industries. They see a growing renewable power sector as a win-win for the country, as Americans shift away from imported, greenhouse gas–producing fossil fuels and, by doing so, help to create green jobs in industries that manufacture, supply, and install renewable technologies.

Many economists and promoters of fossil fuels, however, argue that for the foreseeable future, renewable energy cannot realistically provide more than a small fraction of the country's energy needs. Furthermore, they question whether many of these industries will ever be economically viable without government help. Indeed, they point out, some companies cannot survive even with significant government assistance. For instance, in September 2011, Solyndra, a solar cell maker that had received $528 million in government-backed loans, filed for bankruptcy. The company is one of a growing number of solar panel manufacturers to close down in the last two years. Funneling billions of taxpayer dollars into such uncompetitive industries is a wasteful and unnecessary use of scarce government resources, opponents say.

Wind turbines at the Horse Hollow Wind Energy Project in the gusty wind corridor of West Texas. Currently, wind power provides less than 1 percent of U.S. energy needs.

More Nuclear Power Facilities. In March 2011, Japan's Fukushima Daiichi nuclear power plant suffered meltdowns in a perfect storm of earthquake, tsunami, and equipment failure that led to massive radiation leakage, widespread contamination, and 160,000 displaced people. In the wake of the incident at Fukushima, the U.S. Nuclear Regulatory Commission (NRC) launched a review of American nuclear power plant safety, assigning a task force to conduct short- and long-term analyses of the lessons that could be learned from the situation in Japan. On March 12, 2012, the NRC issued new regulatory requirements for the nation's 104 operating nuclear reactors, including new rules governing how plants should respond to natural disasters like the one that felled Fukushima. American nuclear plants are required to promptly begin implementation of the safety enhancements and complete implementation by December 31, 2016.

Although nuclear reactors in the United States currently provide just under a tenth of the country's total energy and 19 percent of its electricity, no new nuclear reactor projects have been built in the United States since a 1979 accident at the Three Mile Island facility in Pennsylvania. Moreover, the Department of Energy projects that only six new plants will come online by 2035. On the other hand, President Obama publicly supports the continued development of new U.S. nuclear power facilities. And in February 2012, the NRC approved its first nuclear construction license in 35 years. The license gives Georgia Power permission to build two new nuclear reactors at their existing Vogtle nuclear plant in Waynesboro, Georgia, with the delivery of commercial power from the new units to begin by 2016.

Proponents of nuclear energy say that despite Fukushima and a number of other major incidents, nuclear power is safe. Indeed, they point out that in the United States, no deaths have ever been directly linked to nuclear power. Nuclear advocates also contend that it is critical to curbing greenhouse-gas emissions; instead it is the only major source of energy in the United States that does not emit carbon. In addition, uranium—the highly concentrated radioactive heavy metal whose atoms are fissioned to produce energy—is plentiful in the United States, so nuclear energy is viewed by many as a promising solution to the country's long-term energy needs.

Those who oppose nuclear energy say that major accidents at Fukushima, Chernobyl, and elsewhere show that nuclear energy is far from safe. As one protester in the United States recently said: "We should not build things that people cannot control." In addition to these concerns, critics charge that nuclear power does not make electricity cheaper, because nuclear power plants tend to be very expensive to build and safely maintain. Increasing nuclear power significantly would also not reduce U.S. reliance on imported oil, because nuclear power generally displaces other sources of electricity, which is largely generated by abundant coal and natural gas, rather than oil. And finally, nuclear waste produced by reactors remains toxic for centuries, making protecting and storing such material extremely expensive and very risky.

Japan's damaged Fukushima Power Plant on February 20, 2012, nearly a year after the nuclear meltdown in March 2011.

OUTLOOK

The development, more than a century ago, of oil and natural gas as primary sources of energy dramatically changed the way Americans lived, allowing them greater freedom and opportunity. Today, most people take for granted the energy that powers their cars or computers or that heats their homes. But the continued use of fossil fuels on such a large scale presents a host of environmental and other challenges—ranging from concerns about climate change to the growing ecological cost of using powerful new technologies to extract oil, gas, and other resources. It will take clear thinking as well as creative ideas if we are to continue to feed our hunger for energy without irreparably harming our planet.

THE DEBATE: ENERGY

The use of fracking should be greatly expanded.

PRO: These amazing technologies have already increased the country's production of oil and particularly natural gas. Natural gas prices are one-sixth of what they were a few years ago, providing consumers and businesses with a much-needed reduction in their energy costs. Using these new methods, the United States can lessen and even possibly end the nation's dependence on foreign sources of energy.

CON: The energy industry does not really know what effect these new methods will have on the environment. We already do know that hydraulic fracturing has resulted in cases of contaminated drinking water as well as increases in air pollution. And in some places, fracking has even caused small earthquakes. Instead of rushing headlong into another oil and gas boom, we should invest in long-term solutions.

The United States should invest more in renewable energy.

PRO: Renewable energy will eventually become more affordable and be able to compete with oil and other fossil fuels. Until then, however, government must continue to support these vital, burgeoning industries. Doing so will help move the country away from greenhouse gas-producing fossil fuels and create new "green" jobs.

CON: There are no real alternatives to oil, gas, and coal, nor will there be for the foreseeable future. Renewable energy cannot realistically provide more than a small fraction of the country's energy needs. Pouring more money into so-called green industries makes no sense because there is no evidence that they are economically viable.

The United States should once again begin building nuclear power plants.

PRO: Despite a few unfortunate accidents, nuclear energy is safe. Indeed, no one in the United States has been killed or even injured as a result of a nuclear accident. In addition, nuclear power produces no carbon and thus does not contribute to climate change. Finally, the United States has abundant supplies of uranium, which will allow us to provide fuel for widespread nuclear power generation for decades to come.

CON: Nuclear power should not be part of America's energy future. In addition to safety concerns, nuclear energy does not make sense economically. Power plants cost billions of dollars to build and operate and thus provide energy to consumers at a much higher cost than more traditional sources. Finally, nuclear power generates waste that will remain highly toxic for millennia and must be carefully and expensively stored.

HEALTH CARE

INTRODUCTION

The United States spends more than any other nation on medical treatment—more than $2.6 trillion in 2010, which is more than ten times what was spent in 1980. Health care spending now comprises almost one-fifth of the nation's economy. Most policymakers and citizens agree that these soaring medical costs have contributed to a crisis in the health care system. And many believe the fact that nearly 50 million Americans go without health insurance is simply unsustainable for the nation's economy, as well as a moral crisis for the country.

KEY QUESTIONS

- Should the federal government guarantee universal health care?

- Should the United States require health insurers to cover contraception?

- Should the United States enact a pay-for-performance system for medical care?

Many factors contribute to massive health care expenditures. The United States delivers health care primarily through a private health insurance system, which creates a level of administrative bureaucracy that consumes part of every health care dollar spent. A lack of systemic electronic medical records and a transient society means that treatments are often duplicated and diagnoses missed or delayed. Many patients often ask for—and receive—expensive tests and procedures, regardless of whether data suggests they will help. Scientific advances have made new life-saving medicine and treatments more available, but often at very high cost. The two major government-run health programs—Medicare and Medicaid—consume almost a quarter of the federal budget, yet are often run inefficiently. Doctors, who often prescribe excessive treatments or tests, also contribute to the high cost.

In March 2010, Congress passed and President Obama signed into law the Patient Protection and Affordable Care Act, a dramatic and controversial overhaul of the U.S. health care system. Even with the U.S. Supreme Court upholding its constitutionality in June 2012, the law is taking center-stage in the presidential campaign, guaranteeing that the argument over how to "fix" health care—and which of the many contributors is the most to blame—remains front and center in the national debate.

BACKGROUND

The U.S. Health Care System: 1900–Today

Among industrialized countries, the United States is almost alone in maintaining a system of health care that is primarily delivered through a private insurance system. This means that private health insurance companies act as middlemen between doctors and patients. Many of those covered by private health insurance obtain coverage through their employer, with whom they share the cost of coverage; others purchase it on their own.

The U.S. government estimates that approximately 50 million Americans do not have any insurance coverage. For those who are covered, out-of-pocket costs have been increasing dramatically in the form of higher premiums, co-pays, and deductible charges; health care spending now consumes close to 20 percent of the gross domestic product (GDP). Though health care spending is increasing around the world, other industrialized nations—including the United Kingdom, Germany, and New Zealand— spend only 6 to 10 percent of GDP on health care, and all report healthier populations than the United States.

Attempts to Make Health Care Accessible

Beginning in the early 1900s, U.S. policymakers began to recognize that many Americans were unable to afford the costs of doctors or hospital coverage. As early as 1912, some politicians, including Teddy Roosevelt, argued that the United States should have a national health care system, in which health care was made available to all citizens and paid for by tax dollars. Early objectors included associations of medical doctors, who argued such plans would compromise the quality of care delivered. Some employers began to offer private health care coverage as a job benefit. During the first half of the century, the increasingly important labor unions advocated for employer-sponsored coverage and helped grow the percentage of the population who received health care benefits through their employer. Though several U.S. presidents proposed national health care plans—including Republicans and Democrats—none was ever seriously considered by Congress and by 1951, almost 50 percent of the population had some sort of medical insurance.

However, that left a sizeable population of nonworking elderly and disabled Americans, as well as young children in poverty, without any

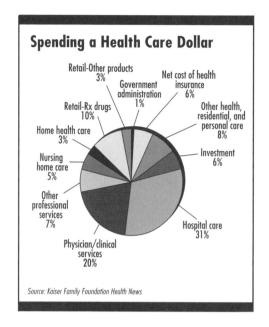

Spending a Health Care Dollar

Retail-Other products 3%
Government administration 1%
Net cost of health insurance 6%
Retail-Rx drugs 10%
Other health, residential, and personal care 8%
Home health care 3%
Investment 6%
Nursing home care 5%
Other professional services 7%
Hospital care 31%
Physician/clinical services 20%

Source: Kaiser Family Foundation Health News

access to health care. In 1965, Congress and President Lyndon Johnson created two new health care delivery systems— Medicare and Medicaid— to address this gap. Today, 49 million elderly Americans receive Medicare benefits and nearly 60 million poor or disabled people are enrolled in Medicaid and CHIP (the Children's Health Insurance Program).

Paying for Good Health

How Insurance Works. Private insurance companies and federal and state governments—not patients—actually write the checks for most health care services. In 2010, approximately 65 percent of American adults had some type of private health insurance, many through their employers. Commonly, workers pay monthly premiums (fees) to participate, and employers pay the additional costs to the insurance companies. Depending on the insurance plan, patients sometimes pay a deductible of hundreds or thousands of dollars before receiving benefits as well as a co-pay each time they visit the doctor. Self-employed workers must buy their own coverage and sometimes band together to receive group discounts.

Still, for most insured people, the total cost of premiums, co-pays, and deductibles is less than they would pay if they got ill and had to pay out-of-pocket for their care. Therein lies the mechanism on which health insurance operates: even though most people will not get significantly ill in any given year, their collective premium payments help pay the costs of those who do incur serious illness and costs. Insurance allows large groups of people to share the risk of contracting a serious and expensive disease or illness.

How Doctors and Hospitals Get Paid. Generally, insurers pay a percentage of the fees that doctors and hospitals charge. Until the 1990s, most insurers used an "after-the-fact, fee-for-service" payment policy. Under this system, hospitals and doctors submitted bills directly to insurance companies and were reimbursed for most of their charges. A system called "managed care" emerged after that, which uses a series of mechanisms intended to control costs and improve care. Although many Americans complained that managed care limited their choices, the system has been credited with controlling the increase in health care costs during the 1990s.

Government Programs

Medicare. Today, about 49 million elderly Americans receive Medicare benefits. One part of Medicare helps pay for hospital care. Medicare beneficiaries must first pay a certain amount—called a deductible—and then Medicare covers the remaining hospital expenses. Each working person in the United States pays a special payroll tax to fund this hospital insurance.

The second part of Medicare, supplemental medical insurance, covers 80 percent of doctors' fees, laboratory tests, and other medical expenses. Participation in this plan is optional and requires additional fees.

Medicaid. Medicaid is a joint federal-state program that helps about 60 million men, women, and children with low or no income pay for health care. The federal government matches state funds for Medicaid. Each state establishes its own eligibility requirements based on income and administers its own program.

PAYING FOR HEALTH CARE

For much of the recent past, patients who receive health care have not been the ones to pay the actual bills. Instead, most covered patients pay monthly or annual premiums to their health insurer, along with a co-pay at the time of service, and then health care providers bill insurance companies. Most analysts agree that this "after-the-fact" payment system results in a "cost screen," meaning that consumers rarely know in advance, if ever, the total costs involved in their medical care and treatment. Without this information, patients cannot comparison shop, and providers do not have to compete for patients by offering lower prices. Because third parties pay large portions of the bills, many policymakers assert that the health care industry has been able to raise prices above that which consumers, employers, and even the government can bear. New policy proposals aim to change this model.

Why Does Health Care Cost So Much?

Expensive Technology and Medication. The development of new technologies has also increased health care bills. New medical equipment is often expensive and requires highly trained and well-paid technicians to operate it effectively. Today, organ transplants are commonplace, dialysis is available for kidney failure, respirators keep people breathing when their lungs fail, and machines assist diseased hearts. Doctors go to great lengths to give patients the best treatment possible, but these efforts are costly.

Prescription drugs are another factor in rising health care bills. For the most part, drug companies fund the research and trials necessary to develop drugs and ensure their safety. Once these medications reach the market, pharmaceutical companies charge consumers hefty sums to offset research and development expenses.

An Older Population. America's older and retired population is increasing dramatically as the "baby boom" generation reaches their sixties. Each older American consumes nearly four times as much in health care services as a young adult. Because of Medicare, very few people over the age of 65 do not have health insurance. However, older Americans still have to pay monthly insurance premiums and a deductible before Medicare picks up the tab. Moreover, elderly men and women tend to use more costly prescription drugs than do younger people.

Personal Health and Patient Responsibility. According to the Centers for Disease Control and Prevention, more than one-third of American adults and more than 12 million American children living today are obese, which is broadly defined as having 20 percent or more body fat than an individual's ideal healthy body weight. Obesity is a serious condition, directly connected to chronic and frequently fatal illnesses such as heart disease, stroke, type 2 diabetes, and certain types of cancer. A 2012 study revealed that the annual medical costs incurred to treat ailments associated with obesity might be as high as $190 billion per year.

Emergency Services for the Ill and Uninsured. Experts estimate that care received in an emergency room costs three to four times as much as that received in a doctor's office or medical clinic. Yet most uninsured Americans wait to obtain medical services until they need emergency care—or they seek out care in an emergency setting because hospitals receiving federal

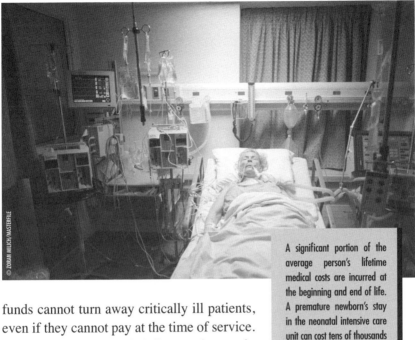

A significant portion of the average person's lifetime medical costs are incurred at the beginning and end of life. A premature newborn's stay in the neonatal intensive care unit can cost tens of thousands of dollars a week, while the life-prolonging drugs and devices used to keep many elderly people alive despite illness and advanced age can be extraordinarily expensive

funds cannot turn away critically ill patients, even if they cannot pay at the time of service. This leaves billions of dollars each year in uncompensated care provided by hospitals (estimates range from $35 billion to more than $50 billion) and those costs are passed onto taxpayers and the insured through what some call a hidden tax in the form of higher premiums, co-pays, and deductibles.

In addition, many uninsured patients do not receive any kind of health maintenance or illness prevention care and thus treatable or avoidable conditions, such as obesity and heart disease, go undiagnosed until they are severe. The Institute of Medicine estimates that 18,000 adults aged 25–64 die each year because of lack of insurance.

Improving the Health Care System

The question of what to do about health care—who should get it, how to pay for it, and what to do about government entitlement programs—is one of the longest-standing and divisive policy debates in the United States.

Expanding Coverage and Lowering Costs. Many Americans believe that there are far too many people without health care coverage. Washington

TRACKING HEALTH CARE "HOT SPOTS"

As more advanced software allows users to sift through massive mountains of data, medical professionals-cum-data analysts have begun tracking medical "hot spots." The term is borrowed from a successful crime-fighting strategy that used data to find high-crime pockets, times, and locations, and then directed key resources toward them, causing crime rates to drop dramatically. Medical "hot spotters" look for places or even particular patients whose extreme medical needs, excessive hospitalizations, and chronic illnesses cost the medical system hundreds of thousands of dollars annually. By identifying where these patients are coming from, say, a particular low-income community or elder-care facility, they can direct intensive medical and social services their way, providing preventative care, monitoring prescription drug compliance, and finding and addressing the social ills—such as poverty, hunger, illiteracy, mental illness, and others— that cause many expensive health problems. The work is labor intensive but early results from cities like Atlantic City, New Jersey, are demonstrating dramatic decreases in costs, proving that the majority of health care dollars are spent on a very small number of patients. Find and help those patients, say supporters, and you will cut costs and improve quality of life.

lawmakers have proposed a number of reform initiatives over the years. In 1993, President Bill Clinton and First Lady Hillary Rodham Clinton championed sweeping health care reform in the hope of achieving health care coverage for all Americans. However, the insurance and drug industries opposed the plan, and the initiative was defeated.

In 1997, Congress passed the Children's Health Insurance Program, the largest expansion of health insurance coverage to children since Medicaid. The program primarily offers insurance to children in families with modest incomes too great to qualify for Medicaid, but without enough money to afford private insurance. Like Medicaid, CHIP is jointly funded by federal and state governments, but the states administer the program within federal guidelines.

Medicare Part "D." In 2003, President George W. Bush and Congress passed an enhancement to Medicare called "Part D," which provides optional coverage for prescription drugs to help reduce out-of-pocket expenses for participants. However, this new benefit, which was left unfunded in the original law, has increased government Medicare expenditures significantly.

State-Level Reform Efforts. States have struggled to address the rising cost of health care and the lack of coverage. Most notable are Massachusetts and Vermont. In 2006 in Massachusetts, the Democratic-led state legislature passed and Republican Governor Mitt Romney signed the nation's first law requiring citizens to have health insurance or pay a penalty. Massachusetts residents must now have a minimum amount of health care coverage, either through an employer-sponsored plan or by purchasing insurance through private or public programs. Subsidies are offered to make sure that care is affordable for all. While many people nationwide support Massachusetts's insistence on an "individual mandate," others, including most Republicans and now Romney himself, say the program will cost far too much.

Tort Reform. Some people believe that abuse of the justice system with regard to medical lawsuits is a significant contributor to the high cost of health care in this country. Many lawmakers throughout the nation favor implementing "tort reforms," which put limits on the types of medical malpractice lawsuits that can be brought and cap the monetary rewards that can be won. Tort reform supporters believe that doctors currently pay

In 2011, Governor Peter Shumlin signed into law an act creating a path to a "single payer" health system for Vermont, the first state in the nation to do so. Proponents believe it will bring publicly-funded health care to every citizen. The law mandates the creation of a five-member board appointed by the governor to set payment rates for doctors and determine which benefits will be covered.

far too much in malpractice insurance fees, which end up being passed on to patients and cause doctors to leave the profession. And they say that doctors' fears of being sued force them to practice "defensive medicine" by ordering medically unnecessary tests to appease patients and shield themselves from any possible liability.

Collective Purchasing. Another cost-saving measure is the collective purchasing power of health insurance companies. Because they pay the actual bills for large numbers of individual patients, they are able to negotiate lower rates and fees with medical providers.

Encouraging Patient Wellness and Responsibility. Research shows that healthy living campaigns—which encourage good nutrition, exercise, and preventative care—are far better from a financial standpoint than is treating the many illnesses that result from unhealthy living down the road. Across the country, efforts to fight obesity are underway, such as New York City Mayor Michael Bloomberg's 2012 proposal to ban large, sugar-laden drinks from being sold in the city. Advocates say the government is well within its rights

Protesters opposed to the Affordable Care Act of 2010, which significantly reshaped the delivery and funding of health care in the United States, make their voices heard outside the U.S. Supreme Court. In 2012, by a 5-4 vote, the Court upheld the constitutionality of the law.

to pursue such measures, given the national crisis over the cost of medical care. Opponents, however, decry such "nanny state" interventions and say people must make their own choices about their health.

The Patient Protection and Affordable Care Act of 2010

Presidential candidate Barack Obama made health care reform a signature issue in the 2008 campaign and in March 2010, after a year filled with drama and contentious debate, Congress passed and the president signed into law the Patient Protection and Affordable Care Act—arguably the most sweeping changes to the U.S. health system in history. Most notable in the legislation, commonly referred to as the Affordable Care Act (ACA), were new rules requiring insurers to provide coverage regardless of preexisting conditions and to offer coverage for children up through age 26 on their parents' plans; the expansion of Medicaid to more people; new Medicare and Medicaid fee structures; and most significantly, a mandate that almost all Americans obtain health coverage—many with the help of government subsidies—or pay a penalty.

The new health care law passed Congress without a single Republican vote. Twenty-six states and several private organizations sued, claiming that the government had overstepped its powers by forcing citizens to purchase a particular product. Four lower appellate courts offered different rulings and in March 2012, the United States Supreme Court heard the case, emphasizing its significance by scheduling six hours of oral argument over three days and addressing several major points about the law. In June, the Court upheld the ACA, ruling that the mandate was authorized by Congress's power to levy taxes. The decision paved the way for the law to be implemented across the country, although opponents vowed to push for full repeal in Congress.

CURRENT ISSUES

Health Care: Right or Privilege? Though most everyone agrees that the current U.S. health care system is financially unsustainable and fails to consistently produce high quality care, there is much argument over how to improve it. At the most basic level, Americans disagree over whether access to health care is a "right"—and thus something to be guaranteed by government. Or is it a privilege—to be earned or purchased—but not an entitlement.

Those who believe that access to health care is a right argue that the government should guarantee that its citizens have health insurance coverage. Most of the developed world ensures this, say proponents, and it is an embarrassment and a shame that the United States has more than 50 million people who lack health insurance of any kind. Creating a system in which everyone is covered spreads the risks and the costs fairly among the entire population. Supporters of universal coverage also argue that eliminating the massive bureaucracy created by the current patchwork of private health care insurers, government-funded programs, and charity care administered by emergency rooms would reduce overall health care spending significantly. Moreover, advocates argue, guaranteeing access to health care means that Americans will avail themselves of it before they are in a health crisis, saving money across the board.

Many Americans believe, however, that health care is a privilege, not a right, and oppose government-sponsored universal coverage. While providing access to health care for as many people as possible is a laudable goal, taking care decisions out of the hands of doctors and placing them into the hands of government bureaucrats, which universal coverage would require, is a terrible trade-off. Under a government-run, universal care system, services will necessarily be rationed; access to the best care will be severely limited; and wait time for services will be long, sometimes fatally so. And if people believe that their care will be paid for by the government regardless, there will be no incentive to take care of their own health and doctors will be free to "over-provide" care, resulting in increased, not lowered, costs overall.

Covering Contraception. As various provisions of the landmark 2010 Affordable Care Act came into effect, fights emerged over contentious social issues. One notable hot-button debate has been about contraception (birth control) and whether or not all health insurance providers must cover its costs for their patients.

In February 2012, President Obama issued an order mandating that all employers must offer health insurance that covers the cost of contraception for their employees. A Center for Disease Control study revealed that between 2006–2008, 99 percent of American women who had ever had sexual intercourse had used at least one method of birth control. Scholars estimate that birth control use saves approximately $19 billion in direct medical costs each year. While some forms of contraception are available

THE POWER OF BIG PHARMA

Despite their prevalence on every TV station, website, and magazine cover in the United States, advertisements for prescription drugs are not seen in most parts of the world. In fact, Bangladesh, New Zealand, South Korea, and the United States are the only nations in the world that allow direct-to-consumer (DTC) advertising of pharmaceutical drugs. Advocates for DTC marketing, which has been legal in the United States since 1997, say it allows patients access to more information about potential treatments and to be better-informed about their health and its care. However, numerous critics believe the practice permits pharmaceutical companies to make unproven claims about the efficacy of their products and puts doctors in the awkward position of being petitioned by patients for drugs they might not have otherwise prescribed. Most European countries have much stricter rules on advertising that go well beyond pharmaceuticals, including proposed or enacted bans on gambling and tobacco advertising, and on any advertising aimed directly at children.

over-the-counter, many, including the birth control pill, require a doctor's authorization and a maintenance prescription. While widespread use of birth control drugs have reduced manufacturing and purchasing costs considerably over the years, a one-month supply of birth control pills still costs between $15-$50 and thus is a considerable and consistent health care cost for many women.

The ability to control one's reproductive system is a necessary—and constitutionally protected—right, say supporters of the contraception mandate. Imposing one's own religious views on all citizens by denying them contraceptive coverage is unconstitutional and endangers women's ability to ensure good health for themselves. People who want to use birth control but who work for organizations that oppose it should not be penalized. Proponents of the mandate also point out that the provision does not deal with abortion services at all; in fact, they say, allowing easier, cheaper access to birth control will likely reduce the number of abortions sought in this country. Besides, argue supporters, there is a clear exemption in place for religious organizations. Not a single church will be forced to pay for any contraceptive coverage, and by virtue of President Obama's accommodation, Catholic hospitals—which employ large numbers of non-

7:19 am

Sandra Fluke, a Georgetown University Law School student, testified before Congress in February 2012 about the need for Catholic schools to provide contraception services to their students. Her testimony received significant media attention, both positive and negative.

Catholic providers—will be able to ask their health insurance companies to cover the costs of the care instead of paying for it themselves.

Compelling organizations to pay for something they find morally objectionable is a complete violation of religious liberty, argue critics of the mandate. In particular, representatives of the Catholic Church say it is outrageous to require them to pay for birth control services—some of which are based on mechanisms that may actually induce abortions rather than prevent conception—when the Church specifically denounces the use of artificial birth control measures and opposes abortion of any kind. The government's ridiculous argument that the rule does not apply to church organizations but to their affiliated agencies such as hospitals—which would include hundreds of Catholic hospitals that routinely treat the poor—is a perfect example of why the government should not be in the business of making distinctions about what is and is not a religious organization. Instead of forcing people to disregard their most deeply held religious beliefs, Congress should be passing much stronger "conscience protection" laws.

Paying for Performance. A significant feature of the current U.S. health care system is that doctors and hospitals are paid for the volume of the care they provide, not its quality. Hospitals and providers generally bill insurance companies at pre-negotiated rates for the services they provide. For example, if a patient requires an emergency cardiac procedure and then contracts an infection while in the hospital, the hospital can bill the insurer (or the government, in the case of Medicare) twice—first for the cardiac treatment and second to resolve the infection.

Many researchers and policymakers propose that health care costs can be reduced while quality of care is increased if providers are encouraged to eliminate unnecessary treatments and work harder to ensure that patients either do not become sick or do not become sick again after treatment; in a nutshell, paying doctors for their performance. These advocates argue that paying doctors for the number of services they provide—not for healing patients—essentially makes patient recovery less desirable from a financial perspective. Other supporters contend that switching from a fee-for-service plan to a type of pay-for-performance mechanism called a "bundled" payment system—which pays a patient's care providers in concert for treating the patient as a whole—will encourage collaboration among the various doctors or hospitals that treat a patient, resulting in less duplication of services, faster and more effective treatment, and mitigation of the exorbitant costs that the sickest and most complex patients often incur. Supporters of such "outcomes-based medicine" cite estimates that such changes could reduce medical spending by up to 30 percent.

Discouraging doctors from using all the tools in their medical kit to combat illness by telling them they will not be paid if they do is a form of health care rationing and totally unacceptable, argue opponents. Besides hamstringing professionals, from a practical perspective if you start reducing fees to doctors and hospitals who treat very sick Medicare patients those doctors will refuse to treat those patients at all for fear of financial risk. Already, it is very hard for Medicare patients to find primary care doctors because reimbursement fees are so low. A much better way to reduce health care spending, say opponents, is to empower consumers with information and money to spend in an open market. Patients therefore will have "some skin in the game" and be encouraged to stay healthy and to shop for the best deals in medical care. Competition in the health care marketplace will then spur lower prices and better quality, as it has in so many other industries.

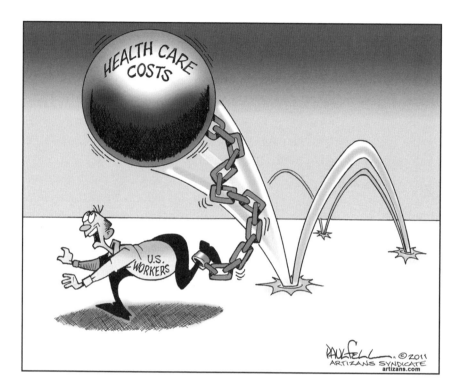

OUTLOOK

The U.S. health care system is a study in contrasts: it delivers some of the most cutting-edge, life-saving medicine in existence, yet fails to cover 50 million Americans. Aspiring doctors from all over the world vie to enroll in the United States renowned medical schools, yet spiraling costs and budget-busting entitlement programs mean that the U.S. system is literally unsustainable. Arguments over who should receive what services and who should pay the bills highlight key philosophical differences about the ways in which government should work and will continue to dominate national conversation for years to come.

THE DEBATE: HEALTH CARE

The United States should guarantee universal health care.

PRO: Health care is a right and the government must ensure that all citizens have access to it. Besides eliminating shameful health disparities between the rich and the poor, enacting universal coverage spreads the costs and risks among the entire population and encourages better health and less costly treatment for all by providing access to preventative care. Eliminating the current bloated, bureaucratic system would provide major cost savings as well.

CON: Health care is a privilege and government-run, universal health care is socialism. Enacting such a plan means that government bureaucrats will make decisions about health care, not trained professionals, and that health care will be rationed, resulting in lower quality care and longer lines to access it. If people have no incentive to care for themselves because they know the government will pay for whatever treatment they need, then costs will soar.

The United States should require health insurers to pay for contraception.

PRO: Requiring insurers to cover the cost of contraception means that women will get care that allows them to control their own physical—and economic—health. Imposing one's religious views on others by denying them access to care is discriminatory. And besides, religious organizations have been granted accommodations to help them meet the requirement without violating their own beliefs.

CON: Compelling religious organizations to purchase a product they find immoral is unconstitutional. Some types of birth control are actually abortion-causing, and others are in opposition to some religious teachings that condemn any artificial birth control measures. Instead of violating religious beliefs by forcing birth control on citizens, the government should be doing more to create and defend "conscience protection" laws.

Paying doctors for their performance will improve care and reduce costs.

PRO: Under the current system, there is no financial incentive to permanently heal patients or to concentrate on preventing illness in the first place, since care providers are paid based on the quantity of treatments they provide. Changing to a "bundled" or "outcomes-based" system draws on best practice research that demonstrates that costs go down when care is more effectively and efficiently managed and, more importantly, overall wellness goes up.

CON: The government should not be allowed to ration care, determining who gets what potentially life-saving treatment. These critical decisions should be left to doctors and their patients and should be a part of a free-market, competition-driven health insurance system. Besides, curtailing doctors' ability to treat patients as they see fit and paying them less to do more means many will choose not to provide care for the poor and elderly, or will leave the profession entirely.

IMMIGRATION

INTRODUCTION

The United States, a "nation of immigrants," has often welcomed new arrivals. Many people credit America's immigrant tradition with building the nation's economic superiority and cultural diversity. To serve the nation's best interests, the federal government creates policies to manage levels and patterns of immigration. These laws establish immigration limits, border security, visa (entry permit) rules, and citizenship requirements.

KEY QUESTIONS

- Should Congress pass the Dream Act?

- Should the federal government allow more immigration of skilled workers?

- Should the National Guard presence along the Mexican border be reduced?

Despite these rules, many people come to the United States illegally, sneaking over the border; using false documents to enter by land, air, or water; or staying in the United States longer than their visa allows. Most come in search of work and a better life or to join family already living in the United States. According to the Department of Homeland Security, 11.5 million people were living in the United States illegally in 2011. More than half are from Mexico.

Although illegal immigration rates leveled off the last couple of years, legal and illegal immigration continue to be contentious topics. In recent years, Congress passed legislation reinforcing the border but failed to pass comprehensive reform addressing needs for temporary workers and dealing with illegal residents. In the absence of federal solutions, state governments have passed their own, often very controversial, laws on illegal immigration.

In 2012, policymakers and citizens continued to argue about all aspects of immigration policy. Major debates included the "Dream Act" (and whether children brought illegally to the United States by their parents should ever be eligible for citizenship), whether to increase immigration limits on highly skilled immigrants, and reducing the presence of National Guard troops at the border.

BACKGROUND

A Nation of Immigrants

The United States was built by immigrants, many of whom were seeking a new life in a new land. That opportunity attracted many people, and at first, anyone could move to the United States. However, the swelling population prompted the federal government to begin making laws to control immigration and preserve the racial, religious, and cultural makeup of the United States. The first law was the Chinese Exclusion Act (1882), which suspended immigration from China for six years. After that, periodic quotas limited the number of entrants of certain nationalities, including Asians, Europeans from southern and eastern Europe, and Latin Americans. Today, U.S. law sets a limit on legal immigration to 675,000 people a year, with preference going to relatives of U.S. citizens as well as immigrants with desirable job skills. The federal government approves a separate limit for refugees.

Categories of Immigrants. U.S. immigration policy spells out which people can enter, how long they can stay, and whether or not they can apply for permanent residence or citizenship. The Department of Homeland Security implements most aspects of U.S. government immigration policy set forth by Congress and the White House, although the Department of State issues visas. There are several categories of immigrants.

Legal immigrants come to the United States seeking to establish permanent residence. They may choose to apply for permanent resident status (popularly known as "getting a green card"). These residents receive protection under U.S. law, but do not hold all the rights and responsibilities of U.S. citizens. Permanent residents may apply for U.S. citizenship after living in the country for five years, and a majority who apply become citizens.

Refugees and asylees come to the United States seeking protection from persecution in their home countries. The federal government limits the number of

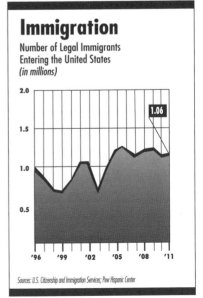

Immigration

Number of Legal Immigrants Entering the United States
(in millions)

1.06

Sources: U.S. Citizenship and Immigration Services; Pew Hispanic Center

asylees. After one year of U.S. residency, these immigrants can apply for permanent resident status.

Nonimmigrants enter and exit the country legally with temporary visas that specify the purpose and length of their visit. These men and women are typically foreign government officers, tourists, business people, or students. Nonimmigrant visas are also provided for temporary workers. Current temporary worker programs provide limited numbers of visas to technical or highly specialized workers and also nonagricultural laborers. Other categories include nurses, farm workers, athletes, artists, and entertainers.

Illegal or undocumented immigrants, by law, can be deported—forcibly returned to their home countries. About 60 percent of illegal immigrants enter the country by crossing a U.S. border illegally or by misrepresenting themselves. The other 40 percent enter the country legally but stay beyond the limits of their visas, or authorizations, to travel to the United States.

Legal and Illegal Immigration. In 2011, the United States admitted more than 1 million legal immigrants. Nearly 30 percent came from three countries— China, India, and Mexico. In 2009, an estimated 300,000 people also entered illegally—a drop from the estimated 850,000 a year from 2000 to 2005. The majority of illegal immigrants come from Mexico. Officials attribute the decline in illegal immigration to factors such as enhanced security and enforcement and the weakened U.S. job market (especially in housing construction). Analysts also believe a decline in the long-term Mexican birth rate and improved economic conditions in Mexico have reduced the northward flow of migrants.

Illegal Immigrants and the Economy. Illegal immigrants make up about 5 percent of the U.S. workforce despite laws that forbid employers from hiring undocumented workers. Illegal immigrants typically possess few skills and work for lower wages. They fill jobs that business leaders say most citizens will not take, such as picking fruit, processing meat, or cleaning toilets. Their low-wage work helps companies keep production costs—and thus prices—down for goods like food and new homes and services like landscaping and housekeeping. Many working illegal immigrants also pay income and Social Security taxes.

However, some economists and citizens worry that undocumented aliens take jobs from native-born Americans and depress wages for everyone by working for so little pay. Many people also believe that undocumented workers pay too few taxes to compensate for the heavy burden they place on public and social services.

NY DAILY NEWS VIA GETTY IMAGES

From 1880 to 1920, more than 23 million immigrants—most of them from southern and eastern Europe—came to the United States seeking a new life. Here, new immigrants arrive at Ellis Island, New York, the nation's main gateway for new arrivals around the turn of the century.

Revising Immigration Policy

The Immigration Reform and Control Act of 1986. Signed by President Ronald Reagan, this law tightened security at the Mexican border and enacted strict penalties for employers hiring undocumented workers. The law also legalized and made eligible for citizenship nearly 3 million illegal residents who had entered the United States before 1982. Some critics blame this "amnesty" (government pardon) for spurring additional illegal immigration over the following decades.

Post 9/11 Measures. Foreign nationals were responsible for carrying out the September 11, 2001, terrorist attacks. All the 9/11 hijackers entered the United States through airports. Three stayed in the United States longer than their visas allowed, eight carried fraudulent passports, and some possessed U.S. driver's licenses. After 9/11, the effort to strengthen homeland security led to greater scrutiny of all visa applications and implementation of visitor and foreign student tracking systems.

Furthermore, because driver's licenses confer important privileges, such as the ability to board airplanes, members of the 9/11 Commission suggested that licenses meet national standards. In 2005, Congress passed the Real ID Act, requiring states to guarantee that all people granted driver's licenses are legal residents. However, the Department of Homeland

Security continues to extend the deadline for compliance because of cost and privacy concerns.

Immigration Reform Deadlocked. In 2004, President George W. Bush proposed a major overhaul of the nation's immigration laws. His plan included increased border security, an expanded temporary guest worker program, and a path to citizenship for illegal immigrants meeting certain criteria—but Congress only agreed on boosting border security. Another attempt at comprehensive reform failed in 2007, and Congress has not considered a major overhaul since.

States Step In. Frustrated at the lack of federal direction, state governments have passed hundreds of new laws to address illegal immigration. Although some states have passed laws to help illegal immigrants—for example, measures to improve access to higher education—most of the laws aim to make life difficult for undocumented residents and their families. In April 2010, Arizona adopted a controversial law that authorized police to check a person's immigration status while enforcing other laws and required immigrants to carry their authorization papers at all times.

Since then, several other states passed similar measures. Alabama's law went even further than Arizona's. The law requires that public schools determine the immigration status of students and makes it a crime for anyone to transport an illegal immigrant. The laws frightened illegal immigrants and even legal migrant workers, causing some to move or not come to work. Farmers in several states reported not being able to find enough farm workers to plant and harvest crops.

THE VISA LOTTERY

The Diversity Visa Lottery, launched in 1995 to enable people from countries with lower rates of immigration to come to the United States, issues up to 55,000 visas every year. Some legislators want to kill this program, arguing that something as critical as immigration should not be conducted randomly. Instead, they say, immigration policy should evaluate potential immigrants' backgrounds and work skills so that immigration meets America's cultural, economic, and humanitarian goals. Critics also worry the lottery program poses a security risk by possibly giving terrorists and criminals legal entry to the United States.

Many of the strict measures face court challenges. The Justice Department sued Alabama, Arizona, South Carolina, and Utah, arguing the states' laws cracking down on illegal immigrants interfered with federal government authority over immigration matters. In 2012, Arizona's case reached the Supreme Court. In *Arizona v. United States* (2012), the Court upheld one provision of Arizona's law—that requiring state police to determine the immigration status of anyone they stop or arrest if the person can be reasonably suspected to be in the country illegally. However, the Court ruled that federal powers regarding immigration policy meant the Arizona law's other provisions could not be enforced.

Major Issues in Immigration Reform

Border Security. In 2005, more than 1 million people were apprehended trying to illegally cross the U.S.–Mexico border. The heavy foot traffic resulted in environmental damage, crime, migrant deaths, and strains on local law enforcement and social services. In response, President George W. Bush deployed National Guard troops, and Congress authorized spending to complete 650 miles of fence and barricades, increase surveillance technology, and add thousands more border patrol agents. For temporary reinforcement, President Barack Obama sent 1,200 National Guard troops to the border in 2010.

Workplace Enforcement. To help employers identify illegal workers who carry falsified documents, the federal government created E-Verify in 2007. The Internet-based program enables businesses to check the eligibility of employees to work in the United States by comparing Social Security numbers to a national database. One-third of states now require some or all employers to use the system.

Deportation Policy. To enforce immigration law, the U.S. immigration and Customs Enforcement Agency has the power to arrest and deport anyone who has entered the United States illegally. Between 2009 and 2011, the Obama administration deported a record 400,000 illegal immigrants annually. The administration says its primary focus is deporting aliens convicted of crimes or considered threats to national security. In 2012, President Obama extended this policy, ordering immigration officials to defer deportations for two years for people younger than age 31 brought to the United States illegally by their parents and meeting other criteria.

Temporary Workers. To legally match foreign workers with businesses that want to hire them in the United States, some officials have suggested creating new temporary, or "guest," worker programs. Most proposals would dramatically increase the number of worker visas and, unlike current programs, allow illegal immigrants already working in the United States to apply. However, guest worker initiatives have languished along with the effort to pass comprehensive immigration reform.

Undocumented Residents. Americans sharply disagree about what to do about the more than 11 million people in the United States illegally. Some favor denying illegal immigrants all benefits and services and making life so difficult that they leave, or "self-deport." Others believe that those who work, pay taxes, and attend college or serve in the military deserve the opportunity to become citizens with full responsibilities and rights.

CURRENT ISSUES

Dream Deferred. Under the "American Dream Act," undocumented children brought to the United States by their parents could achieve conditional legal status and possibly citizenship. To qualify for legal status, applicants must have lived in the United States for a set period of time, graduated from an American high school or obtained a GED, and not violated any other terms under existing immigration law. To be eligible for citizenship, applicants must maintain their legal status and complete two years of college or military service. The bill could enable several hundred thousand young people to achieve citizenship. It passed the House in 2010 but failed in the Senate. In June 2012, President Obama ordered officials to give young illegal immigrants who are in high school or are high school graduates or military veterans a two-year deferral on deportation and allow them to apply for work permits. Although immigration proponents hailed the initiative, both they and critics argued that the only fair and legitimate way to resolve the long-term status of such illegal immigrants is through legislation. Proponents of the Dream Act, including President Obama and most Democrats, have vowed to keep trying to pass some version of it.

Advocates of the Dream Act argue that children brought to the United States illegally should not be punished for the mistakes of their parents. Yet they are—their undocumented status limits their options and leaves them at constant risk of deportation from the only home country they have ever known. Proponents say the Dream Act offers a win-win solution. First, it helps undocumented young people better themselves through college or military service. Second, it benefits the United States by turning illegal residents into productive, contributing members of the economy and society. It makes far more sense, advocates say, to extend a path to citizenship to such young people than to spend money to deport them.

BIRTHRIGHT CITIZENSHIP

All children born in the United States—whether their parents are in the nation legally or not—are automatic U.S. citizens. Some state and national legislators believe this provision encourages illegal immigrants to come to America to have children (so-called "anchor babies") who can later petition for legal status for family members. These critics think automatic citizenship should end. However, they are up against the Constitution's Fourteenth Amendment—which originally had nothing to do with illegal immigration. In fact, when the amendment was adopted in 1868, immigration to the United States was unlimited. However, the nation, still reeling from the Civil War, was rife with discrimination against newly freed slaves. To remedy that, the amendment extended citizenship to all persons born or naturalized in the United States.

DAMIAN DOVARGANES/ASSOCIATED

Children brought to the United States illegally by their parents are illegal residents who cannot work and can be deported anytime. Most of them and a strong majority of Latino voters—a growing voting bloc—favor the Dream Act, which would enable such young people to achieve legal status and possibly citizenship.

By granting amnesty to undocumented children, the Dream Act would wrongly reward lawbreakers, allowing them to jump ahead of legal applicants, argue opponents. The law would also be a magnet for new illegal immigrants. Furthermore, once children become U.S. citizens, they can petition for citizenship for parents and siblings, creating chain migration that legalizes millions of people—an unacceptable outcome. Critics contend that the United States cannot afford to educate and provide social services for people here illegally and their families, even if some are in the nation through no fault of their own.

Opening the Door to Skilled Immigrants. Legal immigration, particularly of skilled workers, also presents a challenge to policymakers. Under current immigration policies, the federal government limits the number of highly skilled workers who receive temporary work visas (called H1-B visas) to 85,000 a year. Furthermore, the number of skilled workers who may receive permanent status (green cards) is limited to 140,000, or about 15 percent of the total number of green cards issued each year. Some say that's not enough to meet America's economic needs and call for raising the limits.

Many policymakers favor lifting the limits because highly skilled immigrants—including engineers, scientists, and mathematicians—strengthen the U.S. economy. Because of them, America leads the world with technological giants like Google and Intel (both cofounded by immigrants). However, companies today cannot find the highly skilled workers they need among America's workforce, which leaves needs unmet or drives some companies to relocate overseas, hurting the economy. Highly skilled immigrants further contribute to America's strength by being productive members of society who earn high salaries and pay taxes. To be globally competitive, America must attract and keep the best and brightest.

Others say that increasing immigration for skilled workers hurts American citizens. They contend that millions of American engineers and other highly educated citizens remain unemployed after the economic downturn. These citizens would be eligible or easily trained for the job openings companies say they can't fill. Critics accuse American companies of seeking to bypass American workers in favor of skilled immigrants who will accept lower salaries. That takes jobs from struggling Americans and lowers wages, thereby hurting everyone. Furthermore, depressing salaries for highly skilled citizens will eventually discourage U.S. students from pursuing doctoral degrees, depriving them of the best opportunities and creating an actual shortage of American skilled workers.

Guarding the Border. In 2011, the number of people caught trying to cross the U.S.–Mexico border illegally had dropped to about 300,000, the lowest level since 1972. The Obama administration claimed the border was more secure than ever (although some analysts believe the weak U.S. economy and tougher immigration measures have also played a big role in dampening illegal immigration). In response, in 2012, the Pentagon began reducing the number of National Guard troops stationed at the U.S.–Mexico border from 1,200 to about 300—a move that sparked debate.

Using National Guard troops to patrol the border is wasteful and ineffective, say critics. Department of Defense rules prohibit troops from searching vehicles, seizing drugs, or pursuing suspects—meaning that Guard members may only watch the border and report trouble. Reducing the Guard forces would free up funding that could be better spent on other aspects of border security. Furthermore, the U.S. economic recession has helped reduce border crossings, making a militarized border—which unduly strains diplomatic relations with Mexico—unnecessary. With more than 18,000 agents, more barriers, and surveillance technology such as

Most illegal entries occur along the nearly 2,000-mile U.S. – Mexico boundary that traverses California, New Mexico, Arizona, and Texas. After peaking in the 2000s, illegal immigration has decreased in recent years, probably due to many factors, including enforcement, a weak U.S. job market, and improved economic conditions within Mexico.

sensors and drones, the border patrol can now secure the border.

Opponents to troop cuts counter that the border is more dangerous than ever. Border crossers are increasingly resourceful, armed, and violent—and horrific and widespread drug cartel violence spilling over the border remains a strong possibility. Given that sections of the border remain unfenced and hundreds of thousands of people are still determined to cross it (and the numbers could increase with economic recovery), a militarized border with more National Guard troops, not fewer, is a necessity. The United States must deploy all the resources at its disposal to keep citizens safe.

OUTLOOK

Immigration—legal and illegal—has resulted in a dramatic shift in the racial and ethnic demographics of the nation, making the politics surrounding immigration reform all the more volatile. Given the controversial nature of the issue, Congress will not attempt to address the issue until after the 2012 elections. Even then, the economic, security, and cultural concerns of immigration policy will likely continue to make reaching consensus difficult.

THE DEBATE: IMMIGRATION

Congress should pass the Dream Act.

PRO: The United States should not punish children brought to the country illegally by their parents. The nation and these young people benefit when they are given the chance to come out of the shadows, better themselves, and become contributing members of society. Furthermore, it's more economical to expand their potential than to deport them.

CON: The U.S. government should never offer amnesty, even to undocumented students. Rewarding lawbreakers would undermine America's rule of law and attract a new wave of illegal immigrants. Illegal immigration places a heavy and unaffordable burden on social services and law enforcement that hurts American society and the economy.

The United States should admit more high-skilled immigrants.

PRO: Increasing the numbers of skilled immigrants would help the American economy. Such workers often help create jobs, either by innovating or starting new businesses. They pay taxes and contribute greatly to American society. Without them, American companies do not have enough skilled workers to effectively compete in the global economy.

CON: Putting Americans to work before hiring foreigners will best help the economy. Millions of citizens seek highly skilled jobs and could be trained if necessary. Companies too often use the skilled worker visa program to get cheaper foreign labor, which depresses salaries and discourages U.S. students from pursuing doctoral degrees.

The United States should reduce the National Guard deployment at the U.S.-Mexico border.

PRO: The U.S. - Mexico border is more secure than ever. The costly deployment of the National Guard—which lacks authority to arrest suspects—unnecessarily militarizes the border and wastes money. With advanced technologies such as cameras and sensors, the now fully staffed border patrol can secure the area more efficiently and effectively.

CON: The border is not secure, and if anything, the number of National Guard troops should be increased, not decreased. Illegal immigrants are increasingly more violent, and spillover violence from Mexico's drug wars could make American border towns combat zones. The United States must use every means, including its military, to protect its citizens.

SOCIETY AND DISCRIMINATION
INTRODUCTION

Freedom and equality are fundamental American values and the foundation of the U.S. system of government. However, putting those principles into practice has taken decades of debate and struggle. When the Constitution was written in 1787, it granted only white male property owners the right to vote. And despite the nation's promise of equality, the persistence of slavery until the 1860s meant that promise was kept for only a few Americans. Gradually, legislators amended the Constitution to abolish slavery, and extend voting rights to nonlandowners, racial minorities, and women. Changes to federal and state laws followed, outlawing the most egregious forms of unequal treatment. But overcoming discrimination in everyday life such as in schools, the workplace, and social situations would prove a greater challenge, prompting protest and political change over the last century.

KEY QUESTIONS

- Should same sex couples be allowed to marry?

- Should the government do more to ensure women receive equal pay for equal work?

- Should voters be required to show proof of identity?

The civil rights movement of the 1950s and 1960s focused on securing equal treatment for African Americans, followed by the women's movement of the 1970s and 1980s, and subsequent efforts by disabled Americans, immigrant groups, and gay Americans in the 1990s and 2000s. Despite these gains, many believe that more should be done to ensure equal opportunity for women and minorities while others argue that the laws are sufficient to protect these groups and the government should not intervene further. This difference of opinion lies at the center of many of today's most controversial current issues, such as whether same-sex couples should be allowed to marry, whether salaries earned by women are fair, and whether people should be required to show photo identification in order to vote.

BACKGROUND

An American Snapshot

The United States is a nation of great racial, ethnic, religious, and geographical diversity. Such differences are often evoked as the nation's greatest strength, but they are also the cause of some its deepest divisions as the country struggles to make good on its promise of equality and freedom for all.

According to the 2010 U.S. Census, 64 percent of Americans described themselves as "non-hispanic whites," with blacks making up 13 percent, Hispanics 16 percent, and Asians about 5 percent of the total population. The number and proportion of Hispanic Americans and Asian Americans grew significantly in the last decade, each increasing by 43 percent between 2000 and 2010.

The Demography of Political Leadership. In the 112th Congress, African Americans, Hispanics, Asians and Pacific Islanders, and American Indians accounted for 75 of the 435 members of the House of Representatives and only 4 of the 100 senators, less than 15 percent of all congressional seats. According to the 2010 census, these same groups added together account for 36.3 percent of the total U.S. population. Women hold only 73 seats in the House and 17 in the Senate, but account for 50.7 percent of the population. Some observers say that these statistics prove that the interests of minority groups and women are not fully represented in federal legislative policymaking. However, others say that political ideology and lawmakers' accountability and responsibility toward their constituents are far more important factors than race or gender in ensuring that the U.S. people are fairly represented.

Working Toward Equality for Women. The effort to secure a woman's right to vote began in the mid-1800s. Advocates known as "suffragists" tried to include women in the Fifteenth Amendment (ratified in 1870), which guaranteed the right to vote to all men, regardless of race. But it was not until 1920, with the ratification of the Nineteenth Amendment, that women were extended the right to vote in all state and national elections. Decades later, the momentum of the civil rights movement helped open other doors for women. Seeking equality in the workplace and education, women's groups won victories when Congress adopted the Equal Pay Act in 1963, requiring

Female protestors known as "Suffragists" march in support of extending voting rights to women. They earned this right in 1920 when the 19th Amendment to the Constitution was ratified.

equal pay for men and women who perform equal work; and in 1972, when the Title IX program barred gender-based discrimination in all education programs receiving federal support. In 1978, Congress amended the Civil Rights Act to prohibit job discrimination against pregnant women. In the 1970s, many women's rights groups also supported the Equal Rights Amendment to the Constitution, which stated: "Equality of rights under the law shall not be denied or abridged by the U.S. or by any state on account of sex." Congress adopted the amendment in 1972, but it fell three states short of the thirty-eight necessary for ratification by the 1982 deadline.

The Civil Rights Movement. Race—particularly the relationship between white Americans and black Americans—has always been a volatile issue in the United States. The original language of the Constitution did not even consider black men to be men: slaves were only considered to be three-fifths of a man for purposes of taxation and population count. During the Civil War, President Abraham Lincoln emancipated the slaves and the abolition of slavery was later ratified in the Thirteenth Amendment. The Fourteenth Amendment, which guarantees due process and prohibits states from denying citizens equal protection under the law, was the most powerful of the Civil War amendments and would become the basis for many future legal attempts to gain additional civil rights for African Americans and other minorities.

However, racial prejudice and discrimination persisted and in the years following the Civil War, southern states implemented "Jim Crow" laws, which segregated public facilities by race. In 1896, the Supreme Court upheld such laws in the case of *Plessy v. Ferguson,* writing that segregation was legal as long as "separate but equal" facilities were provided. Over the next 70 years, some civil rights were slowly extended to black Americans. In 1948, President Harry Truman ordered the U.S. military to desegregate its units. In 1954, in *Brown v. Board of Education of Topeka,* the Supreme Court unanimously ruled that maintaining racially segregated schools for black students and white students was unconstitutional because such schools could not offer equal educational opportunities. The Civil Rights Act of 1957 made it illegal to prevent people from voting in federal elections. However, the act had many loopholes and proved ineffective in securing the universal right to vote.

In the 1950s and 1960s, black Americans launched a civil rights movement based on nonviolent political protests to force legal and social change. This movement resulted in a number of significant legal victories. In 1964, the Twenty-fourth Amendment was added to the Constitution to bar the use of a poll tax (a tax that was often used to prevent low-income African Americans from voting). The Civil Rights Act of 1964 prohibited discrimination in public accommodations, such as restaurants and hotels, in programs receiving federal aid, and in hiring practices. And the Voting Rights Act of 1965 banned literacy tests, poll taxes, and intimidation of voters in any state. Efforts to enforce these laws would remain a challenge for decades.

The Right to Vote. In the 18th century, only white men who owned property were allowed to vote. Women, African-American slaves, free people of color, and Native Americans were excluded from the democratic process in almost all instances. By the mid-19th century, property requirements were dropped. Following the Civil War and the abolition of slavery, in 1870 the Fifteenth Amendment to the Constitution granted black men the right to vote. In 1920, women earned that right when the Nineteenth Amendment prohibited voting rights from being withheld on account of a person's sex.

In 1964, President Lyndon Johnson signed the Civil Rights Act into law, banning many forms of racial discrimination and segregation.

Despite these gains, barriers to voting remained, and at times increased as states sought to control access to the electoral process. Until the mid-20th century, many states established poll taxes, and literacy tests and fostered intimidation and threats of violence in an effort to prevent African Americans from voting. By the 1950s, leaders of the civil rights movement made voting rights a centerpiece of their demands for equal treatment. Voter registration drives and protests in the South sparked violent opposition, but eventually yielded significant gains and the federal government stepped in to force states to uphold the law. The combined effect of the Voting Rights Act of 1965 and the 24th Amendment to the Constitution (1964) was that states were no longer allowed to impose literacy tests, poll taxes, or scare voters away from the voting booth. Following the passage of these laws, the U.S. Justice Department became, and remains, heavily involved in reviewing any new restrictions on voting enacted in several Southern states with a history of racial discrimination.

Taking Affirmative Action. In the early 1960s, President John Kennedy issued executive orders requiring federal contractors to "take affirmative action" to ensure that their hiring practices did not discriminate because of race, color, or national origin. Presidents Lyndon Johnson and Richard Nixon expanded these programs to include gender and to apply to certain organizations accepting government funds; many are still in force today. The policies seek to increase employment and higher educational opportunities for minorities and women and require government institutions to actively recruit qualified minority candidates. Since the 1960s, many colleges and universities have implemented their own affirmative action programs. However, Supreme Court decisions in the 1980s and 1990s defined and limited the scope of affirmative action initiatives in higher education, especially where rigid quotas were adopted.

Equal Rights for Gay Men and Women. In recent decades, gay men and women have become more open about their sexual orientation and, in turn, have sought legal protection from discrimination. Although federal law does not extend civil rights protections on the basis of sexual orientation, some cities, counties, and states have passed laws that ban discrimination against gay men and lesbians. In *Lawrence v. Texas* (2003), the Supreme Court ruled that gay couples had a constitutional right to privacy with regard to their sexual behavior in their own homes.

The legal debates surrounding homosexuality in recent years have focused on family issues such as marriage, adoption, and equal access to health care benefits and social services, and whether gays should be allowed to serve openly in the U.S. military.

Civil Rights for People with Disabilities. Disabled Americans have worked to ensure that civil rights are not impeded due to a person's physical or mental condition. Foremost among civil rights legislation for people with disabilities is the Americans with Disabilities Act (ADA), passed in 1990 with overwhelming bipartisan support. The law banned discrimination against people with disabilities in the workplace and in public places, and defined "disability" as "a physical or mental impairment that substantially limits

In 1990, Congress passed the Americans with Disabilities Act guaranteeing individuals with disabilities equal opportunity in public accommodations, transportation, and employment.

DIVERSITY IN COLLEGE ADMISSIONS

Should colleges consider race as a factor in college admissions? For decades, universities used very specific methods to achieve diversity in their student bodies until a 2003 Supreme Court decision limited those tools severely. Since then colleges can consider race as one of many considerations when deciding whether to admit a student. But in 2012 the Supreme Court agreed to hear a new case that might prevent race from being considered at all. Brought by an applicant who says the University of Texas denied her admission because she was white, the case is being watched closely by those who say race has no place in the admissions process and those who believe that it is essential to achieving true equality of opportunity.

one of the major life activities" such as communicating, hearing, seeing, walking, or dressing or feeding one's self. The law allowed people to sue when they believed they had been discriminated against because of a disability. However, a series of Supreme Court cases since 1990 have significantly narrowed the meaning of "disability" thereby reducing the number and type of workers who receive protection under the ADA.

CURRENT ISSUES

Same-Sex Marriage. The institution of marriage is a contract between two people committed to a lifelong relationship. In the United States, marriage is often accompanied by a religious ceremony, but it is the legal act of marriage that binds a husband and wife together and offers them certain rights in society. The public recognition of this relationship, and the financial, social, and legal benefits that accompany it, have been elevated and protected by the law throughout American history. As a result, the Supreme Court has ruled that the Constitution protects the fundamental right to marry, but it allows states to define the requirements for marriage and to restrict this right for certain compelling reasons. Under this standard of review, the Court has upheld, for example, age limits for marriage. However other state laws that prohibited interracial marriage have been struck down as unconstitutional.

Today, many same-sex couples argue that they should be able to legally marry and enjoy the financial benefits and rights, emotional security, and societal acceptance afforded to married heterosexual couples. In response to state-based efforts to legalize gay marriage, in 1996 Congress passed the Defense of Marriage Act, which specifies that under federal law, marriage may only be between a man and a woman. The law also allows states to deny legal recognition of same-sex marriages performed in other states.

Since this law was enacted, however, many states have chosen to allow civil unions between same-sex couples and others have moved to offer gay couples the right to marry. And public opinions on homosexuality and gay marriage have also shifted considerably: a 2011 Pew opinion poll showed that Americans are equally divided in the question of same-sex marriage, a 20 percent decline in opposition since 1996.

In May 2012, President Obama publicly expressed his support for gay marriage, a historic announcement that gives the polarizing issue potentially greater visibility during the 2012 presidential campaign. When asked about his position previously, Obama replied that he was "evolving" on the issue and had not completely decided.

Despite his endorsement of gay marriage, Obama did not propose any federal legislation to repeal the Defense of Marriage Act, despite his administration's position that it is unconstitutional, and said states should

set their own marriage laws. As of 2012, gay couples can now marry in Connecticut, the District of Columbia, Iowa, Massachusetts, New Hampshire, New York, and Vermont. However, in California, Maryland, and New Jersey, similarly passed laws have or may face referenda and legal challenges and are not currently in effect. State and federal courts have split on the constitutionality of gay marriage, leading many experts to say that only the U.S. Supreme Court can settle the issue of whether same-sex marriage is a constitutional right.

Opponents of gay marriage believe the tradition of heterosexual marriage is the cornerstone of the American family and the best environment in which to raise children. They believe that marriage should be between one man and one woman and that allowing same-sex couples to marry could open the door to other undesirable changes to marriage laws, such as allowing people to have multiple spouses. Other opponents argue that homosexuality is immoral and in opposition to mainstream religious beliefs and therefore should not be sanctioned by the government. They oppose the efforts of certain states to allow gay marriage as an unfair imposition of personal lifestyle choices on a population that does not support it.

Supporters of same-sex marriage believe that gay couples have a fundamental right to enjoy the financial and social benefits of marriage just as heterosexual couples do. They cite the Fourteenth Amendment's guarantee of equal protection under the law as the basis for this right. They believe the government should protect these rights from efforts in some states to eliminate them, as they have done for the rights of African Americans and other minority groups in the past. They believe that love between two people, and the willingness to make a lifetime commitment, should be the major requirement for a legal marriage. Allowing same-sex marriage, these advocates believe, would fulfill the American promise of equality for gay Americans.

Gender and Earnings. Since gaining the right to vote in 1920, women have gained many rights and privileges that were previously denied to them. One area where women still lag behind their male counterparts, however, is in the area of salaries. This "wage gap" has been the subject of recent debate.

Until the early 1960s, help wanted ads often listed separate job opportunities for men and women. In some cases the ads described identical jobs under both the male and female listings but listed different, and lower, salaries for women. This differential was based in part on the

THE END OF "DON'T ASK, DON'T TELL"

Since 1993, gay men and women in the U.S. armed forces served without revealing their sexual orientation in order to comply with "Don't Ask, Don't Tell," (DADT) a policy signed into law by President Bill Clinton. In the years that followed, more than 13,000 service men and women were dismissed from duty as a result of this policy. Over the years, changing American attitudes combined with new challenges posed by the wars in Afghanistan and Iraq caused policymakers to change their minds about this law. In December 2010, at the urging of President Obama, Congress passed legislation to repeal the law. In September 2011, after the military certified it was ready to implement the change, DADT officially came to an end.

belief that women could not perform at the same level as men and that men needed higher wages because they were often supporting families with their pay. However, these beliefs were challenged during World War II when men joined the armed forces and women replaced them in the domestic workforce in large numbers, performing as well as their male counterparts in similar jobs. However, after the war ended, these gains were not sustained. Between 1950 and 1960, women earned on average between 59 cents–64 cents for every dollar their male counterparts earned in the same job.

To address these disparities, in 1963 Congress passed the Equal Pay Act which prohibited employers from paying women less for jobs that require "equal skill, effort, and responsibility, and which are performed under similar working conditions" as jobs performed by men. However the Act allows employers to pay women lower wages if they can show the difference in salary is based on seniority, merit, productivity, or any other factor besides a woman's gender. As a result, the pay gap between men and women still persists.

In 2011, the Bureau of Labor Statistics estimated that women still make on average only 81.2 cents for every $1 earned by men, even though they make up almost half of the workforce. The figures are worse for minority women: African American women only earned approximately 62 cents and Latinas only 53 cents for each dollar earned by a white male. In 2011, Congress considered but defeated a bill known as the "Paycheck Fairness Act" that supporters say would have enhanced remedies for women who

Government statistics show that women earn on average only 81.2 cents for every $1 earned by men.

believe their salaries are lower as a result of their gender. The debate over this bill highlighted the differences of opinion over this current issue and the question of whether government should do more to address the wage gap.

Supporters of the Paycheck Fairness Act and other government remedies for gender wage disparity say that sex-based discrimination is the cause of these problems. They say sexism in the workplace limits opportunities for women and keeps them from receiving promotions, raises, and additional training that could lead to higher salaries. These advocates believe that although women may choose lower paying careers and may prefer part-time work, they often do so because of a lack of family-friendly policies in the workplace. Given the persistence of these problems nearly 40 years after the Equal Pay Act, some believe tougher laws against wage discrimination may be the only way to solve these problems.

Critics of enhancing existing equal wage legislation argue that the pay disparity has less to do with discrimination than it does with the different choices that men and woman make. They point to studies that show that when the differences in education, experience, and job tenure are taken into account, the wage gap narrows. If women choose lower paying professions, or choose to accept certain workplace benefits instead of increased salaries, then that is not something that government can regulate. In addition, the fact that women choose to take time off from work to have children means they may not have the same experience levels as men and do not deserve to be paid more. Opponents argue that government should not force businesses to compensate women for their personal and professional choices.

Identification Required to Vote? The right to vote is central to the idea of a free democracy. The ability to freely elect national, state, and local leaders; support referenda; and weigh in on other important matters is a responsibility and privilege of citizenship. However the Constitution does not affirmatively define who is allowed to vote, and the states hold the power to decide who is eligible to participate in elections and to regulate the process surrounding voting and voter eligibility. As a result, the history of voting rights in America is a complicated one, revealing political, social, and moral differences of opinion among citizens and lawmakers that have changed over time. Throughout the 19th and 20th centuries, the debate over voting rights focused on amending the Constitution and passing related laws to ensure all citizens, regardless of race, gender, or property status, had the right to vote and could exercise it freely.

In the 2000s, the issue of access to voting shifted to a discussion of whether proof of identity should be required in order to vote. Concerned that undocumented immigrants or people seeking to illegally influence the outcome of an election might be attempting to vote, state legislatures across the country began passing laws requiring people to prove that they were eligible to vote before being allowed to enter the voting booth. As of April 2012, 16 states required photo identification in order to vote, with another 16 requiring some form of identification but not necessarily with a photo. Opponents in these states have sued to repeal these laws, leading to a series of conflicting rulings across the country.

Disagreement over the requirement of voter identification often falls along party

Before being allowed to cast a ballot, many state legislatures now require citizens to show some form of identification to prove they are citizens and are registered to vote.

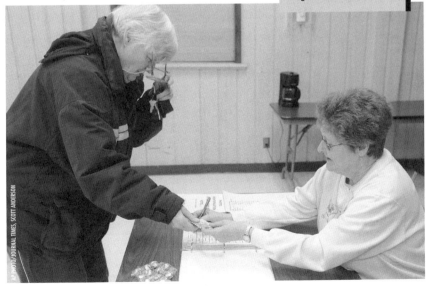

AP PHOTO/JOURNAL TIMES, SCOTT ANDERSON

lines. Republican controlled state legislatures have led the charge to enact these laws while the Obama administration has opposed them. In 2011, Attorney General Eric Holder announced that the U.S. Justice Department would scrutinize any new laws requiring voter identification to ensure that they did not violate voters' constitutional rights, and halted implementation of new voter ID laws in South Carolina and Texas.

Supporters of voter identification laws say they are necessary to prevent voter fraud. Since proof of identity is a necessity for so many activities in modern life—such as traveling, obtaining work, or opening a bank account—it should not be a burden to obtain it. Regulating the process of elections is a power that is reserved for the states and thus state legislatures should be allowed to impose requirements designed to ensure the integrity of elections. Advocates of these laws believe that statistics and anecdotes prove that voter fraud is occurring and that requiring proof of identity in order to vote is the best way to stop it.

Opponents of voter identification laws claim there is no evidence that voter fraud is on the rise. They accuse supporters of the measures of using these laws to suppress voter turnout among minorities, the poor, and the elderly who are less likely to have proof of formal identification or who might be intimidated by the requirement. These critics point to the history of states erecting barriers to voting and question whether recent efforts are also politically and racially motivated. The cost and effort involved in securing state identification is sometimes more than some citizens can afford, and should not be a requirement to exercise their constitutional right to vote.

OUTLOOK

The concerns of Americans and their lawmakers are as broad and diverse as American society. In weighing potential policies with significant impact on society, lawmakers must consider that attempts to treat one group fairly must not come at the expense of other groups or of the nation's values. The debates over same-sex marriage, pay equality for women, and voter identification laws bring to light these ongoing struggles. The nation has a long history of extending rights to make sure that all its citizens share in the freedom and civil rights that are the nation's cornerstones. Whether the United States has met that goal, or whether there is still work to be done, will continue to be a source of debate among lawmakers and citizens alike.

THE DEBATE: SOCIETY AND DISCRIMINATION

Same-sex marriage should be outlawed.

PRO: Marriage in America has been, and should always be, between one man and one woman. Allowing same-sex couples to marry will undermine this important institution and open the door to government approval of other nontraditional relationships that are not favored by mainstream Americans. For those who believe homosexuality is immoral, same-sex marriage is an affront to their beliefs.

CON: Gay men and women should be afforded the same rights as heterosexual couples. The right to marry is a fundamental part of American life and allows access to many legal and financial benefits. To prevent gay couples from enjoying these rights amounts to unfair and unequal treatment under the law and is not in keeping with the American ideal of freedom and equality.

The government should do more to ensure women are paid fairly.

PRO: Studies show that women are paid less than their male counterparts for the same work in the same jobs. The government should address this unfair treatment by imposing more regulations on employers to ensure women are treated equally. This kind of discriminatory treatment is unconstitutional and should not go unaddressed. If the government does not step in, employers will never change.

CON: The law already prohibits women from being paid less as a result of their gender. If there are women who are receiving lower salaries than men it is because there are legitimate reasons for the disparity in pay. Women with less experience or who have chosen to devote more time to their families than their jobs do not deserve the same salaries.

Voters should be obligated to show proof of identity in order to vote.

PRO: Preserving the integrity of elections is an important responsibility of the states. Statistics show that voter fraud, where people who are not eligible to vote are allowed to cast ballots, is on the rise. Documentation proving one's identity is a requirement of modern life and should also be required before voting to protect the democratic process.

CON: Requiring people to show identification before they can vote will prevent people from participating in the electoral process. Not everyone needs or can afford to secure this kind of documentation. States should not give in to political motivations and erect voting barriers that are intended to prevent minorities, the poor, and recent immigrants from exercising their constitutional right to vote.

TECHNOLOGY AND PUBLIC POLICY

INTRODUCTION

In today's world, most technological innovations "change everything." Whether it is a faster smartphone, a smaller, more powerful personal computer, advances in medicine such as micro-surgery, or dramatic developments in computer-assisted engineering and design, just keeping up with the speed of technological innovation is a daunting task for most people.

KEY QUESTIONS

- Should Congress do more to combat online piracy?

- Should the government make broadband available to all Americans?

- Does high-tech domestic surveillance by the government violate civil liberties?

Governments, too, often find themselves left behind as entrepreneurial companies and individuals push the boundaries of what machines and the human mind can do. In many cases, the ethical, legal, and economic questions surrounding the introduction of new technologies are left unanswered, only to be replaced with new questions when the next "big thing" hits the market.

Technology has not only changed how people communicate or how they find information and entertainment, it has changed people's expectations for what the world around them can do. The ability to find answers to questions instantly, to talk or see people on the other side of the globe, and the power to customize experiences has changed human life in ways that are only beginning to be understood.

As the role of technology in our lives has grown, policymakers are struggling with the various ways it affects the economy and our individual liberties—including how far the government should go to criminalize the piracy of copyrighted works and whether more should be done to ensure citizens have access to high-speed Internet connections. In addition, civil liberties advocates worry that technology has made it too easy for the government to spy on its citizens even as others applaud its use to thwart domestic terrorism. All of these questions have led to increased debate about how and where the United States should spend its money to maintain what some see as a technological edge over the rest of the world.

BACKGROUND

Making the Modern World

The 20th century has been called the "fastest moving century." In 1900, people transported themselves by foot or horse and buggy. By the late 1960s, men were walking on the moon. In 1900, life expectancy in the United States was about 47 years; by 2010 it was 78 years. For most of the century, people sent letters, waiting days, even weeks, for delivery. By 2000, people were exchanging millions of instant electronic messages with their families, friends, and business associates causing mail usage rates to drop so significantly that by 2011 hundreds of post offices were slated for closure. While technology succeeded in improving life in extraordinary ways, it also created the means to destroy it on a vast scale. In 1900, there were no military aircraft or missiles. A mere forty-five years later, a single atomic bomb dropped from an airplane leveled an entire city.

Faster and Faster. In the early part of the 20th century, transportation became faster and more convenient. Fifteen years after the Wright Brothers successfully tested their powered biplane in Kitty Hawk, North Carolina, airplanes were being used to carry bombs during World War I. Soon, nonstop commercial flights were carrying passengers around the world. The advent of railroads and trains in the mid-1800s connected scattered cities and towns across America making it possible for large quantities of agricultural products and commercial goods to be transported long distances and for people to travel cross-country more easily than ever before. Although the automobile was actually invented at the end of the 19th century, the advent of the mass-produced Ford Model T and other "motor buggies" between 1908 and 1914 increased the number of cars in America by about 500 percent, to nearly 2.5 million cars. By 2010 there were more than 254 million registered vehicles on American roads.

Following decades of scientific advances, on July 20, 1969, man first walked on the surface of the moon. The U.S. astronauts to accomplish this feat were carried to space aboard the Apollo 11 spacecraft.

For many, the most exciting breakthrough of the 20th century—space exploration—came at the height of the Cold War. The rivalry between the United States and the Soviet Union was largely carried out in laboratories by scientists and engineers, as each side maneuvered for scientific and technological superiority. The 1957 launch of the Soviet satellite Sputnik into orbit marked the beginning of the space race. Only twelve years later, the United States became the first country to send a man to the moon.

Mass Technology for Mass Destruction. In the 20th century, waging war became, in many ways, a contest of technological mastery. World War I (1914-1918) was the first major war to use radio communication and electrical power. New weapons, such as armored tanks, dirigibles (airships), poison gas, airplanes, submarines, and machine guns increased casualties and brought the war to civilian populations. In 1945, the world witnessed an even more devastating fusion of technology and war, when the United States dropped atomic bombs on the Japanese cities of Hiroshima and Nagasaki. Despite bringing about the end of World War II, these bombs destroyed both cities, killing as many as 250,000 people. By 1970, the United States and the Soviet Union had accumulated more than 70,000 nuclear warheads. Today, the existence of nuclear bombs and other

In 1942, a machine called ENIAC (Electronic Numerical Integrator and Computer) was invented to compute artillery range tables during World War II. Considered to be the first supercomputer, ENIAC took up 1,500 square feet of space, weighed 30 tons, and contained 18,000 vacuum tubes.

BETTMANN/CORBIS / AP IMAGES

technologically sophisticated weapons, such as biological and chemical agents, continue to threaten all nations.

The Information Age. Innovations in communication accelerated after World War II. The development and marketing of numerous technological breakthroughs—from television to mobile phones, and transistor radios to the Internet—changed the methods and speed of communication and information dissemination around the world.

See It Now. Television became a major agent of social change in the 20th century. Derisively called the "idiot box" by social critics, television also exposed audiences to other peoples and places, and brought historic events including wars and space travel into millions of homes. Very few households had a TV during the 1930s, soon after television broadcasting made its debut. By 2000, there were roughly 1 billion TV sets throughout the world.

A PC in Every Home. In the 1950s and 1960s, computers were large, bulky mechanisms used primarily by governments and large corporations. The invention of the microprocessor in 1971 enabled engineers to shrink both the size and cost of computers, making them affordable and practical for everyday business and household use. Over the next two decades, computer technology rocketed ahead on every front. By the mid 1990s, the personal computer had become a standard item in most homes and offices across America.

Life in the 21st Century. Though the last 100 years brought incredible changes and advancement, the pace of innovation has actually sped up over the past decade. The inventions characterizing life in the 21st century—smaller computer chips, faster processors, nanotechnology—are constantly advancing, presenting a daunting challenge for the public and lawmakers who must continually evaluate the consequences of these new technologies on society.

The Internet: Shrinking the World. The paramount importance of the personal computer in people's lives was solidified with the popularization of the Internet, once just a data network used by the U.S. Department of Defense and a handful of universities. As of March 2011, more than 2.2 billion people around the world—or nearly 33 percent of the world's population were using the Internet. Billions of people are surfing the Web on optical fibers, cable television lines, radio waves, telephone lines, and increasingly via handheld electronic devices other than computers, such as cellular telephones. No industry has gone untouched by the power of the Internet. Business models are erased and redrawn to adapt to this technology, and many Internet users have embraced the technology for their own purposes, setting up personal websites, online communities, and blogs. Recently, the power of the Internet was seen in the way dissidents used online social networks to organize protests and bring about the downfall of long-established dictatorships in Northern Africa and the Middle East in 2011 as part of the Arab Spring.

While the growth of the Internet has sparked exciting developments in technology and communication capabilities, users must contend with annoying, destructive, and even offensive and criminal elements including electronic viruses, spam mail, and unwelcome or objectionable material from hate groups and pornographers. The low-cost lure of the Internet allows people of every stripe to spread messages of any kind to anyone with an online connection. All branches and levels of government are continually challenged to address the complex issues surrounding these new realities.

Innovation and Regulation. Throughout the 20th century and into the present, breakthroughs in technology required the government to impose

HOW MUCH INFORMATION
IS TOO MUCH INFORMATION?

Online technology allows websites and Internet service providers to track and store information about the habits of their users. This information about what books people read, what products they buy, and what websites they visit is extremely valuable to companies who are eager to tailor their advertisements and marketing techniques to the preferences of potential customers. But as the sophistication of these tools increases, some privacy advocates argue that things have gone too far. In 2011, Facebook and Google came under fire from their users for making it easier for advertisers to target content directly at them using this collected information as a guide. Opponents of these online marketing techniques say that the complicated opt-out procedures on these sites only confuse consumers and make it too easy for private information to be widely shared. Proponents of online marketing tools say these safeguards are sufficient and that consumers appreciate receiving tailored information about products and services they are likely to want. As these marketing tools increase in complexity, the government may try to do more to further regulate these practices.

IAN NICHOLSON/PA WIRE

In the 2010s, the technology industry changed course again as devices like Apple's iPad, which function like laptops but have the portability and convenience of a smartphone, began to dominate the market.

regulations to curb potential crimes from these innovations and to protect law-abiding users. For example, in 1986 Congress passed the Computer Fraud and Abuse Act, which among other things, made it a federal crime to plant a virus in a computer network, traffic in passwords and other personal information, or use a computer to defraud or threaten others. In 2000, the Children's Internet Protection Act was passed, which requires elementary and secondary schools to install blocking software on their computer networks to filter objectionable material. In 2005 the Supreme Court ruled in the case of *MGM Studios v. Grokster* that companies distributing and promoting software used to illegally copy and transfer copyrighted material are liable for that infringement.

Still, the accelerated pace of technological change—especially over the past decade—makes it more difficult to reach consensus on regulation. The government, for example, might want to use regulations to ensure that personal privacy will be protected from Internet service providers that might sell a person's search history to marketers and others. The business community, on the other hand, generally believes that government regulations curb the incentive to innovate and slow the delivery of exciting and ever faster services to their customers. Finding balance between these competing interests is increasingly difficult.

CURRENT ISSUES

Internet Piracy. The U.S. Constitution authorizes Congress to create laws to give authors and inventors exclusive rights over how their writings and discoveries are used. The purpose of establishing these copyright and patent protections is to stimulate creativity and innovation. These laws are based on the belief that people will be more likely to invest the time and effort in creating something new if they know that laws will protect that investment and prohibit others from duplicating or borrowing it without their consent. Most of today's copyright laws were passed in 1976; some were revised in the late 1990s to reflect changes brought on by the digital age of computers that made it much easier to copy and share written and visual works such as books, movies, and songs.

Today, the sale of copyrighted works is big business as multinational media corporations make billions of dollars each year on the sale and licensing of creative works that can now be distributed to a worldwide audience instantly. But these advancements also mean that it is easier than ever before to illegally copy and sell movies, songs, video games, and books without ever returning a portion of the profits to the people who created, published, or produced them. This practice of "pirating" copyrighted goods has grown exponentially in recent years. Although losses are difficult to estimate, media companies claim they lose tens of billions of dollars annually as a result of this theft. As the universe of potential media consumers grows—in particular as developing nations acquire the wealth

VOTING ON THE INTERNET

In 2010, a total of 33 states allowed their citizens to cast votes in government elections using the Internet. What began as a way to allow citizens traveling overseas and members of the military deployed in other countries to more easily cast their ballots, has grown into a method more frequently used by states and localities to administer elections. Supporters of the practice say that with more Americans gaining access to computers, and voter turnout rates dropping, the Internet can provide an important tool to enhance participation in the democratic process. Opponents of online voting say that votes cast online are not secure and could be tampered with, increasing the potential for election fraud. As security techniques improve, it will be interesting to see whether citizens demand, and governments allow, these kinds of voting experiments.

and technology to participate in international commerce—the debate about how to combat Internet piracy has taken center stage.

In 2011, Congress proposed two bills known as the "Stop Internet Piracy Act" (SOPA) and the "Protect Intellectual Property Act" (PIPA), each designed to combat this problem. SOPA and PIPA would have required U.S. Internet service providers and search engines to block access to sites suspected of generating illegal content. In early 2012, as Congress prepared to debate the legislation, Internet giants such as Wikipedia and Google organized protests against these proposals, saying they amounted to government-mandated censorship of online content. They recruited millions of their users to sign petitions, contact lawmakers, and temporarily shut down their sites to express displeasure with the idea. The resulting outcry caused lawmakers to withdraw the proposals within days, but the challenge of how to combat online piracy remains an issue.

Advocates for media companies and creators of copyrighted content say the government needs to do more to combat online piracy. When someone makes and sells an illegal copy of a movie or a song, they are not only stealing revenue from the individuals and corporations who own that work, they are undermining the purpose of copyright law, which is to create a safe and secure environment for innovation and creativity. Allowing online pirates to go unpunished is unfair, and the government should require search engines and service providers to do more to help track down and prevent this illegal behavior.

Opponents of proposed laws like SOPA and PIPA do not advocate the violation of copyrights, but are concerned that these laws go too far in criminalizing activities that are essential to the free exchange of ideas that the Internet depends on to thrive. Requiring entire websites to be taken down could cut off access to legitimate content, and would unfairly involve Internet companies in the determination of which content is legal and which is not. These advocates believe that content on the Internet is speech and that the First Amendment's protections would be undermined if regulations like those proposed by SOPA and PIPA become law.

The Digital Divide. In the 1990s, as Americans discovered the power of the Internet, millions of users accessed the web through dial-up connections that utilized existing phone lines and modems to connect to an online service provider. But dial-up access can be unreliable and slow, and as the amount of information and images being shared began to increase, many were looking for better alternatives. Within a few years, newer, faster methods of connectivity were beginning to take hold, including digital subscriber lines, but all used existing infrastructure designed originally to transmit telephone calls, and none were capable of keeping up with the amount of online data being transmitted and received.

By the 2000s, the most common method of accessing the Internet in the United States was through a "broadband" connection. This type of high-speed connection—usually accessed via a cable, satellite, or wireless provider—can transmit multiple types of data (such as television programming, voice calls, and Internet content) at the same time and is much faster and more reliable than earlier methods. In 2011, more than 62 percent of Americans had access to a broadband Internet connection in their homes and millions more were able to access it at work or at school. But given the expense of installing and subscribing to broadband services, rates of broadband access are lower among residents of rural communities and among nonwhites with lower incomes. This disparity is causing some to worry that America is suffering from a "digital divide." And although the United States has a relatively high rate of Internet access, which compares well to most industrialized nations, it lags slightly behind some of the emerging economies in Asia like Singapore, South Korea, and Taiwan, creating concern that this digital divide is also a threat to U.S. economic competitiveness.

Faster Internet connections via broadband access ballooned in the 2000s, but some Americans are being left behind. School systems in particular have had a hard time keeping pace with emerging technologies.

Given the growing importance of the Internet to education, employment, and government, some lawmakers began to call for more investment in broadband access to ensure that all Americans have access to the Internet's information and services. President Obama made increasing access to broadband a priority in his budget requests to Congress and ordered the Federal Communications Commission to develop a "National Broadband Plan" to develop solutions to this challenge so that eventually 98 percent of Americans would have access to this service in their communities. The president's 2009 economic stimulus package included $7 billion to improve broadband access and in 2011 he called for an additional $5 billion. But opponents of these plans say they are too expensive and they question the government's role in subsidizing these costs.

Supporters of government investment in broadband access argue that high-speed Internet is to American life today what telephone or television was decades ago: it is an essential service that no American can afford to be without. These advocates of government investment say profit-making corporations are unlikely to foot the entire bill for extending broadband service to rural communities and increasing access among low-income Americans. Since access to reliable and fast Internet connections is necessary to fully realize educational opportunities and participate in the economy, the government is wise to invest in these services to ensure all Americans have access.

Opponents of government spending on broadband access say that in this time of growing deficits and the national debt, the nation cannot afford this massive investment of infrastructure. While fast Internet service is a convenience of modern life, it is not a fundamental right that the government must guarantee. These experts say that telecommunications companies are best equipped to finance and manage these investments in infrastructure and that as demand and competition for these services increase, additional communities will receive service and prices for broadband access will drop. But until then, the government should not spend any more money on these projects.

Domestic Surveillance. The terrorist attacks of September 11, 2001, changed the way federal, state, and local governments look at national security and the protection and safety of U.S. citizens. Before 9/11 there was the belief that the way to fight terrorism was to meet the terrorists on their home turf. But after 9/11 the focus turned to preemption—stop the terrorists before they can organize and attack. This means not only fighting sustained wars overseas (Afghanistan and Iraq), but also using technology to track, monitor, and expose potential terrorists or criminals here at home.

Outdoor security cameras, like this one on a utility pole in New York's Times Square, are becoming a more common sight in cities and towns across America as law enforcement officials struggle to combat terrorism and crime.

The use of technology to keep the United States safe is highly controversial. Federal, state, and local governments have employed battlefield level technology to fight terrorism at home including the use of infra-red scanning devices to track license plates, hidden cameras in most public locations such as parks and museums, powerful computers to store databases of information culled from online activity, and the monitoring of credit card purchases and cell phone calls of millions of U.S. citizens.

An example of this type of domestic surveillance is the Department of Homeland Security's Suspicious Activity Reporting Initiative (SAR) also known as the "See Something, Say Something" campaign. Under SAR, law enforcement officials and ordinary citizens can report suspicious activity directly to the FBI that will hold the information in a database and compile additional information to build a file in the hopes of potentially capturing terrorists before they attack.

Proponents of high tech domestic surveillance claim that keeping America safe far outweighs any concerns some might have about the violation of civil liberties and privacy that those millions being monitored or screened might experience. Supporters of domestic surveillance— including the last two presidential administrations—say that the work of more than 3,400 federal, state, and local law enforcement agencies and private companies in maintaining a "close watch" on American society for the last decade has kept us safe from further attacks. They point out that the May 1, 2010, attempt to ignite a car bomb in Times Square brought several elements of domestic surveillance together to thwart the attack, capture the suspect, and bring him to justice. Without the aid of detailed databases, surveillance cameras, and the vigilance of ordinary citizens, proponents say, the United States might have experienced another devastating terrorist attack in New York City.

Opponents of domestic surveillance say that regardless of the good that may come from it, the government should not pry into the private lives of American citizens without probable cause that some wrongdoing is taking place. These critics claim that the government is using warrantless searches—in direct violation of the Fourth Amendment—to spy on citizens without their knowledge who have done nothing wrong, but simply use their cell phones, buy items online, or take pictures of sunsets over the U.S. Capitol. They claim that the use of high-tech domestic surveillance techniques need to be balanced with protecting the civil liberties of citizens. Without such a balance, the very cornerstone of the U.S. judicial system, innocent until proven guilty, is lost.

OUTLOOK

The explosion of science and technology during the 20th century has enriched lives and expanded the possibilities for human progress. At the same time, it has led to new conflicts that will continue to challenge human ingenuity and force citizens and policymakers alike to consider the ethical, moral, and political ramifications of new discoveries and develop a framework for integrating what is possible with what Americans hold to be right. The speed with which technology develops—and how quickly human habits and behaviors change to conform to it—creates even greater difficulty for governments whose decision-making processes are not designed to respond to rapid changes in the landscape. The ability to create flexible laws and policies that can adapt to new circumstances may be the only way that these traditional systems can keep up with the increasing pace of change.

THE DEBATE: TECHNOLOGY AND PUBLIC POLICY

Congress should do more to combat online piracy of copyrighted materials.

PRO: Copying and selling creative content without permission is stealing and the government should do more to stop it. Since most online piracy originates outside the United States, the only way to address the problem is to hold American companies accountable for enabling this illegal activity. Online piracy is costing businesses and copyright owners millions of dollars and Congress needs to take action.

CON: The Internet is an important tool that enables the free exchange of ideas between millions of people worldwide. Although illegally copying and selling copyrighted material is wrong, governments should not require search engines and Internet service providers to be piracy police, since it could interfere with users' access to legitimate online content.

The government should make high-speed Internet connections available to all.

PRO: Broadband connectivity and the high-speed Internet access it enables are essential services that ensure Americans can get the information they need to be educated, productive citizens. It is unfair that this service is still not available to millions of Americans in rural areas or without the money to pay for it. Government would be wise to invest in broadband connectivity so all Americans can benefit from it.

CON: High-speed Internet access is a privilege, not a right. Although broadband connectivity has made the Internet faster and more powerful, expanding this service is more appropriately paid for by telecommunications companies and business interests. The government cannot afford to spend billions on expanding broadband access to more people when the nation is already struggling with growing deficits and the national debt.

High-tech domestic surveillance by the government is a violation of civil liberties.

PRO: Americans have come to expect that their government is there to protect them, not spy on them when they have done nothing wrong. High-tech domestic surveillance shatters the fundamental faith that most Americans have in the Bill of Rights and basic liberties found there. As Benjamin Franklin once said, "Those who would give up essential liberty to purchase a little temporary safety deserve neither liberty nor safety."

CON: Increased technology has given the United States increased security. It has been proven time and again how having information about individuals on file can prevent further terrorist attacks. The United States now has the means to do so and if that means that certain liberties are pushed temporarily aside then that is a small price to pay to prevent another catastrophic loss of American lives at home.

DEFENSE

INTRODUCTION

In the decade between the end of the Cold War and the terrorist attacks in September 2001, the U.S. military downsized and reduced its massive nuclear stockpile. U.S. armed forces remained active overseas, helping to restore and keep peace in troubled lands. Without a large, overarching threat, however, U.S. leaders were slow to formulate a new military strategy.

KEY QUESTIONS

- Should the U.S. government cut military spending?

- Is the U.S. military currently equipped to confront unique and differing challenges around the world?

- Should U.S. armed forces be involved in nation-building?

The terrorist attacks on September 11, 2001, presented the nation with a new and urgent threat to its national security. The United States attacked Afghanistan in October 2001 to overthrow the Taliban government that harbored the terrorists. Congress and the White House increased defense spending and boosted domestic safety efforts. President George W. Bush declared that the United States would strike preemptively, and without international backing if necessary, to confront possible threats from terrorists or hostile states. This policy resulted in the invasion of Iraq in 2003, even though U.S. forces were still engaged in Afghanistan.

Despite ongoing instability in Iraq for the next 3 years, the United States eventually turned the security of that nation over to its citizens and the last U.S. troops left Iraq in December 2011. The fighting, however, continues in Afghanistan. The administration of Barack Obama expects to shift the mission of U.S. forces there from a purely combat role to an advisory one by 2014. And although the capture of suspected terrorists has provided the U.S. military with information that ultimately lead to the killing of al-Qaeda leader Osama Bin Laden and other terrorists in the last few years, even these military operations raise difficult legal, moral, and budgetary questions about the role of the U.S. military in a changing and increasingly dangerous world. Most recently, the Obama administration proposed cutting defense spending for the first time in more than 10 years as a way to streamline the U.S. military into a more efficient and effective fighting force, one that is better able to meet the national security challenges of the 21st century.

BACKGROUND

U.S. Defense Policy

The Cost of Defending the Nation. Approximately 1.4 million men and women serve on active duty in the U.S. Air Force, Army, Navy, Marine Corps, and Coast Guard. Another 1.2 million serve in the National Guard and Reserve forces. These troops, with their weapons and equipment, support the nation's military goals and protect and defend its vital national interests, including the sovereignty and territorial integrity of the United States and the lives and well-being of its citizens. To achieve these goals, the United States has the largest military budget in the world. For fiscal year 2013, President Obama requested more than $525 billion to maintain the United States's military might. This is, however, about a one percent decrease from 2012 and the first such decrease in military spending since 1998. The Obama administration justified the cuts claiming that in a time of trillion dollar deficits nothing, not even the cost of securing the nation, can be considered "off the table." This is especially true given the shifting role of the U.S. military.

After World War II, U.S. forces were trained to defend against one principal threat, the Soviet Union. This costly and sometimes frightening conflict, called the Cold War, shaped worldwide defense strategies and international relations for more than forty years. The U.S. defense policies of the Cold War—deterring nuclear attack, protecting

> The United States spends more money on defense than any other nation in the world; about $525 billion in FY 2013 alone. The Pentagon anticipates cuts to the defense budget in coming years that would mean the reduction of more than 100,000 combat troops, fewer air squadrons stationed worldwide, and a smaller Navy fleet.

allies, and containing communism—required a large military budget. The Korean and Vietnam Wars—fought to stop communist expansion into those Asian peninsulas—increased defense spending even further. But after the breakup of the Soviet Union in 1991, Congress reduced spending on defense. In the 10 years following the terrorist attacks in September 2001, however, defense spending increased dramatically. But with the war in Iraq ended and America's involvement in Afghanistan coming to a close, defense spending has decreased once again. As the Pentagon moves away from Cold War strategizing and plans for a future with a leaner, more efficient armed forces, the purpose and the goals of the U.S. military will continue to be debated with every budget cycle.

Nuclear Weapons. During the Cold War, the United States and the Soviet Union produced tens of thousands of nuclear bombs to deter one another from attack. Each side still has between 5,000 and 7,500 nuclear devices today (with Russia controlling the stockpile of the former USSR). Both have agreed to reduce their arsenals to between 1,700 and 2,200 active warheads by the end of 2012.

A World without Nuclear Weapons? In a speech in 2009, President Obama outlined his vision of putting "an end to Cold War thinking" and having "a world without nuclear weapons." That dream, however, has met a harsh reality. In 2010, the administration released its Nuclear Posture Review, a document required by Congress that determines U.S. nuclear policy for the next decade. In it the Obama administration tempered its lofty rhetoric with a more pragmatic approach to U.S. nuclear weapons policy, announcing that the primary nuclear threat to the United States was from rogue states or terrorist cells obtaining nuclear weapons. It also stated that while the main focus of U.S. nuclear weapons policy is deterrence, it would not hesitate to use these weapons should a nation or terrorists use powerful biological or chemical weapons against the United States that result in numerous civilian casualties.

Nevertheless, the Obama administration appears committed to setting the United States and the rest of the world on a path toward reducing nuclear weapons. In March 2012, President Obama indicated to his then Russian counterpart, Dmitry Medvedev, that should he be reelected in 2012, and with the installation of Vladimir Putin as the new Russian president later that year, he would have more flexibility to discuss reductions in Europe's missile defense systems. If President Obama were to win such agreements from Europe's leaders it would likely lead to further decreases in the U.S. and Russian nuclear arsenals.

Defending and Supporting Allies. After World War II, the United States helped create and lead the North Atlantic Treaty Organization (NATO), a military alliance meant to defend Western Europe against communist aggression. Today, NATO's 26 members include Canada, most western European countries, Greece, and Turkey, as well as several new members from Eastern Europe. All members are legally required to help defend one another's current borders. The United States is also committed by treaty to defend other allies around the world, including Japan and South Korea. But with the fall of the Soviet Union in 1991 (and the break up of NATO's counterpart, the Warsaw Pact), there is a debate in the international community about the relevancy of NATO today. Currently, the alliance nations collectively focus on issues such as cybersecurity, global disarmament, and terrorism but questions remain as to what should be the ultimate goals of NATO in the 21st century.

Use of Force to Achieve Policy Goals. During the Cold War, the United States wanted to "contain" communist influence and expansion. Consequently, U.S. leaders often used military force to support pro-American governments fighting communist-backed invasions or insurrections. For example, in 1954, when communist guerrillas and the army of North Vietnam threatened South Vietnam, the United States began a nineteen year military commitment—first with a handful of advisers and eventually a military force of more than 500,000 soldiers—with high human, political, and monetary costs. Efforts to contain communism also led to U.S. military interventions in the Korean War (1950-53), Guatemala (1954), Lebanon (1958), Cuba (1961), the Dominican Republic (1965), and Grenada (1983).

Persian Gulf War. After Iraq invaded Kuwait in August 1990, U.S. and allied troops organized a successful counter assault, first with an air attack in January 1991 followed by a ground campaign in February. After just 100 hours of fighting, however, Iraqi forces were overwhelmed and a cease-fire was declared as the Iraqi army retreated. As a condition of Iraq's surrender, dictator Saddam Hussein agreed to a United Nations (UN) resolution to disarm.

Kosovo. From March 1998 to March 1999, a war for autonomy was fought between the Kosovo Liberation Army and Serbian troops in the Serbian province of Kosovo. When NATO-brokered peace efforts broke down in March 1999, the United States—as part of a large NATO military force—

began air attacks on strategic Serbian targets. After two months of bombing, Serbian president Slobodan Milosevic accepted NATO's conditions and ended the conflict.

Afghanistan. In October 2001, the United States attacked Afghanistan's Taliban government for its refusal to turn over the al-Qaeda terrorists responsible for the September 11 terrorist attacks. The U.S. military, with help from Afghan opposition forces, overthrew the government, captured or killed al-Qaeda members, and disrupted numerous terrorist bases in that country.

However, the country struggled with a weak government, a thriving opium drug trade, and increasing attacks from Taliban insurgents. As a result, U.S. and NATO forces increased and by 2011 more than 94,000 U.S. troops and 42,000 NATO troops were serving in Afghanistan. In February 2012, however, after France announced its intentions to withdraw its troops from Afghanistan by 2013, Secretary of Defense Leon Panetta announced that U.S. troops there would shift from a combat role to an advisory one the same year. Such a change in mission, he said, would help the Afghan military and police forces make the transition to self-reliance, paving the way for an eventual withdrawal of American troops by 2014.

In 1991, U.S. and allied troops expelled Iraqi forces from Kuwait. More than a decade later, the United States, believing Iraq was harboring weapons of mass destruction, invaded it and overthrew the government of dictator Saddam Hussein.

Iraq. After U.S. officials judged Iraq to be in violation of UN resolutions to give up its

chemical, biological, and other weapons, the United States, Great Britain, and a coalition of allies invaded Iraq in March 2003, overthrowing the government of dictator Saddam Hussein. However, violence from rebels, extremist, and rival ethnic, religious, and political groups kept parts of the country in chaos for years. At one point more than 170,000 U.S. military personnel were stationed in Iraq.

Today, Iraqi security forces—trained by U.S. and NATO military personnel—have taken over the police and military duties formerly filled by coalition forces. As a result, on December 15, 2011, Secretary Panetta oversaw the lowering of the U.S. forces-Iraqi flag for the last time at Baghdad International Airport. The war, Panetta declared, was over and the world could look forward to an "independent, free, and sovereign Iraq." A few days later—after eight years, 4,500 American lives, 30,000 wounded soldiers, and tens of thousands of Iraqi lives lost—the last convoy of U.S. combat troops rumbled across the Iraq–Kuwait border. Currently, only about 150 U.S. military advisers remain in Iraq.

Defending Against Terrorism

The use of terrorist tactics by groups and individuals who disagree violently with U.S. foreign policy initiatives—especially U.S. support of Israel—has increased in the last twenty years. Car bombs, suicide bombers, and coordinated attacks against U.S. targets both at home and abroad present a new challenge to U.S. policymakers and the rest of the world.

The al-Qaeda terrorist network, founded and funded by Osama bin Laden, was responsible not only for the September 11, 2001, terrorist attacks, but also for the 1998 bombings of American embassies in Kenya and Tanzania and for the attack on the U.S. Navy destroyer *Cole* docked in Yemen in 2000. Intelligence experts believe that al-Qaeda and other terrorist groups are seeking biological, chemical, or even nuclear weapons.

Although the U.S. homeland has not seen another major attack since 2001, there have been several thwarted attempts since then and al-Qaeda remains for many a serious national threat. In 2011, however, the United States could claim it had successfully removed one such threat to its national security—Osama bin Laden.

Since the invasion of Afghanistan, Taliban and al-Qaeda leaders including Osama bin Laden were believed to be hiding in the ungoverned mountainous region of Waziristan, Pakistan, along the border with Afghanistan. However, after years of intelligence gathering and surveillance, it was determined that Osama bin Laden was actually living in a fortified

In December 2011, the U.S. forces flag used in Iraq was lowered for the last time as U.S. armed forces prepared to leave that nation after an eight year war.

compound in Abbottabad, Pakistan. President Obama ordered a raid on the compound and on May 1, 2011, he announced to the world that Osama bin Laden had been killed. Although bin Laden's death can be considered a "victory" in the U.S. effort to combat terrorism, the United States continues to use a multi-tiered approach to deter future terrorists.

Protecting the Homeland. Before the September 2001 attacks, responsibility for domestic security was divided among many different government agencies. In 2003, Congress and President Bush created a new cabinet department, the Department of Homeland Security (DHS). DHS merged twenty-two federal agencies and now coordinates immigration, border control, customs, transportation security, emergency response, and the Coast Guard, among other functions.

Preemption. The United States and its allies went to war with Iraq in 2003 in a preemptive strike. The war in Iraq represented a broad and explicit expansion of the controversial idea that a nation can make war in self-defense even when no attack has been launched on it or no clear threat made against it. In this case, it was the search for "weapons of mass destruction" described by President Bush. Iraqi dictator Saddam Hussein was eventually captured and tried and executed by an Iraqi court but his suspected biological and chemical weapons and potential nuclear weapon development sites were never found.

Gathering Intelligence. An important element in the U.S. anti-terrorism policy is the information, or intelligence, gathered by U.S. intelligence organizations. But intelligence efforts failed to head off the terrorist attacks in 2001, and predictions that Iraq had an arsenal of lethal weapons of mass destruction were proven incorrect. In light of these failures, lawmakers called for comprehensive reform of U.S. intelligence-gathering capabilities. In 2005, new legislation created the position of Director of National Intelligence to oversee and coordinate the nation's intelligence-gathering efforts.

In 2002, the United States began moving captured suspected terrorists to a new detention and interrogation facility at the American naval base in Guantanamo Bay, Cuba. "Gitmo," as it is known, soon became controversial over the guidelines and legal limitations governing the detention and interrogation of suspected terrorists, or "enemy combatants." The "enhanced interrogation techniques" used at Gitmo and other U.S. military facilities to gain information on terrorist activities eventually caused a public outcry in the United States and around the world. In a July 2006 decision, the U.S. Supreme Court ruled that these detainees should be protected under the Geneva Conventions, the 1949 international law that prohibits "cruel treatment and torture." President Obama, upon taking office in 2009, vowed to close Gitmo within a year.

But questions over what to do with terrorist suspects held there— whether to move them to U.S. prisons, try them in civilian or military courts, or release them—forced the administration to reconsider its position. Today about 170 prisoners—some of whom have been there for over 10 years—remain at Gitmo without trials. In 2011, President Obama ordered that military trials for those still held begin as soon as possible.

CURRENT ISSUES

The U.S. Military Budget. The cost of maintaining U.S. national security across the globe is huge. From buying new weapons systems to paying salaries for active U.S. service personnel and retirement benefits for those who bravely served, the United States spends hundreds of billions of dollars every year. For many, the benefits far outweigh the costs. To stay

DRONES

The use of military drones—or unmanned aircraft—has increased in recent years. These small, quick, light-weight aircraft can travel long distances, oftentimes at low altitudes to elude enemy radar. They have been used as observation and surveillance posts and to deliver missiles or bombs to precise locations without the need for ground-based observers to help target incoming strikes.

The drones are operated from remote and safe locations by highly trained military personnel who, through the use of onboard video cameras, can "virtually see" where they are going. The similarity to video games is apparent—except that when one presses the "fire" button it is for real. In fact, military recruiters have been known to scout video arcades in shopping malls and other gaming locations looking for the best gamers as potential new enlistees.

a step ahead of the rest of the world, many experts say the United States must continue to spend money on weapons research and development, recruitment, and training. Others, however, question the costs and wonder how the government can continue to justify huge defense budgets in the face of massive deficits.

In January 2013, President Obama and Defense Secretary Panetta unveiled the first defense budget in more than a decade to show an overall cut in military spending. In addition to $525 billion for fiscal year 2013 (a one percent drop from 2012), the budget anticipates about $500 billion in cuts over the next 10 years, as required by the Budget Control Act passed by Congress in 2012. That will mean, among other things, a reduction of more than 100,000 combat troops, mothballing a number of large battleships, reducing the number of air squadrons stationed worldwide, and the closing of military bases in the United States.

Supporters of the budget cuts say they represent a major change in U.S. military strategy. These supporters claim that the U.S. military needs to shift its attention from the defense of Europe to new threats in Asia and elsewhere. This change in global military strategy requires a smaller and more mobile military force than the one currently deployed, mostly at European bases. According to these supporters, defense budget cuts reflect this change in strategy by shrinking the overall size of the U.S. military while at the same time investing in less expensive but highly effective tools for U.S. soldiers to carry out their missions such as a greater emphasis on the use of cyber capabilities to fight wars and the further development of unmanned but deadly drone aircraft to conduct missions deep inside enemy territory. In addition, defense budget cutters say that the current political climate calls for reducing government spending in all sectors, including defense. Secretary Panetta stated that the proposed decreases in the defense budget are the right thing to do in these tough fiscal times. He claimed the cuts would affect all 50 states either in the form of base closures or loss of jobs for defense contractors. Panetta said the new budget is a test to see if deficit reduction is all talk and no action on Capitol Hill. Those who support the budget cuts also believe it is time for the Department of Defense to be more accountable to the American people. They claim that if the U.S. military cannot keep America safe with $525 billion then it is time for the country to rethink the "bang it is getting for its buck."

Those who oppose the budget cuts claim that they are a threat to national security and that the United States will quickly lose its superpower status. They say the Obama administration has not learned from the nation's history, in that every time the United States has decreased defense spending after a major conflict, it is soon facing a major international threat woefully unprepared and under armed. In addition, these critics believe that the United States is not preparing itself for potential "big wars" with rivals such as China or North Korea. On the contrary, these opponents say that defense spending needs to be increased so that aging jets, battle cruisers, and tanks can be modernized with the latest technological advancements. Finally, critics of the proposed cuts say that besides making the nation more vulnerable, these cuts—especially the closing of U.S. military bases—harm local economies and cost many civilians their jobs because their employers depend on nearby base personnel to patronize their businesses. These cuts, critics claim, will only continue to fuel the continuing economic downturn for years to come.

A 21st Century Military? World War II ended more than 60 years ago. The Cold War has been over more than two decades. Yet despite the new budget proposals made by the Obama administration, some believe that the U.S. military is still fighting—and still preparing to fight—similar wars. These critics claim that contrary to what President Obama is saying, U.S. armed forces will continue to be based in large, highly mechanized units that, while possessing extreme firepower, cannot respond to a worldwide crisis quickly. They point out, for example, that the United States still maintains

Secretary of Defense Leon Panetta believes that defense spending over the next 10 years will produce a U.S. military capable of responding to any crisis quickly.

11 aircraft carrier battle groups (a total of up to seven escort and support ships that operate with the carrier). Russia has one and China has none, nor is it expected to have an operational aircraft carrier for another 20 years. These critics say that the United States will never fight a war again that requires such a large military force. They claim that the United States continues to build and support these weapons as a way to keep military contractors, such as ship builders and aircraft manufacturing companies, operating. And while the funding of many of these weapons systems keep these companies alive and provide thousands of Americans with jobs, the ships, military aircraft, and missiles they produce are simply no longer needed. What these critics say is needed, is a military comprised of smaller units equipped with the latest in battlefield technology that is able to move quickly into a crisis situation and succeed without little loss of American or civilian lives. Those who call for change to a 21st century U.S. military, point to the Navy SEAL operation against Osama bin Laden in 2011 and the special-forces operation that rescued two U.S. aid workers in Somalia in 2012 as examples of the type of armed forces the United States must develop on a more widespread basis than is currently being proposed.

Others disagree and point to the 2001 invasion of Afghanistan and 2003 invasion of Iraq as examples of the need for a mechanized military. Neither of these operations would have been contemplated, they claim, had the military not had the hardware and the firepower to undertake them. These proponents say that an uncertain world where potential threats exist at every corner still requires manpower, or "boots on the ground," to maintain a significant U.S. military presence. And ground troops require the type of weapons systems the Pentagon has traditionally funded—armored vehicles, air cover, and highly fortified ships to protect harbors and sea-lanes. While these proponents of a large military do not discount the need for highly trained and fast moving forces to engage in future combat missions, they believe that the United States still faces serious threats from current and rising superpowers—such as China—to continue to develop and maintain the latest in military technology and hardware.

The U.S. Military as Nation-Builders. In the past, the role of U.S. armed forces was clear—fight to protect the national interest. U.S. military forces were trained, for the most part, to defeat the enemy. What happened after the battle or the war was left to other parts of the government or to the private sector. But today the military faces a multi-prong task—fight the war but also train those who follow to take up the fight while maintaining the peace and policing the streets. Accordingly, these multiple goals leave many wondering what the role of the U.S. military should be in the future.

Some say that the U.S. military should not be involved in what is known as nation-building, which includes everything from building schools and roads to training a new military force to take over once the United States leaves. In 2000, George W. Bush famously campaigned against the idea of a nation-building role for the U.S. military, claiming that the military was there to defend the United States and that we should not have "some kind of nation-building corps from America." Some experts agree with this view and state that military commanders are not properly trained to develop the skills needed to handle the often delicate negotiations with local political and religious leaders that are required to rebuild a nation after it has been devastated by war. These people believe that diplomats and others, such as private relief organizations, are better equipped to deal with the varied aspects of nation-building. In addition, training military officers and other military personnel for these tasks will rob them of valuable time to learn the skills of commanding a fighting force and using new weapons and technology that will give U.S. forces an edge on the battlefield.

Others believe that the mission of the U.S. military has dramatically changed since World War II. They say that as far back as the Vietnam War, the U.S. military has been involved in nation-building activities where one

A major part of the decade-long U.S. mission in Afghanistan has been to train fledgling local defense forces and build support with local tribes. Here, Afghan children look at U.S. soldiers establishing a new base in Kandaksai, Afghanistan.

of the stated goals of that war was to "win the hearts and minds" of the Vietnamese people and convert them to the ideals of freedom and democracy. Today, these experts claim, is no different. In Iraq and Afghanistan, U.S. armed forces were asked to serve in several capacities—as defenders of the nation and as promoters of peace. These people say that what is needed is that the U.S. armed forces be reorganized with an entire career path laid out not in fighting and winning wars but in the advising and training of those who will follow. Soldiers cannot be expected to do both jobs, these experts say, and instead a special advisory career field needs to be created within the armed forces that allows U.S. personnel with an interest in nation-building to find a home in the military.

OUTLOOK

The United States is still the most powerful military nation in the world, but that alone does not guarantee safety. National security policymakers face many challenges today; among them the changing mission of U.S. armed forces and concerns that terrorists may be plotting new attacks on the United States. The president and Congress will need to work together to reassess the threats to U.S. national security and determine the best way to meet those threats. At the same time, decision-makers will need to agree on the best way to fund an adequate defense against these new threats that will keep America safe.

THE DEBATE: DEFENSE

The U.S. government should cut military spending.

PRO: The United States faces new threats from new enemies. Cuts in defense spending need to reflect these new global realities and the need for a leaner but still effective U.S. military. Troop levels should be reduced in Europe, less money spent for Cold War–era weapons, and bases here and abroad that are no longer needed, closed. The new military strategy for the new century focuses on smaller forces and short-term commitments; such a strategy will cost much less than one rooted in Cold War mentalities.

CON: Now is not the time to cut defense spending. Although it has been more than 10 years since the 2001 terrorist attacks, U.S. policymakers should not be lulled into a false sense of security. The world is still a very dangerous place. With rising threats in the East such as China and North Korea, and terrorists still plotting against the United States, America needs to maintain its military superiority over the rest of the world. The security of the nation is the upmost responsibility of the government. To cut back here is to put the nation in grave danger.

The U.S. military is currently equipped to confront unique and differing challenges around the world.

PRO: U.S. armed forces use state-of-the-art equipment to confront our enemies. The highly trained soldiers, and the commanders who lead them into battle, combined with the firepower of U.S. weapons systems, makes the U.S. military the best fighting force in the world. Without advanced fighter jets, armored personnel carriers, and aircraft carriers the military could not carry out its mission — protect American lives and interests at home and abroad.

CON: The U.S. military is preparing to fight a war it will never fight. The days of battlefields filled with tanks and artillery are over. The U.S. military must prepare for a war where small, highly trained forces are able to move quickly and with surprise to attack the enemy. Money currently being spent on huge weapons systems is being wasted. That money could be better spent on training and equipping units like the one used to find and kill Osama bin Laden.

U.S. armed forces should be involved in nation-building.

PRO: The role of the U.S. military has changed dramatically in the last 60 years. Military personnel can no longer be counted on to be simply soldiers who fight wars. They must also be trained to be counselors, teachers, trainers, and even construction workers. Today's conflicts involve military personnel to take on different roles at different times in order to rebuild a nation torn apart by war. The military must prepare for and train its recruits for these modern day battles.

CON: The main role — the only role — of the U.S. military is to fight and win wars. Asking military personnel to take on nation-building tasks goes beyond the stated mission of the armed forces. It is better to leave the job of nation-building to the experts—the diplomats, teachers, and relief organizations that know how to handle these sometimes politically or religiously sensitive situations. Let the soldiers be soldiers; leave the nation-building to others.

DEMOCRACY AND HUMAN RIGHTS

INTRODUCTION

Democracy is a form of government in which citizens rule themselves either directly or through elected representatives. In 2012, there were 117 electoral democracies, representing 60 percent of world governments. In 1989, just 41 percent of all governments were democratic. As democracy has spread, so, too, have its core concepts. Many people have come to believe democracy's premise that individuals possess certain rights and liberties, including freedom of expression and the right to equal and dignified treatment.

KEY QUESTIONS

- Is promoting democracy in the U.S. national interest?

- Should foreign aid be reduced?

- Should the United States be advancing international women's rights?

To describe and secure the fundamental rights of every person, world leaders have signed several agreements, including the 1948 United Nations (UN) Universal Declaration of Human Rights. These laws assert that everyone should have basic necessities like food and shelter as well as security. Nevertheless, international agreements have not stopped some governments from imposing autocratic rule or committing brutal atrocities against their own people.

American efforts to promote democracy and human rights faced many challenges in 2011. Starting in late 2010, citizens in the Arab world—one of the least democratic regions of the globe—protested for freedom and democracy. Rulers threatened by the demonstrations unleashed violence against their people but many still fell from power. The grassroots quest for democracy and human rights inspired Americans but also prompted worries that potential instability and unrest in the region might be harmful to the U.S. national interest. Meanwhile, as the United States faces budget deficits at home, many Americans are questioning the amount and effectiveness of foreign aid—one of the major tools for promoting democracy and human rights.

BACKGROUND

Democracy

Government by the People. The United States is the world's oldest continuous democracy. After the signing of the U.S. Declaration of Independence in 1776, the ideals of representative government—government by the people—began to take root elsewhere, especially in Western Europe. From the mid-19th century through the 20th century, the idea of self-determination received a boost as European nations like Great Britain, France, and Spain relinquished their colonies in Africa, Asia, and Latin America and allowed them to govern themselves. Then, in 1991, when the Soviet Union collapsed, many former Soviet republics and eastern European countries held democratic elections and began converting to market economies. The collapse of the Soviet Union had a ripple effect beyond Europe, putting pressure on authoritarian (power concentrated in one person or an elite group) and autocratic (unlimited power with one person) governments to change. Today, most Latin American countries have democratically elected governments, and people are calling for democratic reform across the Arab world.

American leaders have long believed that the global spread of democratic government benefits the United States, as well as people around the world. Throughout its history, the United States has given other nations aid or pursued military strategies abroad to encourage the establishment of stable democracies.

Rebuilding Europe. In the aftermath of World War II, U.S. officials devised the Marshall Plan, a multi-billion-dollar aid program to help rebuild the democracies of Western Europe and bolster them against the communist influence of the Soviet Union. In addition, the United States worked to establish democracy in postwar Japan.

The Cold War. From the end of World War II through the collapse of the Soviet Union in 1991, American policymakers focused on containing authoritarian communist regimes and supporting democracy among many U.S. allies. To stop the spread of communism, the United States became involved in the Vietnam and Korean Wars, and also supported anti-communist rebels in nations like Afghanistan and Nicaragua.

In 2011, the repressive military government of Burma (also known as Myanmar) released political prisoners and planned for parliamentary elections. In response, Secretary of State Hillary Clinton (here with Burma's President Thein Sein) made a high-profile diplomatic visit to Burma to encourage the government to pursue additional reforms.

Nation-Building. In the 1990s, the United States became involved in nation-building missions in Bosnia, Haiti, and Somalia. The term "nation-building" has come to describe the process of using the military to bring civil order and improved government to countries struggling to emerge from war or other unrest. Some policymakers and citizens argue that such missions are costly and unnecessary.

Post 9-11. Since the September 11, 2001, terrorist attacks, terrorism replaced communism as one of the top security concerns of the United States. Many analysts think that terrorism grows out of political and economic oppression and unstable nations. To build a world safer for U.S. interests, President George W. Bush made supporting democracy a stated goal of the United States, and pursued it both through nation-building and encouraging democratic elections.

Wars and Nation-Building. The war in Afghanistan, launched by the United States in October 2001 to overthrow Afghanistan's Taliban government that harbored al-Qaeda terrorists, turned into nation-building. However, despite a new constitution and free elections, the country's fledgling democracy remains weak and unstable because of tribal tensions, political corruption, the opium drug trade, and attacks from Taliban fighters. After American-led coalition forces withdraw in 2014, some fear democratic progress could evaporate, especially if the Taliban returns to power. The Taliban adheres to strict fundamentalist Islamic law and previously denied women and girls basic rights.

After the 2003 invasion of Iraq to topple the regime of dictator Saddam Hussein, the U.S.-led coalition shifted efforts toward helping Iraq build a stable democracy. U.S. leaders hoped that Iraq would become a democratic role model for other countries in the Middle East, and American forces exited the country in 2011. However, despite parliamentary and general elections, the Iraqi government continues to struggle to resolve differences among its factions, quell violence, and protect human rights.

Elections in the Middle East have not always produced results favorable to U.S. interests. In 2006, members from the terrorist group Hamas gained a parliamentary majority during democratic elections in the Palestinian Territories where the United States offered development assistance money in support of democracy. Likewise in Lebanon, the terrorist group Hezbollah won a majority in parliament in a series of elections. These outcomes complicated and moderated the push for democracy. In a 2009 speech in Cairo, Egypt, President Barack Obama stressed that no system

AID TO PAKISTAN AND EGYPT UNDER FIRE

Pakistan receives $3 billion in U.S. annual economic and military aid—and some lawmakers are calling for reducing it. They argue that Pakistan failed to adequately support the hunt for al-Qaeda leader Osama bin Laden and secretly helps terrorist groups and militants. Others responded that the nuclear-armed Muslim nation remains a crucial if imperfect partner in countering terrorism and Islamic extremism. Similarly, aid to Egypt was also scrutinized in 2012 after the military-ruled transitional government charged 19 Americans with fomenting anti-government protests through their work with pro-democracy nongovernmental organizations. Some U.S. lawmakers said the move called into question Egypt's commitment to democracy and its partnership with the United States, and many called for rescinding the annual $1.5 billion in military and bilateral U.S. aid. Others urged patience, stressing the importance of maintaining influence and relations with a critical ally and the most populous nation in the Arab world.

Election observers watch as a voter casts his ballot in Egypt's 2012 parliamentary elections. The United States, European countries, and nongovernmental organizations send observers to support democracy and help ensure elections are free and fair.

of government should be imposed upon one nation by any other, but that the United States remains committed to governments that reflect the will of the people.

Uprising in the Arab World. In December 2010, a fruit vendor in the North African nation of Tunisia set himself on fire to protest government oppression. His simple but powerful act spurred other Tunisians to rise up in protest. Their actions then sparked protests for greater freedom and democracy across the Arab world. Throughout the spring of 2011, sometimes referred to as the "Arab Spring," citizens frustrated with corruption, rising food prices, and oppression took to the streets. U.S. policymakers, although generally supporting peoples' free will, struggled with how the United States should respond to crises that took different forms in a strategically important region.

North Africa and Yemen. As protests grew in the North African nations of Egypt, Libya, and Tunisia and the Middle Eastern nation of Yemen, the United States exerted diplomatic pressure to encourage dictators to step down. In Libya, where Colonel Moammar Gaddafi fought back, the United States supported a European-led military effort to shore up Libya's rebels, who overthrew Gaddafi in August 2011, later killing him. The future stability of these nations is uncertain. Libya has planned elections, but the oil-rich nation remains rocked by civil disorder and militia violence.

Elections in Tunisia and Egypt have brought Islamist parties (supporters of Islamic religious fundamentalism and legal principles) to power. Yemen remains highly unstable because of corruption, violent tribal feuds, and al-Qaeda militants who have sought sanctuary in the nation's remote and largely ungoverned provinces. Many observers worry that democracy may not prevail in these nations.

Bahrain. Protests against the ruling monarchy have been mostly suppressed with military support from neighboring Saudi Arabia. Some critics have called on the United States to exert more pressure on the rulers for reform. However, the U.S. government considers Bahrain—the base for the U.S. Navy's Fifth Fleet that patrols the Persian Gulf—a crucial ally.

Syria. The government of President Bashar al-Assad has violently cracked down on protesters since the spring of 2011, killing more than 5,000 civilians and bringing the country to the verge of civil war. After the failure of a UN resolution calling for Assad's resignation, some U.S. and international leaders called for creating a coalition to channel aid and weapons to the opposition. However, as of spring 2012, the United States and its European allies had resisted calls for military intervention in the crisis.

Human Rights

What Are Human Rights? The term "human rights" encompasses a broad range of liberties that supporters believe belong fundamentally to all people, regardless of culture, religion, or government, generally:

- Individual Security. Protection from genocide; slavery; torture; cruel, degrading, or inhumane punishment; arbitrary arrest or imprisonment; and invasion of homes. Access to fair trials.
- Basic Needs. The ability to secure basic human needs, such as goods, clothing, shelter, education, and health care.
- Civil and Political Liberties. Freedom of speech, press, and association, and freedom of movement within, to, and from a person's country. The ability to take part in one's government directly or through elected representatives. Freedom from discrimination on the basis of race, color, ethnic origin, religion, social status, and gender.

Human Rights Documents. To avoid repeating the tragedies of World War I and World War II, leaders from many countries met in 1945 to create the United Nations. In doing so, they assessed their core values on human

dignity and developed statements calling for protection of the basic rights of every person.

The first global human rights documents were the UN Charter, approved in 1945, and the Universal Declaration of Human Rights, approved by the UN in 1948. A centerpiece of global human rights standards, the Universal Declaration of Human Rights is largely based on Britain's Magna Carta, France's Declaration of the Rights of Man and of the Citizen, and the U.S. Bill of Rights.

Current Human Rights Concerns. In the U.S. Department of State's 2010 annual report to Congress on "Country Reports on Human Rights Practices," it cited three significant trends behind the dramatic changes in the Middle East and North Africa.

- The growth and influence of nongovernmental organizations promoting democracy and human rights issues around the world.
- The growth of the Internet, mobile phones, and other communication technologies that allow instantaneous global communications.
- An escalation of violence, persecution, and discrimination against vulnerable groups (including minorities and women).

The report also identified the most serious human rights violations around the world. Other governments cited for abuse were Afghanistan, Bahrain, Belarus, Burma, Cambodia, China, Congo, Cuba, Iran, Iraq, Ivory Coast, Libya, Nicaragua, Nigeria, North Korea, Pakistan, Russia, Syria, Ukraine, Uzbekistan, Venezuela, Vietnam, and Zimbabwe.

Democracies and Human Rights. The violation of human rights is not limited to authoritarian governments. Many countries hold elections but restrict fundamental rights and liberties. And even the United States draws the fire of human rights advocates. They criticize the United States for its indefinite detention of war prisoners held at the U.S. naval base in Guantanamo Bay, Cuba, and for America's use of drones (unmanned aerial vehicles) to carry out attacks on suspected terrorists abroad, which critics argue violates the U.S. prohibition on assassinations.

Foreign Aid

The United Sates uses a variety of foreign policy tools to support democracy and advance human rights. They include diplomacy, public outreach, sanctions, military intervention, and foreign aid.

Foreign aid became an important feature of U.S. foreign policy after World War II. The emergence of the Cold War—the post-1945 power

GAY RIGHTS AND HUMAN RIGHTS

Many nations in Africa and the Arab world forbid homosexuality and some punish it with prison sentences, flogging, and even death. In 2011, President Obama and Secretary of State Hillary Clinton announced that U.S. foreign aid and diplomacy would be used to fight discrimination abroad against lesbian, gay, bisexual, and transgender people. "Some have suggested that gay rights and human rights are separate and distinct," said Clinton in December 2011, "but in fact, they are one and the same." Critics argue that U.S. foreign aid should be used to promote national security—not a social agenda. Furthermore, they contend that promoting gay rights could present foreign policy problems by violating other peoples' deeply held cultural and religious beliefs and irritating important allies like Saudi Arabia and Turkey.

struggle between the United States and the Soviet Union—prompted an increased emphasis on foreign aid. At first, the goal was political: to stop the spread of communism. However, by 1960, many Americans began to take a more humanitarian view of foreign aid, and in 1961, Congress created the United States Agency for International Development to improve the standard of living in developing countries. Today, the United States annually gives aid in the form of money, goods, services, and technical expertise. U.S. goals in providing foreign assistance include promoting development, strengthening allies and fragile states, providing humanitarian assistance, supporting U.S. strategic interests, and addressing global health problems like HIV/AIDS.

There are several types of foreign aid:

Development Assistance. Many development programs aim to help nations transition to democratic governments and establish market economies to improve living standards. Aid monies support initiatives like building the roads, schools, hospitals, power plants, and other infrastructure that countries need to grow.

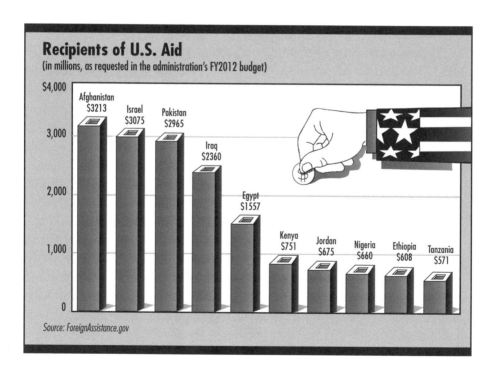

Recipients of U.S. Aid
(in millions, as requested in the administration's FY2012 budget)

Afghanistan $3213
Israel $3075
Pakistan $2965
Iraq $2360
Egypt $1557
Kenya $751
Jordan $675
Nigeria $660
Ethiopia $608
Tanzania $571

Source: ForeignAssistance.gov

Humanitarian Assistance. Humanitarian assistance generally offers immediate short-term relief. When famine, civil war, or other disasters strike countries, the U.S. government sends aid to feed the hungry, treat the sick, and shelter the homeless.

Military Aid. When the United States wants to strengthen the armed forces of friendly governments, it provides military assistance. Such programs enable allies to buy U.S.-made weapons, airplanes, and vehicles and to train soldiers for their national defense.

Although U.S. aid goes to more than 100 countries, a large portion goes to a small group, determined largely by U.S. national security priorities. Because fighting terrorism and creating stability in the Middle East and Asia are major goals, Afghanistan, Iraq, and Pakistan have received some of the largest amounts of U.S. foreign aid in recent years. Several African nations receive large sums to help fight HIV/AIDS.

CURRENT ISSUES

Democracy and the National Interest. The United States has long advocated for democracy around the world and reemphasized its commitment to freedom after the invasion of Iraq. As the Arab world continues to struggle with democratic reform, Americans again debated whether promoting democracy serves the U.S. national interest.

Supporters contend that when government officials are held accountable through free and fair elections, they tend to act in the best interests of their people—honoring human rights and civil liberties and respecting the borders of neighboring countries. Advocates also think that when new democracies adopt free-market reforms, increased international trade benefits the U.S. economy. Although transitions from autocratic to democratic governments can be violent and difficult at first, democracy will prevail, insist supporters. Some proponents insist the United States has a moral obligation to support for all people the same rights and freedoms that Americans have.

Promoting democracy does not necessarily protect U.S. national interests—and it may in fact harm them, say those who argue that security and stability must sometimes take precedence. These critics point to the problems with democratic transitions all across the Arab world. They contend that healthy democracies require populations committed to

In 2011, to combat a devastating drought and famine in Ethiopia, Kenya, and Somalia (pictured) affecting more than 10 million people, the United States pledged more than $150 million in emergency aid.

the success of their state, as well as a basic rule of law and fair courts, at a minimum—and without those building blocks, violence could erupt. Failed transitions can become big problems for the United States, requiring costly nation-building efforts or the rise to power of groups hostile to American interests or allies.

Assessing Foreign Aid. The United States spent about $50 billion in foreign economic and military assistance in 2011, about 1 percent of the budget. As U.S. policymakers struggled to reduce America's ballooning budget deficit and national debt in 2012, many looked to cut foreign aid spending. Some citizens and policymakers believe that the United States spends too much and receives too little in return for its foreign aid dollar.

Critics of foreign aid point out that the United States has almost always given the most money of any nation in terms of dollar amounts, and, as lawmakers look for budget savings this amount must be cut. They argue that foreign aid is a poor investment that fails to promote U.S. interests around the world. Many aid recipients vote against the United States in the United Nations, for example. And too often, aid goes to corrupt and undemocratic governments that never use the money to help their people or build democratic institutions. Critics point to Afghanistan, struggling to deliver basic civil services and provide its own security despite generous U.S. aid. Opponents believe that money spent by private organizations better achieves specific goals and helps those in need.

Advocates note that foreign aid only accounts for one percent of all federal spending, and in fact, the United States should spend more. Proponents argue that aid is a much cheaper and more effective way to achieve U.S. economic and security goals than is military intervention. They argue that humanitarian and global health aid saves millions of lives and promotes goodwill toward Americans. Development assistance helps weak governments become more stable and less hospitable to terrorists. U.S. aid helps nations become market economies and U.S. trading partners, which benefits American companies and the U.S. economy.

Empowering Women. In developing countries, women and girls suffer disproportionately from poverty and lack of rights, education, and health care. In some nondemocratic nations, women cannot work or hold political office, or even drive cars. They have little say in matters of marriage, divorce, and childcare and little protection from domestic violence. In 2010, the Obama administration began an unprecedented expansion of U.S. aid programs and diplomacy aimed at empowering women and girls in developing nations. Efforts address education, job training, business grants, gender-based violence, and health care (including family planning). Overall, the administration's emphasis on empowering women has raised questions about how active the United States should be in pursuing this agenda.

Democracy and liberty cannot exist if half the population is oppressed, say proponents of women's rights. Education and small business support can lift women from poverty by enabling them to serve in business and government. Plus, better health care enables women to plan for and raise healthy families.

Under the Taliban, girls' schools in Afghanistan were closed, and women were banned from working outside the home and also forced to wear the burqa. Women's rights have improved in some areas since the October 2001 US-led invasion, particularly access to education, with 2.7 million girls now in school.

Economies grow, communities become safer and more stable, and all of society benefits when women have rights, say supporters. Empowering women also fulfills America's commitment to human rights and bolsters democracy.

Opponents counter that different cultures and religions envision democracy and women's roles in society differently, and, except in instances of violence against women, the United States must not impose its values and beliefs on other cultures. Meddlesome business, health, and education programs could do more harm than good by upsetting firmly ingrained cultural traditions, destabilizing societies, and promoting values not shared by other peoples. Social change will be more lasting and successful when it comes from within societies themselves, critics say. Critics argue that America's commitment to human rights should stop short of promoting a social agenda or favoring one gender.

OUTLOOK

U.S. policymakers will continue to face the ongoing challenge of how to promote democracy and human rights around the world in ways that also protect U.S. national security as well as world stability. The Arab world—and the difficult democratic transitions underway there—will remain a focal point. Are elections there and the rise to power of Islamist parties good for Arab citizens and good for regional stability? When should the United States get involved and support citizens rising up against dictators? How the United States can—and whether it should—try to shape the outcomes and evolutions will continue to be topics of intense debate.

THE DEBATE: DEMOCRACY AND HUMAN RIGHTS

Promoting democracy around the world is in the U.S. national interest.

PRO: More democracy eventually creates a safer, more stable world. Governments held accountable by their people tend to cooperate with other nations and support America's core interests and values. Such nations also deny terrorists a base from which to plan and carry out attacks. Nothing could be more important to the U.S. national interest.

CON: Transitions to democracy can lead to violence, instability, and worst of all, governments hostile to U.S. interests. Failed transitions can also lead to costly U.S. nation-building efforts. Before promoting democracy, U.S. policymakers must ensure that resulting governments will be stable and supportive of U.S. interests, energy supplies, and allies.

The United States gives too much foreign aid.

PRO: The United States must cut spending, and the $50 billion in foreign aid is a good place to trim. Although some monies are well spent, too much goes to corrupt governments that pad their own pockets without helping their citizens. Foreign aid would be more effective coming from private organizations.

CON: As a percentage of the federal budget, the United States gives surprisingly little foreign aid. Those dollars help weak governments build democratic institutions and market economies, both of which benefit U.S. interests. It is also far cheaper to spend money to promote economic development than to send armies later to rescue a failed nation.

The United States should advance international women's rights.

PRO: Women in developing countries suffer disproportionately from violence, discrimination, poverty, lack of health care, and education. Not only does the United States have a moral responsibility to support their human rights, it has an interest promoting democracy, which can only occur when women as well as men participate.

CON: The primary goal of U.S. aid should be to promote U.S. interests in security and stability, not promote social agendas. Not all cultures and religions share American beliefs and values regarding the role of women in society. American interference threatens cultural norms and risks creating greater instability in developing countries.

THE GLOBAL ENVIRONMENT

INTRODUCTION

The environment—Earth's soil, water, and atmosphere—recognizes no political boundary. Streams and rivers flow from one nation to the next, fish and animals cross oceans and land masses, and the emissions released into the air by industrial and agricultural production stretch across countries, continents, and oceans. But tackling significant environmental challenges—man-made or otherwise—is challenging because of this very lack of boundaries. What one country views as a pressing priority, another may choose to downplay or ignore.

KEY QUESTIONS

- Should the United States do more to address global climate change?

- Should the Environmental Protection Agency be abolished?

- Should the Clean Water Act be strengthened?

Today, many people believe the greatest threat to the environment is the warming of the earth and the varied climatic changes it is producing. Much of this warming is occurring because of energy production; specifically, the burning of fossil fuels and the resulting production of greenhouse gasses, which trap heat inside the earth's atmosphere and raise the earth's temperature. Yet, energy fuels work and life in the modern world and helps economies grow. Today, most energy comes from burning fossil fuels—coal, natural gas, and also oil, which powers most forms of transportation.

The volatility of oil prices and the United States's dependence on foreign sources of oil, coupled with ongoing worry about increasing global temperatures, has created a contentious debate among U.S. policymakers and citizens about whether the United States is doing enough to protect the environment and maintain energy security. Recent environmental disasters and mounting evidence that human-induced global warming is damaging the ecosystem enrage many who fear disastrous environmental and economic consequences in the very near future. Others point to the world's precarious economies and argue that increased regulations are simply too costly and too damaging to economic growth in a time of serious financial strain.

Locally, more Americans are paying closer attention to the safety of their food and water sources. All the while, because of the nature of environmental challenges, the world's nations struggle to work together to address them, while still advancing their own national and economic agendas.

BACKGROUND

Energy and the Environment

Energy makes the world go, spurring economic development and progress toward higher standards of living around the globe. The United States successfully harnessed energy resources to fuel its own economic development in the 20th century and became the world's wealthiest nation. But global energy consumption also has significant environmental consequences. The byproducts of creating and using energy can adversely affect the soil, air, and water as well as human health and the earth's climate.

Fossil Fuels. The earth's supply of fossil fuels is nonrenewable, meaning they will eventually be exhausted. Yet, in the United States, more than 80 percent of consumed energy comes from burning fossil fuels—coal, oil, and natural gas—that have been stored underground for thousands of years. Most other nations also depend heavily on these fuels. Oil, when refined into gasoline or diesel, fuels cars, trucks, aircraft, trains, and ships. Power plants burn coal—historically cheap and plentiful in the United States—to provide electricity to factories, businesses, and homes. Burning coal and oil releases small dirt particles into the air that cause smog. The burning also releases compounds responsible for acid rainfall. And the process is blamed for emitting significant amounts of gases, particularly carbon dioxide, that many believe contribute to global warming.

Alternative Energies. Alternative energies such as wind, solar, and nuclear power can also provide electricity. Cars can run on fuels made of plant materials (like corn or potentially even algae) or on electric batteries. But while these alternatives offer cleaner emissions, they may not be widely available or may have their own environmental costs, such as radioactive nuclear waste or the need for increased use of harmful pesticides and fertilizers to produce plant-based energy.

Climate Change. Over the last century, levels of carbon dioxide, nitrous oxide, methane, and several other gases in the atmosphere have risen. Most scientists now blame human activities—such as the burning of fossil fuels and the growth of massive and intensive agricultural systems—for the increases. Experts believe these gases, along with water vapor, form a layer that traps the sun's heat, thereby raising the temperature of

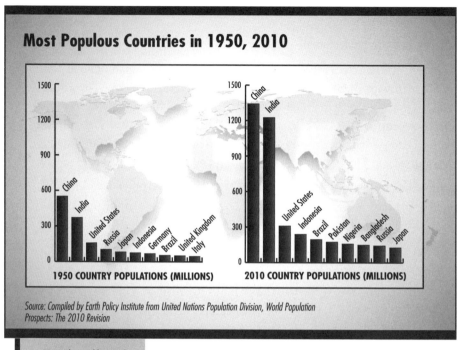

Most Populous Countries in 1950, 2010

1950 COUNTRY POPULATIONS (MILLIONS)

2010 COUNTRY POPULATIONS (MILLIONS)

Source: Compiled by Earth Policy Institute from United Nations Population Division, World Population Prospects: The 2010 Revision

In 1804, the world's population hit one billion. Just 200 years later, according to UN estimates, the world's seven billionth person was born on October 31, 2011. Sub-Saharan Africa—currently home to 900 million people—is seeing the most rapid growth, with that number projected to triple by the end of this century.

Earth's atmosphere and creating what many call a "greenhouse effect."

According to scientists, because of the greenhouse effect, Earth's average surface temperature has increased over the past century by around 1.4 degrees Fahrenheit, with most of the increase occurring over the last thirty years. According to the National Oceanic and Atmospheric Administration, 2010 tied with 2005 as the warmest year of the global surface temperature record, begun in 1880. Furthermore, scientists say that average global temperatures will continue to increase. Already, ice cover in the Arctic and Antarctic regions has thinned or collapsed, startling scientists with the speed and scope of the melting. Scientists expect that rising average temperatures will further melt polar ice caps and flood coastal areas, cause increased drought and famine, extend the reach of tropical diseases, cause mass extinctions of plant and animal species, and alter weather patterns around the world.

There remains a group of political commentators and politicians and a small number of scientists, who continue to hold that the earth is not warming in a dangerous way, or believe that human activity is not contributing to documented warming. They object to government efforts to curtail emissions, arguing that there is no reliable, consistent proof that such regulations are needed. However, the overwhelming consensus of the scientific community is that global warming, due in large part to emissions from human activity, is occurring and is dangerous.

Taking Action

Since the 1960s, governments around the world have taken steps to address environmental problems. These efforts include a mix of carrot and stick approaches. Some countries, especially in Europe, have raised taxes on fossil fuels and increased penalties for excessive carbon emissions, often directing that revenue toward developing high-speed rail or toward environmental cleanup. Other governments have offered tax incentives to companies that use "greener" technology. Individual citizens are encouraged to develop healthier environmental practices through tax credits for purchasing energy-efficient cars or home appliances. Seemingly low-tech changes such as the growth of teleworking, whereby employees do their jobs from home using the Internet, have helped reduce the number of cars on the roads each day.

Clean Air and Water. The U.S. government has also passed a series of laws aimed at protecting the environment, including the Clean Water Act (1972, amended in 1977) and the Clean Air Act (1970, amended in

GLOBAL CLIMATE CHANGE AND FOOD SUPPLY

Many experts believe that a global increase in droughts and floods can be attributed to global climate change, though the link between hurricanes and tornadoes and a warmer atmosphere is more difficult to determine. Regardless, global climate change is having a major impact on agricultural systems across the world. Worldwide, traditional rainy and dry seasons are changing and most growing climates now receive more "super hot" days during the growing months. Because crops are highly attuned to heat and light to activate their genetic growing mechanisms, even small changes can have dramatic effects. Initially, agronomists believed that global warming might have an upside with regard to feeding the world, because Carbon Dioxide (CO_2) is a powerful fertilizer. However, recent controlled experiments are showing that the potential bump in crop production because of increased CO_2 will likely be less than expected and may even be offset by the extremes of heat and rain — or lack thereof — resulting from a warmer environment.

1990), which established parameters for reducing pollution and increasing the health of America's air and water. The executive branch also issues directives governing different aspects of environmental policy, including logging, mining, and power plant emissions of mercury and ozone.

Encouraging Fuel Efficiency. Gasoline-powered automobiles are a major producer of carbon dioxide and other air pollutants. In 2011, the Obama administration crafted a deal with the top U.S. automakers to institute new standards that will increase fuel efficiency to a fleet-wide average of 54.5 mpg by 2025. Supporters, including most of the U.S. car industry, say that while these increases may add several thousand dollars to the initial price of a car, they will save owners three times that over the life of the vehicle and produce a significant decrease in dangerous emissions, dependence on foreign oil, and illness due to pollution-related causes. And knowing what the future rules will be across the board allows carmakers to safely invest in research and development on more fuel-efficient technologies without fearing they will be priced out of the competition.

Reducing Emissions. Carbon dioxide (CO_2) emissions remain the greatest contributor to earth's warming, yet because CO_2 emissions are such a massive part of the industrial economy, Congress has not passed legislation regulating them. Instead, they have called for voluntary reductions and technological advances to halt growth in national greenhouse gas emissions by 2025.

Frustrated by this lack of concrete national limits, some states and cities have adopted their own policies in recent years. In 2011, President Obama ordered the Environmental Protection Agency (EPA) to begin imposing some regulations on emissions, an effort which prompted angry outcries and initiated legal action by some Republicans and members of the business community. However, because of the poor economy and significant pushback from many members of Congress, President Obama decided to overrule EPA Administrator Lisa Jackson when the agency recommended new limits on some emissions, infuriating environmental activists in the process.

In February 2012, the United States announced a new multinational effort that takes a different approach by taking on the reduction of gases other than CO_2—gases that are much shorter-lived in the atmosphere yet make up 30-40 percent of overall emissions. The thinking behind the strategy is that by tackling these gasses—including soot (also referred to as black carbon), methane, and hydrofluorocarbons—results will be seen and felt quickly. In fact, scientists predict that action on these emissions now can reduce global temperatures by 0.5 degrees Celsius by 2050 and prevent millions of cases of lung and heart disease by 2030. The Obama administration has committed $12 million to seed the program.

Global Cooperation on Current Challenges

Developing Versus Developed Nations. Since the 1940s, world leaders have met periodically to negotiate international treaties addressing different environmental problems. A major sticking point in recent years has been how to regulate both developed and developing nations and how to help poor countries prepare for environmental change and "green" their economies by developing and using industrial technologies that are both environmentally friendly and economically sound.

Without a doubt, developed nations produce the greatest amount of damaging CO_2 emissions, with China and the United States contributing about 40 percent of total annual emissions. And arguably it is the developed world that produced the emissions

The nation of Bangladesh (shown here after flooding in 2004) is a prime example of a country that produces very low emissions, yet could soon face catastrophic effects from global warming. Scientists predict that water will cover nearly one-fifth of its land mass if sea levels rise even a few feet, forcing nearly 20 million people to be resettled by as soon as 2050.

AP PHOTO/RAFIQ MAQBOOL

over the past 150 plus years that created the problem. Understandably, rapidly industrializing nations (including China and India) strongly resist embracing tighter restrictions just as their nations' economies are beginning to play a dominant role on the world scene. But many in the United States and other developed countries refuse to bear tougher restrictions than industrializing nations, claiming they will lose jobs and wealth to those countries with fewer obstacles to growth.

An ironic twist to current threats from global warming is that many of the areas predicted to be hardest hit by increased temperatures are those least able to afford it. Coastal and island nations around the world will see great damage from rising sea levels as ice caps melt, and shifts in weather patterns will produce damaging droughts—or flooding—in nations where local agriculture still feeds the majority of people. Representatives from many of these countries—which, not surprisingly, produce few harmful emissions—demand that something be done to prevent a catastrophe created by other nations.

A school bus is pushed through the front of a building after a tornado swept through Henryville, Indiana, in March 2012. Climatologists believe that current scientific evidence suggests global warming has played a role in the increase and severity of hurricanes, (but there is a less clear connection to tornadoes.

Current Events and Environmental Policy

Man-made Disasters and Mother Nature's Fury. Public opinion about the environment and efforts at environmental policymaking are frequently affected by world events. Over

the past few years, extreme weather events and man-made disasters have provided fodder for environmental activists seeking greater regulation over potentially harmful human activity.

In April 2010, British Petroleum's Deepwater Horizon oil rig, located in the Gulf of Mexico about 40 miles off the coast of Louisiana, experienced a massive blow-out, eventually pushing billions of barrels of crude oil from the sea floor into the Gulf and onto coastlines. This tragedy immediately brought renewed opposition to offshore oil drilling, which President Obama ordered halted. He has since reversed course, allowing some offshore drilling to proceed.

Less than a year later, the Fukushima nuclear complex in Northeast Japan was severely damaged by a massive earthquake and subsequent tsunami, leaking radiation into the surrounding community, waterways, and farmlands. In the immediate aftermath of the disaster, critics worldwide argued that nuclear power should be shunned entirely and Germany vowed to close all its plants by 2022. However, the U.S. Nuclear Regulatory Commission recently approved the first new nuclear reactor in the United States since 1978 and some European countries such as France and Poland are still committed to maintaining or developing a nuclear energy industry.

Wild weather across the world has also had catastrophic consequences in many places. The United States endured a series of deadly and destructive tornadoes and hurricanes, and parts of Europe saw record cold temperatures in early 2012.

Meanwhile, controversies over attempts to balance environmental protection and energy exploration have triggered partisan battles in the United States. President Obama has struggled to continue his campaign pledge to green the economy—which often requires considerable upfront investment to reap the benefits of job growth, cleaner technologies, and more dependable sources of energy—during the worst economic recession in 80 years. In 2011, his administration faced significant criticism when once-promising solar energy company Solyndra, which had received large amounts of federal subsidies, went bankrupt and it was revealed that taxpayers would be the last to be repaid.

Finally, the debate over hydraulic fracturing—a method known as "fracking" that provides access to natural gas trapped deep in shale rock—has grown more contentious as energy executives and local citizens and environmental activists square off over whether the practice pollutes groundwater and harms humans and animals, or helps to provide a fifty-year supply of energy for the nation.

All of these crises and debates—combined with ongoing economic difficulties at home and abroad—directly affect the conversation about environmental policy and have caused both elected officials and ordinary citizens to reconsider priorities and policies.

CURRENT ISSUES

Reducing Greenhouse Gases. Because of the nature of the atmosphere, and because rivers, oceans, and other water systems do not heed political boundaries, most environmental issues are not contained in any one country. Since the 1940s, world leaders have met periodically to negotiate international treaties addressing different environmental problems with work over the past few decades mostly devoted to reducing carbon dioxide emissions and slowing planetary warming. However, UN-led efforts have been extraordinarily contentious and slow, with repeated international conference efforts—most recently in Durban, South Africa—resulting in little, if any, immediate action.

Still, many people believe that the United States must take a lead in fighting global warming and must do so immediately. Recently, there has been renewed talk of instituting a "carbon tax," in which industry pays a per ton fee for harmful emissions. Such plans have had support from members of both parties. Penalties start out low, to mitigate harmful impacts on consumers and allow companies to green and innovate their production methods, but gradually grow higher, to allow the market to drive the most effective, most efficient companies to prosperity. Some suggest that the tax revenue from the carbon tax could then be distributed to low and middle income-Americans to help offset increases in energy costs as the nation shifts away from fossil fuel-driven energy production. Other proponents of a U.S. lead in reducing global warming suggest stronger caps on allowable emissions, requiring greater energy efficiency in all industries, and increased investment in alternative energies. They say that the time to make change is now and that the threat is real and urgent. They point to recent dramatic weather events worldwide—many with punishing economic impact—as evidence of the danger.

Combating global warming is a laudable goal, say opponents, but not at the expense of jobs and the economy in a time of such significant financial distress for so many. A carbon tax is just that—a new tax— which hurts business and average citizens, and hits the poor particularly hard. Regardless of the seemingly small amount of the initial tax, as the economy grows, the government will increase the tax on businesses, who will ultimately pass along the cost to the consumer. Instead, say carbon tax opponents, the best way to promote environmental health and a robust economy is to remove costly government environmental regulations and to open all avenues of domestic energy production, including untapped oil fields, offshore drilling, and nuclear power. Allowing the private sector the opportunity and flexibility to develop new ways to tap traditional energy sources as well as to fully explore new ones will help ensure environmental and economic health.

Challenging the EPA. The nation's leading environmental regulator is the Environmental Protection Agency, an executive branch agency established in 1970 by President Richard Nixon to bipartisan support. It is tasked with conducting environmental research and assessment and carrying out laws passed by Congress or directives issued by the president in the name of protecting human and environmental health. The EPA works closely with state and tribal governments to carry out these duties. The major tasks of the EPA include ensuring that the Clean Air and Clean Water Acts are enforced, which they do through issuing regulations, policing polluters, and taking offenders to court.

However necessary, environmental protections can also be costly. When businesses want to build new factories or plants, environmental reviews are undertaken to assess the impact on surrounding waterways, air, and land. These studies take time and money, and sometimes result in a denial to build. Similarly, when individual landowners want to divide, sell, or develop their land, they are often subject to review as well. The government argues that these steps ensure that all citizens are protected from potentially damaging environmental impacts. Opponents of such rules say that they unfairly limit Americans' rights.

Recently, critics of regulations have become more vociferous in their opposition to the Environmental Protection Agency. They argue that the regulations issued by executive agencies like the EPA are clear examples of overzealous regulators who are creating de facto new laws, never intended by Congress, which severely limit individual citizens' property rights and freedom to prosper. While many Americans believe protecting the environment is important, they caution that it should never come at the expense of jobs and economic growth. Creating massive new bureaucratic systems to tax energy production and restrict access to energy sources, such as the EPA's 2011 proposed smog limits, is destructive in today's dire global economy. The EPA as it currently exists, critics conclude, should be abolished.

Supporters of environmental protections respond that unregulated industrialization during much of the 20th century brought this country environmental disasters like disease-causing smog, lakes and rivers so badly polluted they caught fire, and the devastation of countless animal habitats and ecosystems. Furthermore, say supporters, EPA regulations help prevent hundreds of thousands of deaths each year from pollution-caused or exasperated heart disease, asthma, and other illnesses. Healthier citizens and cleaner land and water, combined with greener technologies, will generate significant economic benefits through reduced health care costs and increased economic profits.

Keeping the Water Clean. According to recent polling, the American public is very concerned about the safety and health of its water systems, with the issue topping the list of environmental concerns in a 2011 Gallup poll. The nation's major mechanism for protecting waterways is the Clean Water Act, which became law in 1972 and was intended to give the newly formed Environmental Protection Agency the authority to clean up and prevent

RECYCLING TOILET WATER

In October 2011, a California public radio news blog ran a cartoon showing a dog drinking from a toilet bowl. The accompanying caption read "ten million dogs can't be wrong" and it illustrated a story with a high "yuck" factor: the move in some municipalities across the country to reclaim and treat waste water (that is, water from toilets) and then use it for tap water. The recent efforts, which used to receive almost universal condemnation, are part of a growing acknowledgment that water is a precious and expensive commodity and a recognition of new technologies that allow waste water to be so thoroughly cleaned that supporters argue that it is essentially like new.

water pollution, in particular the dumping of highly toxic industrial waste into U.S. rivers and lakes.

However, the language of the original law—and several Supreme Court decisions about it in the past ten years—has left uncertainty among regulatory agencies, state and local governments, and industry about which waterways are subject to oversight. Meanwhile, the Republican party and, in particular, the Republican-controlled House of Representatives, have become increasingly hostile to environmental regulation, claiming it has a destructive impact on job growth and economic recovery.

In April 2011, President Obama issued a "guidance" to the EPA, which spelled out more clearly that small waterways, streams, and lakes are to be covered by the law. Republicans in the House and the Senate, backed by members of the agriculture, construction, mining, and oil industries, responded by proposing bills that would have removed significant water oversight and action power from the EPA and given it to the states, essentially overturning four decades of clean water law.

Those who support strengthening the Clean Water Act say that doing so is necessary to maintain the safety of the waters Americans use every day. Recent investigations have revealed significant levels of dangerous pollutants in many sources of drinking water across the United States, including toxins that cause cancer and other disease. Clean water advocates point with alarm to the fact that confusion over the law's jurisdiction has caused criminal enforcement efforts against polluters to drop precipitously while pollution levels have increased at the same time. They argue that ceding control of water pollution to states is dangerous because states are more likely to be influenced by industry advocates and have often been lax in enforcing water laws already on the books.

Critics of the current clean water law argue that states are equally disposed to wanting to protect their water systems, and at the same time are deeply conscious of the damaging effects of massive regulation on jobs and the economy. Proponents of curtailing EPA jurisdiction over water say that they are trying to restore an appropriate balance to the state-federal partnership for enforcing the law. While the intent of the original legislation may have been noble, the ambiguity of the words "navigable waters" in the Clean Water Act has caused significant and damaging economic consequences for too many businesses and ordinary Americans. This is another example, according to critics, of why massive and complex federal laws are a bad way to run an economy and a nation.

OUTLOOK

Political debate over whether environmental protection can go hand-in-hand with job growth and economic recovery will continue to define environmental policymaking for the foreseeable future. As the search for new sources of energy goes on, the coming years will require difficult decisions regarding environmental and energy policy. Unusual coalitions of advocates—both domestically and globally—may help forge new solutions, or offer more of the same current stalemate.

THE DEBATE: THE GLOBAL ENVIRONMENT

The United States should do more to reduce greenhouse gas emissions.

PRO: Global climate change is a planetary emergency, and efforts to fight it will fail without U.S. participation. Addressing climate change now will be far less costly than addressing the catastrophic consequences of unchecked warming later. A carbon tax will force both conservation and innovation and will be implemented in a way so as to give businesses time to adjust without raising costs significantly for consumers.

CON: If climate change is really a problem that humans can address, then it demands creative solutions and technological innovation, not higher taxes. And a carbon tax is just that: a tax that will be passed on from business to consumer, born disproportionately by the lowest-income citizens. Instead, the United States needs to remove regulations and obstacles to energy exploration and innovation in the private market.

The EPA should be abolished.

PRO: The human contributions to global warming are unproven and the risk to economic growth too great to allow the government the vast regulatory power it now wields. With the global economy still struggling, this is the absolute wrong time to be placing new economic demands on small businesses and average citizens. The EPA acts as if it has the power to make laws, a right reserved only to Congress and the states.

CON: The EPA was established to protect ordinary citizens from the health, economic, and environmental damages wrought by unfettered industrialization and development. Without its work over the past forty years, the United States would be a sicker and dirtier nation, and even more dependent on an unsustainable, fossil-fuel based economy.

The Clean Water Act should be strengthened.

PRO: Before serious environmental legislation like the Clean Water Act was passed, American rivers, lakes, and streams were dirty and polluted, a direct health risk for millions of Americans. Forty years of Clean Water Act enforcement has helped improve these conditions significantly, but millions of Americans still have unclean drinking water and more pollution is occurring all the time. The EPA needs a clearer and improved mandate to help it protect U.S. waters.

CON: Enforcement of the Clean Water Act under the Obama administration has resulted in serious overreach with damaging economic consequences. It is silly to suggest that if given more oversight power that states cannot or will not work to protect the water systems within their own boundaries as well as those that flow through multiple states. The Clean Water Act needs to be overhauled to reflect the appropriate federal-state roles for environmental protection and to ensure that job growth is the nation's number one priority.

GLOBAL SECURITY

INTRODUCTION

In an increasingly interconnected world, nations and international organizations often take collective action to protect global security—combatting threats against the safety of societies and individuals. Global security has been a goal of U.S. foreign policy for many years. The United States fought in World War I to "make the world safe for democracy" and World War II found the United States and its allies fighting to prevent the spread of hatred and destruction around the world. After the war, global security was defined by the Cold War—the struggle between the East (communist nations, mainly the Soviet Union and China) and the West (democratic nations, mainly the United States and its European allies).

KEY QUESTIONS

- Is the United States adequately prepared for cyberattacks?

- Should the United States continue to sell weapons to volatile regions of the world?

- Should military action be used to stop Iran's nuclear ambitions?

Over time, Cold War hostilities were replaced by global cooperation, fueled by economic interdependence, and advances in technology, communications, and transportation. This process of globalization, combined with the fall of communism in 1991, created a multi-polar world where an individual nation's success is intricately connected to the rest of the world.

According to the United Nations, "every state requires the cooperation of other states to make itself secure . . . it is in every state's interest to cooperate with others to address their most pressing threats." Those threats are varied and touch most nations directly. Nuclear weapons, global poverty, terrorism, civil wars and ethnic tensions, widespread disease and epidemics, unstable financial markets, and climate change challenge old alliances, old assumptions about how the world works, and old beliefs.

Today, U.S. leaders speak and act in terms of global security under the belief that a safe and secure world will mean a safe and secure United States. U.S. policymakers use many tools including diplomatic pressure, international conferences, securing global loans and economic agreements, and relying on international and private organizations to achieve its security goals.

BACKGROUND

Global Security in Historical Perspective

The Cold War. After World War II, U.S. national security strategy focused almost exclusively on the Soviet Union and the threat of communist expansion in the free world. The United States enacted several initiatives during the Cold War as part of this strategy.

The policy of containment sought to prevent the spread of communism overseas and keep it contained to the Soviet Union and its immediate post-World War II allies. The United States enacted this policy through direct military involvement in the Korean (1950-1953) and Vietnam (1961-1975) Wars and through military assistance to guerilla forces fighting communist-backed armies from Turkey (1947) to Cuba (1961) to Afghanistan (1980s).

Nuclear deterrence resulted in an escalating arms race between the United Sates and the Soviet Union during the Cold War. As each nation built larger, more powerful, and more accurate weapons the two superpowers reached a point known as Mutually Assured Destruction. Under this doctrine, the United States and the Soviet Union felt assured that neither of

During the Cold War, the United States and the Soviet Union engaged in a deadly arms race building more powerful and deadlier nuclear weapons as each nation tried to outpace the other.

them would ever use their nuclear weapons, as doing so would result in the complete annihilation of the attacker.

Finally, the United States entered into several collective security alliances during the Cold War. Immediately after World War II, the United States and its European allies formed the North Atlantic Treaty Organization (NATO) against the growing Soviet threat in Eastern Europe. The United States entered similar alliances over the next 50 years and although some of these alliances ultimately failed to achieve their objectives, the message was clear—an enemy of communism was a friend of the United States.

During the late 1980s, democratic reforms slowly began to take root in many East European nations, leading eventually to the collapse of communism throughout the region, the dismantling of the Soviet empire, and the end of the Cold War.

Many thought the end of the Cold War would usher in an era of peace, global prosperity, and international cooperation. President George H.W. Bush declared a "new world order" was needed, one "in which freedom and respect for human rights find a home in all nations." The end of the Cold War, however, exposed deep issues just simmering beneath the surface of the superpower conflict. Ethnic tensions broke free in newly liberated nations in Eastern Europe and the world's nations could not prevent a full-scale war and genocide in Yugoslavia that resulted from years of pent-up ethnic rage. U.S. citizens, expecting a "peace dividend" from a shift in Cold War military spending to domestic programs, were disappointed to find the United States still funding long-range bombers and a space-based missile defense system. And in December 1992, President Bush, in one of his last acts as president, ordered 25,000 U.S. troops to oversee famine relief efforts in Somalia after civil war and drought had left thousands there in desperate need.

The Clinton Years. Although President Bill Clinton embraced the concept of global security, the United States, as the world's remaining superpower, was often forced to take the lead when troubles arose. In 1994, U.S. troops were used in Haiti to help restore democratic control after a military coup. In 1999, the United States led NATO air strikes in Bosnia in an attempt to end years of ethnic violence in that part of Europe. Eventually, the Clinton State Department was instrumental in bringing the warring factions together at Wright-Patterson Air Force Base outside of Dayton, Ohio, where a peace agreement known as the Dayton Accords was signed.

THE HIGH COST OF SECURITY

It is difficult to accurately estimate the exact cost of keeping the United States secure in the post-9/11- world, as such a figure would have to include not only the price of, for example, increased border patrols, but also the money lost because of the terrorist attacks themselves. Nevertheless, one estimate pegs the cost of keeping America safe over the past decade at $3.3 trillion. This total includes the wars in Iraq and Afghanistan, the creation of the massive Department of Homeland Security, and numerous expenditures made by the federal government, state and local governments, and private sector businesses in increased security for buildings, employees, and customers. Also included in this $3.3 trillion figure are some consequences of the 9/11 attacks that may not be so obvious. For example, the Rand Corporation estimates that since 2001, U.S. businesses have lost $100 billion in productivity due to extra waiting time in U.S. airports.

During the Clinton presidency, increased globalization of the world's economies and cultures brought greater global cooperation. In 1993, the governments of Canada, Mexico, and the United States and agreed to the North American Free Trade Agreement, which removed most trade barriers among those three countries. In 1995, the World Trade Organization was established to set the rules for fair trade among its 153 participating nations. In December 1999, the first G-20 Economic Summit was convened with the finance ministers and leading economists from the worlds top 20 economies meeting to discuss international economic cooperation. And the North Atlantic Treaty Organization admitted former Warsaw Pact countries such as Czech Republic, Hungary, and Poland the in 1999.

Global Security and 9/11. The terrorist attacks on September 11, 2001, defined U.S. security policy over the next decade. The administration of George W. Bush committed the United States to a "global war on terror" whose aim was to "preserve and promote the way of life of free and open societies" by ridding the world of terrorist threats. As part of this campaign, the United States engaged in two wars. In 2001, the United States invaded Afghanistan because its government had supported the terrorists who staged the 9/11 attacks. Then in 2003, with assistance from 48 other nations, the United States led an invasion of Iraq claiming its leader, Saddam Hussein, possessed weapons of mass destruction. In this case, the United States justified the invasion on the doctrine of preemption—that the United States could attack any nation it deemed threatening, even if the threat was not imminent.

The United Nations and long-time U.S. allies France and Germany did not back the invasion of Iraq. Nevertheless, U.S. leaders went ahead with the war claiming it was justified for global security reasons. While supporters believed this brand of strong U.S. leadership was needed to eradicate the terrorist threat, it nonetheless created an image of the United States as a nation willing to act on perceived threats with or without the support of the majority of nations.

A New Era of Engagement. President Barack Obama took office in 2009 determined to erase the harm he and others perceived this strategy had brought to the United States, both at home and abroad. He pledged to end the war in Iraq, to bring some relief to a war weary nation and a U.S. military stretched thin from years of fighting two wars. To the rest of the world, Obama promised a "new era of engagement" with a deeper respect for other cultures and the sovereignty of nations. Reflecting this new approach, Obama delivered a speech to the Muslim world from Cairo in June 2009 pledging a new beginning between the United States and Muslims.

Palestinians watch President Obama's speech to the Muslim world on June 9, 2009. The president promised a new beginning for the relationship between the United States and Muslims around the world. The unprecedented speech was translated or closed captioned in more than a dozen languages.

Despite the softening rhetoric, the United States has not closed its eyes to the mounting threats to global security nor turned aside all of the Bush administration's strategies. The war in Afghanistan continued under President Obama, although all U.S. combat troops are scheduled to leave in 2014. Terrorists are still hunted around the world and the use of drone aircraft for these operations has risen dramatically. And President Obama agrees with his predecessor when he states that the "gravest danger to the American people and global security continues to come from weapons of mass destruction, particularly nuclear weapons."

President Obama has, however, expanded the scope of global security to include many other threats such as cyberterrorism, the continued U.S. dependence on fossil fuels that limits U.S. foreign policy options, especially in the Middle East, and global climate change. As Obama stated, "the very fluidity within the international system that breeds new challenges must be approached as an opportunity to forge new international cooperation."

Global Security Challenges Today

One of the lessons of the September 2001 terrorist attacks is that one does not need a large standing army to attack a nation today. For example, a person with an off-the-shelf PC can launch a cyberattack interrupting a nation's air traffic control system. A simple vial of bubonic plague stolen from a research lab can be released on a crowed subway train. A small amount of plutonium sold by a former Soviet republic can be used to start a nuclear weapons program. A group of men armed only with machine guns and a few swift boats can capture a huge oil tanker on the high seas and hold it for ransom.

And the attack does not even need to come from another nation or group of individuals. A deadly virus, immune to current antibiotics, could move quickly from small village to large city due to the interconnectedness of people today and the ease of global air travel. According to the FBI, globalization creates a global security threat environment "more complex and diverse than ever before."

Cyberattacks. Today the world is electronically connected in ways barely dreamed of just a few decades ago. It is estimated that about 2 billion people worldwide use the Internet everyday. Although governments maintain highly secure Internet facilities the fact remains that today's mischievous hacker can easily be tomorrow's cyberterrorist. Computer

ANONYMOUS

Anonymous is not one person or even one group of people but instead is a loosely held together online hacking collective that many believed started in 2003. Until recently, most of the online activities associated with the Anonymous name have been of a crude humor or mischievous type. But starting in 2008, hackers calling themselves Anonymous began to organize worldwide protests against what they saw as infringements on Internet freedom from corporations and governments. Anonymous was heavily involved in planning the online protests over the Stop Online Piracy Act when it was being debated in Congress in 2011. Hackers calling themselves Anonymous took down the Universal Music Group website for several hours in January 2012 to protest its attempt to track illegal music downloads. In the same month Anonymous hacked into the Department of Justice and FBI websites to protest their involvement in shutting down the hugely popular (but still illegal) Megaupload.com website. Anonymous does not appear to be going away any time soon. As Anonymous hackers state: "We are Anonymous. We are Legion. We do not forgive. We do not forget. Expect us."

criminals continue to hone their skills and many times successful hackers go undetected. For example, an individual sitting at a terminal in one country can, using the Internet, hack into a computer network in another country to carry out an attack on U.S. computers and thus cover his tracks. Hackers can send a computer virus across multinational networks and as the virus is passed from one computer to another it reproduces on its own, disrupting computer programs, communications, and financial transactions across international borders. The extent of just one cyberattack could have far reaching implications for the nation attacked and the rest of the world.

Weapons Proliferation. Despite modern technological advancements in weapons systems, most armies around the world are still largely dependent on conventional arms—warplanes, artillery, tanks, rifles, small arms, and ammunition. Nations selling these weapons are dependent on the income such sales bring. While the sale and spread of conventional weapons appears, on the surface, as "business as usual," such proliferation takes on new meaning in the post-9/11 world. Nation to nation sales often lead to further transactions—from nations to individual rebel groups, for example.

Once heavily armed, these rebel groups can stage successful revolutions in their homelands (such as Libya in 2011), furthering the instability of a region and disrupting the balance of nations throughout the world.

Nuclear Proliferation. In addition to conventional weapons, the spread of nuclear weapons and dangerous materials remains a global threat. With the breakup of the Soviet Union in 1991, large numbers of nuclear warheads and materials were scattered across former Soviet republics. Some officials fear that economically strapped nations—especially Belarus, Kazakhstan, and Uzbekistan—might not be able (or willing) to prevent hostile nations from buying or stealing these materials. Also, some nations operating outside of conventional norms and shunning international law or safeguards, are pursuing their own nuclear goals. Two of these "rogue" nations—Iran and North Korea—are, some say, a major threat to global security, making the safeguarding of nuclear material a global responsibility.

High-Seas Piracy. Although is sounds like a throwback to a bygone era of swashbucklers and sailing ships, piracy on the high seas is a very real and very dangerous global security issue today. The International Maritime Bureau reported 439 large container shipping vessels and oil tankers were attacked in 2011,

Nearly one billion people in the world do not have enough to eat every day to lead productive lives. Food security refers to global efforts to end world hunger and ensure that nations are equipped to supply their citizens with the necessary amount of food to maintain a healthy lifestyle.

many of them taking place off the east and west coasts of Africa. Bands of heavily armed pirates use fast boats to surround and board the slower moving ships and capture crewmen and the ship itself, which they hold for ransom from the ship owners. More than 800 crewmen were held hostage in 2011 prompting the European Union to take aggressive measures—including using warships as escorts and surveillance aircraft—to police shipping lanes in international waters. In addition, many ship owners have hired private security firms to protect their investment, which includes stationing armed guards on the ships and installing razor wire around the sides of the vessels to prevent pirates from boarding.

Food Security. It is estimated that nearly one billion people—one-sixth of the world's population—suffers from chronic hunger, meaning they are so undernourished they cannot lead productive lives. Ending chronic hunger is a global security goal because, according to the U.S. State Department's Office of Global Food Security "without enough food, adults struggle to work, children struggle to learn, making sustainable economic development difficult to achieve." Food security refers to programs that provide nations in need with technical assistance to assure that citizens are able to grow or buy enough food to lead healthy and economically productive lives. Currently the United States and many other nations are involved in efforts to reduce world hunger including investing in small-scale agricultural production in the hardest hit nations, improving irrigation and water management systems, and implementing nutrition education programs for children and women in areas where hunger persists for generations.

CURRENT ISSUES

Protecting Cyberspace. Much of what the U.S. government—and global society in general—does, is now done in cyberspace where computers track commercial aircraft in the skies, process millions of social security checks each month, regulate water filtration systems in most cities, process millions of financial transactions each day, and automatically turn on switches to help cool and maintain nuclear reactors. Much of this activity takes place over the Internet. Some computer security experts in the United States see a dire danger in this. They point out that the same Internet that allows a customer to purchase items online is the same Internet that is used to monitor the safety of the U.S. nuclear arsenal or control air traffic. Since

Internet regulation is so inconsistent from nation to nation, some experts equate global cyberspace with the American "wild west" where hackers roam freely and bring down important government computer operating systems with the click of a mouse. A July 2010 Government Accountability Office report on global cybersecurity states that "global interconnectivity provided by the Internet allows cyber attackers to easily cross national borders, access vast numbers of victims at the same time, and easily maintain anonymity."

Some experts believe that the United States—and most of the world—is woefully unprepared for what some describe as "cyberwarfare." These analysts point to several incidents where computer terrorists successfully displayed their ability to create havoc in an otherwise civilized cyberworld. In 2007, the Eastern European country of Estonia, one of the world's most "wired" nations, was victim of a nationwide cyberattack that left many of the government's operations at a standstill for several weeks. In 2011 media giant Verizon reported that more than 174 million users had their accounts hacked.

While these experts admit that so far no major international incident has resulted from cyberterrorism, they warn it is only a matter of time before power grids are taken down

The National Cybersecurity and Communications Integration Center readies for cyberattack exercises. Some experts say it will be several more years before the government installs systems capable of defending against attacks such as those being simulated in these operations.

or commercial services are interrupted enough to cause economic chaos around the globe. These experts point out that U.S. computer systems—in both the public and private sectors—are targeted by cyberterrorists more than any other systems in the world and that the attacks are increasing and becoming more and more sophisticated. According to these experts, defensive computer programming efforts and training in cybersecurity is far behind the international hackers' abilities. They cite the example of teams of hackers recently hired by the Department of Defense to try to break into some of their systems; in all cases, the hackers succeeded. According to these critics, unless U.S. policymakers take cyberterrorism more seriously, the United States will find itself losing on the cyberwar battlefield.

Others believe that the threat of cyberterrorism, while real enough, is exaggerated. They point out that to date there have been no "casualties" in a cyberattack. People have been inconvenienced, systems breached, information compromised, but no one has died as the result of cyberterrorism. These experts ask if cyberattacks are becoming more widespread and sophisticated, why are they not more successful? Obviously, they say, the answer is we are doing something right. These analysts cite numerous efforts by the Obama administration to address cybersecurity including the appointment of the White House Cybersecurity Coordinator to organize efforts across multiple government agencies, the launching of the National Initiative for Cybersecurity Education by the Department of Homeland Security with the goal of creating a "cyber-savvy citizenry and a cyber-capable workforce," and the official designation of October as National Cybersecurity Awareness Month with numerous government agencies involved in educational and awareness programs.

Arming the World. The United States is by far the largest arms dealer in the world, both in sheer numbers of weapons sold as well as profits. In the fiscal year ending in September 2011, the Pentagon reported arms sales exceeded $34 billion. The numbers and the deals continue to rise. In December 2011, the United States completed an arms deal with Saudi Arabia, a major U.S. ally in the Middle East, of more than $30 billion, with the Saudis purchasing military planes, helicopters, missiles, bombs, and other conventional weapons. Saudi Arabia was not the only country in the Middle East to receive substantial arms deals recently. India, Iraq, Israel, Kuwait, Oman, Taiwan, and United Arab Emirates all agreed to billion dollar deals in 2011.

The United States is the largest exporter of conventional weapons worldwide, totalling more than $34 billion in 2011. Many of these arms end up in the hands of rebel forces not always in agreement with U.S. policies.

The United States is also the world's largest contributor of military aid to foreign countries. The aid comes in many forms and is most commonly given in the form of congressionally approved grants to foreign governments to purchase American-made weapons, services, and training. Afghanistan, Egypt, Iraq, Israel, Jordan, and Pakistan are the largest recipients of this aid. While military aid is usually tied to strategic foreign policy decisions, critics say the United States is contributing to the proliferation of major weapon systems in countries that are unstable and could provoke neighboring countries and regimes to arm as well.

Proponents of the U.S. arms trade cite the financial benefits — selling arms generates revenue for weapons contractors at a time when budget shortfalls are a major problem. Additionally, many of these weapon systems are designed and constructed in the United States, generating jobs and keeping communities intact. Supporters also argue that arms deals are a way for U.S. leaders to balance strategic interests and other critical issues related to global security. For example, large arms sales to Saudi Arabia balances military power in the volatile Middle East and keeps Saudi Arabia a close U.S. ally.

Some critics argue that the United Nations should regulate the international arms trade, while others think that the United States should not be in the business of arming the world at all. Arms sales, according to this group, actually create more problems for the United States in the long run. While many of the deals are made with U.S. allies, critics note that the same arms end up in countries with brutal regimes that use them to stage attacks against neighbors or to oppress their own people. Although these nations may be considered allies now, many experts cite the recent Arab Spring democracy movements in Egypt and elsewhere as evidence that governments can change hands quickly and possibly be ruled in the future by leaders hostile to U.S. interests.

A Nuclear Iran? Iran is a signatory to the United Nations Nuclear Nonproliferation Treaty of 1968, which seeks to stop the spread of nuclear weapons and the use of nuclear technology for nonpeaceful purposes. At the same time, it stands firm by its rights to acquire these materials to develop its nuclear energy industry. Iran, however, is believed to be operating a parallel clandestine nuclear weapons program. Many claim that a nuclear-armed Iran would be a major security threat to the region, especially to Western allies and interests. Currently, two schools of thought dominate the debate on how to deal with a possibly nuclear-armed Iran—sanctions and diplomacy versus a military attack on Iran's nuclear facilities.

Many believe that economic sanctions against Iran will eventually force that nation's leaders to the negotiating table to work with the United States, Israel, and other countries to find a diplomatic—and peaceful—solution to Iran's nuclear program. These sanctions are imposed by many nations and include mostly bans on sharing nuclear energy development technology but also oil refinery equipment transfers, prohibitions against banking and financial transactions, and freezing Iranian assets in overseas banks. Those who support this approach point out that after several years of sanctions Iran has signaled that it is willing to begin talks. Although this does not necessarily mean an agreement will be reached, those who support sanctions say that is a step in the right direction. Those who back diplomacy say that any type of military action against Iran would increase tensions in the already volatile Middle East and could easily lead to escalated hostilities. Sanction supporters say that more are needed to further force Iran into a corner where negotiation is the only possible way out.

Others disagree and say that the time to negotiate has ended. Critics of further sanctions contend that diplomatic efforts to negotiate Iran down from its nuclear precipice have been ongoing for much of the past decade, producing nothing but time for Iran to continue its nuclear weapons development program. These experts argue that the only option left is striking militarily against Iranian nuclear facilities. Proponents of military action point to Israeli strikes against nuclear reactors in Iraq in 1981 and in Syria in 2007 as the type of successful operation that could be conducted against Iran. In both cases the attacks halted each nation's nuclear programs and did not lead to further military action. Supporters of military action at this time believe that an Iran armed with nuclear weapons poses a greater threat that any retaliation from Iran and its allies or any fallout from the diplomatic community. Those who support attacking Iran believe that time is running out for the West and its vital oil interests in the Middle East to delay military action on the thin hope that Iran will suddenly come to its senses and sit down and talk.

Iranian President Mahmoud Ahmadinejad listens to a technician at a uranium enrichment facility north of Iran's capital of Tehran. Many fear that a nuclear Iran will lead to further instability in the Middle East and may force Israel or others to take aggressive military action against Iran in order to maintain their security.

AP PHOTO / IRANIAN PRESIDENTS OFFICE

OUTLOOK

In the two decades since the end of the Cold War the world has become a very different place. The safety and security of the United States is now wrapped up in the safety and security of the rest of the world. From the threats posed by nonstate actors to environmental disasters looming on the horizon, how the United States responds to these and other concerns is of primary importance to U.S. lawmakers. While the United States remains the lone superpower in the world for the time being, there is little to guarantee that such status equals the amount of international influence the United States once enjoyed.

THE DEBATE: GLOBAL SECURITY

The United States is adequately prepared to defend itself against cyberattacks.

PRO: There has been no successful cyberattack on U.S. computer systems, nor will there be in the future. U.S. defensive capabilities only grow as the hackers get more desperate. Besides, most terrorist organizations would never resort to cyberattacks, as taking down a computer system lacks the fear-inducing "shock and awe" response from the public terrorists seek that car bombings or other activities achieve.

CON: Cyberattacks occur on a regular basis at the Pentagon, FBI, and other high-tech agencies in the U.S. government. The fact that they have been successfully repelled simply means that the attackers have not found the vulnerabilities in U.S. computer systems. Federal air traffic computers date back to the 1960s and many cybersecurity experts in the government have not been trained in the latest technology and techniques used by the best international hackers.

The United States should continue to sell arms to nations in volatile regions of the world.

PRO: The United States makes the best military, surveillance, and satellite equipment in the world. It serves the global interests of all nations to make sure certain nations of the world have access to the latest and best defense tools. Keeping defenders of the peace well armed deters other nations and terrorist groups from attacking. Additionally, the money U.S. manufacturers make from arms deals generates jobs and huge profits.

CON: By selling weapons, the United States is making it easier for countries to take military instead of diplomatic action. Some of the very weapons sold by the United States have actually been used against U.S. forces and its allies. It is hypocritical for the United States to be promoting peace in the Middle East while selling arms to many of the nations in that part of the world. Such a two-faced stance only increases tension in that region.

Military action should be used to stop Iran's nuclear ambitions.

PRO: With Iran so close to having nuclear weapons capability, the time for talk is over. Iran is providing weapons to insurgent groups around the world and makes no secret of its desire to "exterminate" Israel. A nuclear Iran poses a severe threat to global security and requires swift military action on the part of free nations around the world.

CON: Economic sanctions against Iran are working. Increasing sanctions now will help to force Iran to the negotiating table, which will enable U.S. leaders and others to peacefully halt not only Iran's nuclear weapons development but also its aggression throughout the Middle East. Military action will only heighten tensions in the area and increase the possibility of retaliation from Iran and its supporters.

INTERNATIONAL TRADE

INTRODUCTION

Trading goods and services with other nations is vital to economic well-being. Companies that sell—or export—U.S. goods overseas bring money into the U.S. economy. Meanwhile, goods made in foreign countries—or imports—give consumers more choices, resulting in competition and cheaper products. Trade policy influences prices for everything from T-shirts to food to iPhones.

KEY QUESTIONS

- Are free trade agreements good for the U.S. economy?

- Should the federal government support U.S. manufacturing?

- Should the United States enforce fair trade?

Trade is also a cornerstone of international relations. Good trading relations often foster improved cooperation on other issues, such as security. Leaders frequently use trade as a diplomatic tool. For instance, they may give better trade privileges to friendly nations or impose trade sanctions on others. Over the last few decades, as international trade has increased, so has foreign investment. Overseas companies have bought shares in U.S. firms. Likewise, U.S. businesses have hoped to profit from growth in countries such as China and India. In addition, foreign countries have loaned great sums to the U.S. government, funding the national debt. Today the largest foreign creditor to the United States is China. These forms of trade and economic integration, along with social and technological forces, have broken down barriers between nations, creating "globalization."

In the United States, free trade opponents cite the loss of U.S. jobs when American businesses build factories or hire service workers abroad, a trend called "outsourcing." On the other hand, supporters argue free trade strengthens both the U.S. and world economies and promotes American interests and democracy. In this competitive global environment, many of today's debates center on how to promote American exports and preserve and create American jobs.

BACKGROUND

Trading with the World

Why Do Nations Trade? When a nation tries to produce most of the goods and services its people require, its economy grows slowly. The economy grows faster when a country exports its most plentiful or most easily produced goods to other nations and imports goods that others can produce more easily. Many countries have a comparative advantage—such as natural resources, a temperate climate, skilled labor, or technical superiority—that enables them to make certain products at a lower cost than other countries. Comparative advantage allows each country to profit by trading the goods and services it produces most efficiently for those that other countries are better able to produce.

Protectionism. Trade agreements among nations generally establish favorable rules of trade and typically reduce trade barriers. Free trade, or trade without restrictions, however, has been rare throughout history. Most countries use various tools of trade to protect certain industries or to encourage consumers to buy domestic goods and services. This policy is known as "protectionism."

Policymakers use the following tools to control trade:
- *Tariffs* are taxes on imports that increase the price of foreign-made products.
- *Quotas* limit the amount of specific products that can be imported.
- *Subsidies* are payments and other government supports that give a domestic industry a market advantage.
- *Anti-dumping* rules prohibit other nations from selling goods below the real-market value.
- *Trade embargoes* are bans on trade used to entice other nations to change their behavior.

Coordinating World Trade. Despite enforcing some protectionist measures, many U.S. leaders believed in expanding international trade. Following World War II, the United States took the lead in urging the nations of Western Europe to coordinate their trade policies. Furthermore, they encouraged the formation of international bodies and agreements to oversee world economic and trade issues.

Top U.S. Trading Partners (2011)

in billions of dollars

Canada

China

Mexico

Japan

Germany

United Kingdom

South Korea

Brazil

France

Taiwan

Imports to the U.S.

Exports from the U.S.

0 50 100 150 200 250 300 350 400

Source: U.S. Census Bureau.

The International Monetary Fund. Delegates from forty-four nations met in 1944 at Bretton Woods, New Hampshire, to discuss international trade and monetary issues. They created the International Monetary Fund (IMF) in 1945 to provide short-term loans and help stabilize international exchange rates. Today, 188 countries belong to the IMF.

The World Bank. Also founded at the Bretton Woods Conference, the World Bank makes long-term loans to help poor countries develop economically and reduce poverty.

GATT and the World Trade Organization. In 1947, twenty-three noncommunist nations signed the General Agreement on Tariffs and Trade (GATT), establishing a code of conduct for trade. Under the provisions of GATT, a growing number of nations sought to increase world trade by reducing trade barriers. In 1994, GATT members approved a sweeping new trade accord that eliminated import tariffs on thousands of products, phased out quota systems, and established a new global body—the World Trade Organization (WTO)—to settle trade disputes. The WTO's judicial system for resolving trade disagreements has the authority to impose tariffs or sanctions on member countries. Currently, there are 153 nations in the WTO.

Controversy has swirled around the WTO ever since its inception. Critics believe the WTO's broad mandate favors wealthier nations, and strips power from citizens and individual governments. Others credit the WTO for settling trade disputes without trade warfare.

With each member wielding a veto, negotiating new trade rules among 153 countries is always a struggle. The most recent series of WTO trade talks is known as the Doha Round, for the city in Qatar, where they began in 2001. The Doha Round was intended to expand trade globally, emphasizing prosperity for the least developed countries. After ten years, talks stalled over disagreements between developed countries and emerging economies. By 2012, WTO head Pascal Lamy admitted that the Doha Round would not yield a "big package," as originally planned.

The Group of Eight (G-8). Since 1975, a group of major industrial democracies has been meeting to discuss economic issues, trade relations, and foreign exchange markets. The G-8 consists of Canada, France, Germany, Italy, Japan, the United Kingdom, the United States, and most recently, Russia. In 1999, members of this body created the Group of Twenty (G-20), another international organization that helps build consensus on matters of financial stability and worldwide economic growth. By including developing countries such as China, India, Korea, Mexico, and Turkey, leaders wanted to integrate these fast-growing economies into global decision-making.

Trade Blocs. Over the past decade, international trade has been further boosted by free trade blocs—international groups formed to further reduce tariffs and other barriers to trade among member nations.

The North American Free Trade Agreement. In 1994, the North American Free Trade Agreement (NAFTA) created the world's largest free-trade area at that time. Under NAFTA, Canada, Mexico, and the

China is the United States's second-biggest trading partner. From China, the import of greatest value is computers. Our biggest export to China is soybeans. Here, an Iowa farmer kneels in his soybean harvest.

AP PHOTO/CHARLIE NEIBERGALL

United States have gradually eliminated barriers on agricultural products and manufactured goods and removed restrictions on cross-border investments.

The European Union. In 1957, six nations in Western Europe created the European Economic Community (EEC). The EEC, which later became the European Union (EU), abolished import restrictions among member countries and devised common agreements for marketing their products outside Europe. In 2002, twelve European nations replaced their individual currencies with a single currency called the euro and created a unified economy. Countries using the euro now number seventeen. The EU, currently the world's largest economic zone, consists of 27 countries and more than 500 million people. The EU's gross domestic product, a measure of economic might, is more than $17 trillion, or about 20 percent of the global economy. In July 2013, Croatia is set to become the 28th member of the EU.

The Dominican Republic–Central America Free Trade Agreement. In 2004, President George W. Bush negotiated a free-trade agreement between the United States, the Dominican Republic, and the Central American countries of Costa Rica, El Salvador, Guatemala, Honduras, and Nicaragua. Similar to NAFTA, the zone will reduce barriers to trade. Congress approved the agreement in 2005, and by 2007, all countries had ratified the agreement known as CAFTA-DR.

WHERE IS YOUR iPHONE MADE?

iPhone components are made all over the world, but they come together for assembly in a plant in Shenzhen, China, called Foxconn Technology—the largest exporter in China. Recently, Apple has come under criticism for the working conditions in this factory, even though about 40 percent of the world's electronics are manufactured there. Unlike American plants, this company is run like a city. Many of its hundreds of thousands of workers are migrants, poor young people between 18 and 25 years old, who live in dormitories near the assembly line and send money home to their families. They work twelve-hour shifts, six days a week, and earn an average of $14 per day. Because of media attention following a spate of worker suicides, the U.S. Fair Labor Association inspected the facility and found many violations of Chinese law and industrial code. Consequently, Foxconn announced it would reduce the number of hours that employees work and increase wages.

Trade Issues in the United States

Free Trade. Throughout its history, the U.S. government has used protectionism to control trade and promote domestic industries. However, over the past few decades and through presidential administrations of both parties, the U.S. government has advocated lifting trade restrictions with some countries. The United States made regional and bilateral trade agreements that opened markets in Africa, Asia, Latin America, and the Middle East. Officials hoped that free trade agreements would promote global economic growth and spur other countries to enter into similar trade deals. Given the remarkable economic growth of China, for example, and its pursuit of increased trade with African nations and the EU, such policies accomplished some of their goals. The effects of free trade within the United States, however, have been controversial. Passing new trade agreements has proven contentious.

Protectionism. Even though lawmakers have pursued free trade agreements with some countries, they occasionally implement protectionist measures. In some cases, tariffs or quotas are needed to punish another country for unfair trade practices. Especially during economic downturns or periods of high unemployment, protectionism can be necessary to shield a domestic industry and jobs. For example, in 2009, President Barack Obama enacted three-year tariffs on Chinese-made tires because the Chinese were illegally "dumping" state-subsidized tires in the U.S. market. The WTO upheld the U.S. action in 2010, and by that time U.S. tire production and related jobs were rebounding.

The Trade Deficit. Since the mid-1970s, the United States has imported more goods than it has exported. The trade deficit total (including goods and services) was $558 billion in 2011, up from $500 billion in 2010. Simply put, the trade imbalance means that the U.S. economy is consuming more than it is producing. This trend yields both positive and negative consequences. Increased imports create lower prices, which dampen inflation and bring prosperity for American shoppers. However, after decades of free trade policies, most experts agree that the massive rise in imports, without a corresponding increase in American exports, has contributed to U.S. job losses.

Canada, the United States's largest trading partner, is also its biggest supplier of crude oil. Shown here is a pumpjack in Alberta. The greatest exports to Canada are cars, trucks, and vehicle parts. In 2011, $597 billion in goods were exchanged between the two countries.

Foreign Investment. Throughout 2008, a number of economic factors converged to trigger noteworthy increases in foreign investment. Record-high fuel prices enriched oil-producing nations, so those governments searched for stable investment opportunities — often in the United States. Governments of other growing economies, such as China and India, also sought safe U.S. investments. Simultaneously, a tumble in the U.S. housing market weakened banks and mortgage lenders, which sought huge infusions of cash to stay solvent.

Around the same time, the Chinese government, which had been buying U.S. government securities since the 1980s, invested increasing sums in Treasury bonds and other U.S. government debt, which helped bankroll economic bailout packages. By late 2008, China had overtaken Japan as America's largest creditor.

Foreign governments owning large stakes in U.S. banks and U.S. government debt have caused concern. The entire U.S. economy could be vulnerable if those investors withdrew their funds suddenly or if they operated fraudulently. Others welcomed the cash and argued that such investment promotes economic interdependence, which they say encourages all players to act in the best interests of the world economy.

The Great Recession and the Auto Bailout. In 2008, as the United States suffered its worst economic downturn since the Great Depression, its "Big Three" automakers—Chrysler, Ford, and General Motors—were hit hard. After General Motors and Chrysler repeatedly asked for government assistance, in late 2008 President George Bush agreed to loan the companies billions of dollars in exchange for reorganizing their businesses. Over the years, U.S. auto manufacturers had not kept pace with their tough foreign competition. When President Barack Obama took office in 2009, his administration managed the details of the bailout agreement. Even with government loans, GM and Chrysler still had to declare bankruptcy, and they emerged with fewer brands and plants. The leaner companies have begun to show profits, however. Ford, which did not take any government money, rebounded fastest, and returned to profitability in 2009. Some policymakers debated the wisdom of such loans, arguing that private investors should have rescued Detroit or that the companies should have declared bankruptcy from the outset. Others point out that the auto bailout saved millions of U.S. jobs during a critical economic downturn.

CURRENT ISSUES

Free Trade and the U.S. Economy. When the United States started running large trade deficits with Japan in the 1970s and 1980s, free trade policies came under attack. More recently, with job losses associated with the global recession, free trade has again become unpopular among many voters. In late 2011, Congress finally ratified three bilateral trade pacts with Colombia, Panama, and South Korea, which had languished for five years. Because the unemployment rate at that time remained high, at just under nine percent, these new free trade agreements faced criticism from those who wanted to protect American jobs.

Conceding that the economy has been recovering, albeit at an anemic pace, free-trade advocates assert that, now, more than ever, the United States needs expanded trade. They believe that, on the whole, such agreements provide solid benefits to workers and consumers. Reducing tariffs and quotas on imports offers consumers greater choice and lowers the prices of goods. In addition, foreign competition spurs U.S. productivity, resulting in greater efficiency and profits. Together, these forces make goods more affordable and improve the quality of life. Supporters also point out that free trade agreements promote U.S. exports, which are crucial in

OCCUPY THE PORTS DAY

On December 12, 2011, the Occupy Oakland movement—the Oakland, California, arm of the Occupy movement, which protests social and economic inequality—took its activism up and down the West Coast. In addition to blockading the Port of Oakland, they pushed their campaign against the wealthiest 1 percent to ports from San Diego to Anchorage. Thousands of protesters disrupted commercial activity among shipping and trucking companies. Occupy group planners chose these sites because they represent wealthy multinational corporations run by well-paid chief executives. In addition, a large stake in these ports is owned by the investment bank Goldman Sachs, which they denounce. Some longshoremen, truckers, and union leaders, however, criticized the port blockades because they cost workers a day's pay. While Occupy supporters said they were standing up for the rights of the port workers, labor leaders said that the Occupy movement used the labor issue to get publicity and to advance Occupy's own cause.

boosting jobs at a time of high unemployment. Finally, proponents blame technology—which favors highly skilled workers—rather than free trade for the growing wage gap between low- and high-income workers.

Critics of free trade think those agreements have enabled corporations to "outsource" manufacturing and, increasingly, blue-collar jobs to countries where labor is cheaper. These job losses, opponents contend, create long-term unemployment for thousands of Americans, resulting in lost productivity and higher government expenditures for social service benefits. Furthermore, opponents assert that when factories relocate to developing countries such as China and Mexico, federal and state governments lose tax revenue. In short, critics argue that it is corporate chief executive officers and wealthy investors who profit from free trade— not U.S. workers or the U.S. economy as a whole. Therefore, they argue, free trade has contributed to the growing wage gap between the rich and poor. Instead of pursuing new free trade agreements, detractors say the U.S. government should directly address joblessness by helping train workers and create jobs.

Supporting Manufacturing. Some analysts believe that economic troubles originate not with free trade itself, but rather the trade imbalance. In 2011, the United States ran a trade deficit in goods and services of $558 billion. Although the exports of U.S. goods and services in 2011 were the highest ever, they were exceeded by record imports of goods and services the same year. Economists say that as long as free trade continues to increase in favor of imports, the U.S. economy will struggle. They estimate that for every $1 billion in trade deficits, America loses between 10,000 and 20,000 jobs.

Many policymakers and business leaders advocate renewing American industry, particularly companies that produce tradable goods because, conventional wisdom says, they tend to create more jobs than the service sector. Such proponents cite programs such as the auto bailout package, which they say returned Detroit's "Big Three" to profitability and saved millions of U.S. jobs in the recession. In his 2012 State of the Union Address, President Obama challenged American business leaders. He said, "Ask yourselves what you can do to bring jobs back to your country, and your country will do everything we can to help you succeed." His recommendations included tax cuts for American manufacturers and

"WHAT DID THEY USED TO MAKE HERE?"... "JOBS."

minimum taxes (not tax breaks and tax deductions) for multinational companies that offshore jobs. The Obama administration had already established programs that encourage investment in U.S.- based businesses, high-tech research, and product development.

Proponents argue that creating jobs and growth in U.S. industry is the best way to increase exports and ensure economic security. Supporters point out that tax incentives and other investment programs are long overdue, especially considering that governments in China, Germany, and South Korea, have been actively promoting their industries for years. America runs significant trade deficits with those same countries, suggesting that those policies do encourage increased production and prosperity. The fact that General Motors and Chrysler are now reporting profits is proof, they say, that government investment in manufacturing can work. In addition, supporters contend that manufacturing accounts for about 65 percent of all research and development in the United States—propelling advances that give U.S. businesses technological and scientific advantages over their foreign competition. Finally, proponents argue that manufacturing deserves special support because it is largely responsible for the huge increases in productivity in the economy—a contribution that is more valuable than most service industries.

Opponents of government intervention in manufacturing do not disagree with its aims of job creation and economic improvement. Rather, they doubt that government-led initiatives can be efficient or successful. First, many critics contend that the U.S. government, already heavily in debt, cannot afford to essentially dole out money to companies—many of which are already sitting on profits they have hoarded since the recession. Other detractors say that manufacturing is the wrong focus. Rather, America's competitive advantage is in high-skilled services, such as finance and engineering. About 70 percent of the U.S. workforce is employed in the service industry, signaling that America has already shifted away from manufacturing and toward a service dominated economy. Instead of promoting tradable goods, the government should be supporting tradable services, or those which can be provided across borders. Finally, opponents point out that even with efficiency gains, factories do not employ as many workers as they did in the past. Thus, they cannot be relied upon to create the millions of jobs the economy needs.

Enforcing Fair Trade. Some experts think the U.S. trade deficit derives in part from unfair trade practices. For example, U.S. solar panel manufacturers have complained that China was dumping its solar panels, heavily subsidized by the Chinese government, on the American market at below cost in order to drive U.S. companies out of business. President Obama said in his State of the Union Address in 2012, "I will not stand by when our [trade] competitors don't play by the rules.... It's not right when another country lets our movies, music, and software be pirated. It's not fair when foreign manufacturers have a leg up only because they're heavily subsidized." With that speech, Obama announced the formation of a Trade Enforcement Unit, part of the federal bureaucracy that investigates unfair trading practices.

Supporters of trade enforcement argue that American workers are the most productive in the world and produce the best products. Provided the playing field is level, they believe that American businesses will win against foreign competitors—increasing exports and creating U.S. jobs. The World Trade Organization and other multilateral organizations have rules specifying proper trade practices, and member nations must be held accountable, proponents assert. They note the example President Obama gave in his State of the Union Address, wherein the United States stopped a surge in imports of Chinese subsidized tires, thereby saving a thousand American jobs. Supporters contend that more active enforcement along these lines will preserve and increase U.S. jobs.

In 2012, the Department of Commerce said that Chinese subsidies allow solar panel factories to illegally dump these underpriced goods, undermining U.S. companies. It is imposing tariffs on such Chinese imports and making a case to the World Trade Organization. Here, a worker in Nantong, China, makes cells for solar panels.

Critics of trade enforcement disagree on several fronts. First, they warn that repeated U.S. challenges regarding trade issues—as have been taken against China—risk retaliation and the escalation of tensions generally. Opponents also point out that WTO rules are complex and unclear, and the outcomes will not necessarily favor the U.S. position. Meanwhile, the process is lengthy and bureaucratic. In the case of the solar panel industry, for example, most of those U.S. companies had already declared bankruptcy by the time the government complained about Chinese subsidies. They say that any decision will probably come too late to revive the industry in the United States. Finally, detractors of trade enforcement say that a "level playing field" does not guarantee U.S. success. As an example, they cite Germany, with which the United States still runs a trade deficit despite its fair trading practices.

OUTLOOK

As the world's largest economy, the United States will continue to import goods and services from around the world. At the same time, less developed countries in Africa, Asia, and Latin America will continue to expand their economies and seek access to the U.S. marketplace. A great challenge for policymakers is balancing free trade—and the friends and influence it wins the United States—with continuing efforts to restructure the American work force. Should U.S. businesses return to factory-style production or continue developing the information and service sectors? Will companies have greater success in emerging, high-technology fields or in traditional manufacturing? What kinds of training and job skills will be required? Whatever the answers, policymakers agree that increasing U.S. exports is key to providing a stable economy and creating jobs for the American people.

THE DEBATE: INTERNATIONAL TRADE

Free trade agreements are good for the U.S. economy.

PRO: Free trade opens more markets for U.S. goods and services, creating more jobs in the United States. Inexpensive imports mean greater choice, lower prices, and a higher standard of living. Also, competition spurs improvements in U.S. productivity, generating profits for U.S. businesses.

CON: Free trade agreements have encouraged U.S. factories and businesses to move operations to less-developed countries where labor is cheap. As a result, American workers lose their jobs, or must accept lower wages. Plus, the U.S. government loses tax revenues and must pay greater unemployment benefits because of such outsourcing.

The federal government should support U.S. manufacturing.

PRO: The trade deficit, not free trade policies, accounts for the loss of U.S. jobs. Tax incentives will spur manufacturing and increase American exports. New U.S. jobs will be created and the economy will rebound. Manufacturing deserves special treatment because it spearheads productivity growth and underwrites research and development.

CON: The government cannot afford to give corporate handouts when its debt and budget deficit are rising. Instead of helping manufacturers, policymakers should promote services like engineering, law, and finance—wherein the United States already has a comparative advantage. Such exports would build on America's shift to a service economy.

The United States should enforce fair trade.

PRO: American workers are the most efficient in the world. If trading partners do business fairly, then U.S.-made products will win in the marketplace, increasing sales and exports. U.S.-based manufacturing jobs will grow. Trade agreements have rules, and enforcement of those rules will pay off in greater exports and job creation.

CON: Trade enforcement has many pitfalls, including possible retaliation. WTO rules are murky, and the process for filing complaints is lengthy. Whole industries can die before a decision is made. It is better to make long-term plans to support industries than to appeal to the WTO when they are already suffering.

AFRICA

INTRODUCTION

The African landmass is tremendous in size and in the diversity of its geography, resources, people, and problems. The continent has been marred for centuries by slave traders and European and American imperialism.

When Europeans colonized Africa, they purposely created states that divided peoples and deepened conflicts. One legacy is today's civil wars and tribal conflicts—from Somalia to Sudan, from Nigeria to Mali and Democratic Republic of Congo. Terrorism now plays a role in many violent clashes, threatening innocent local civilians as well as regional stability and U.S. national security. Furthermore, to quell insurgency, rulers themselves sometimes resort to abusing their people.

From the 1950s onward, when African nations became independent, the United States supported new democratic governments. Some democracies have been successful while most have struggled with corruption and economic stagnation. In some cases, elected leaders have rigged ballots to maintain power for decades. Tired of dictators and poverty, people across North Africa protested in late 2010 and 2011. These citizens ultimately overthrew longtime leaders, first in Tunisia, then in Egypt and Libya. Whether those democratic uprisings will spread into Sub-Saharan Africa is uncertain, and the fate of democracy across the continent remains tentative.

Some observers find hope in Africa's rising economic prospects. Many African countries are rich in natural resources. Sudan and Nigeria are among the world's largest producers of oil. Gold, diamonds, and copper are mined across the continent. As nations like China and India seek sources of energy and raw materials, African countries have new partners in growth. Some U.S. companies hope to promote trade with Africa to compete and to prosper. Many African leaders hope increased trade and foreign investment will provide jobs, new industries, and long-term economic growth that will support improved quality of life for people across Africa.

BACKGROUND

Geography Shaped by a Desert

The African continent is divided by the largest desert in the world, the Sahara. For millennia, North Africa sometimes referred to as the Maghreb, which includes the Sahara Desert and nations such as Algeria, Egypt, and Libya, has been influenced by Mediterranean and Islamic cultures. Because of the strong influence of the Middle East, North African countries are predominantly Muslim and their official language is Arabic. Sub-Saharan Africa—the area lying south of the Sahara—has a much greater diversity of climate, geography, culture, religion, language, and history.

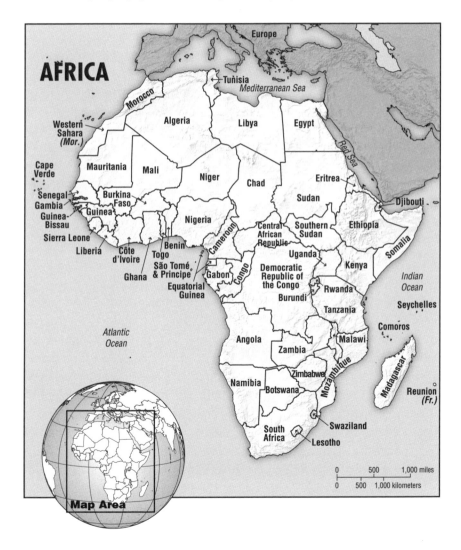

European Colonies in Africa

The Scramble for Africa. In the late 1800s, European countries began carving up Africa. Land was partitioned among Belgium, France, Germany, Great Britain, Italy, Portugal, and Spain. By 1920, there remained only three independent countries on the continent. European leaders colonized Africa for several reasons. Great Britain, for example, wanted control of southern Africa to protect British shipping lanes to India. Most colonizing empires hoped to gain wealth from raw materials. After World War II, Africa's people demanded their freedom. Europeans had also found that administering distant territories was expensive, and that expected profits had not materialized. Within a short time, dozens of African states gained independence.

The Legacy of Colonialism. Scholars trace many of today's problems to aspects of colonial rule. Colonial boundaries, for example, were not designed along religious, tribal, or linguistic groupings. Rather, European countries expressly sought to divide and conquer African peoples. Rival populations found themselves living under the same government, magnifying tensions. In addition, individual groups were often dispersed among several separate countries, causing conflicts along and across borders. When European empires retreated, many of their established boundaries remained. Consequently, ethnic conflict remains a pervasive and devastating legacy.

Post-Colonial Leadership and the Arab Spring

When African countries gained independence in the 1950s and 1960s, the United States encouraged the growth of democracy, which it continues to do today. Elections were held across the region, but the promise of freedom has languished. In many cases, elected officials have resorted to authoritarian or military rule to quell unrest and to extend their power. Corruption and nepotism are rampant. Also, experts note that African leaders have tended to hoard riches and invest them either in military buildups or in banks and property outside of Africa, rather than at home.

Beginning in December 2010 and continuing throughout 2011, people across North Africa demonstrated against their corrupt, authoritarian governments in what has become known as the Arab Spring. A popular uprising among youths in Tunisia forced President Zine El Abidine Ben Ali to flee in January 2011 after twenty-three years in power. The Tunisian revolution sparked prodemocracy action throughout North Africa and

European colonizers exploited Africa's natural resources—especially its precious metals and minerals. Here people gather outside a gold mine in Cape Town, South Africa, around 1888.

the Middle East, resulting in government concessions or reforms in Algeria and Morocco and the overthrow of strongmen Hosni Mubarak in Egypt and Moammar Gaddafi in Libya. Deeper in Africa, minor demonstrations were also held in Mauritania, Sudan, and Western Sahara. In response, Sudan's President Omar al-Bashir, who has led the country for twenty-three years, conceded not to seek reelection after his current term expires in 2015.

It is uncertain whether the Arab democratic movement will spread further throughout Sub-Saharan Africa, where in 2012 at least twelve countries were scheduled to hold democratic elections. The success of these ballots will be judged on whether international observers consider them to have been free and fair—and whether new leaders take the reins in countries like Angola and Cameroon. Case studies below show the broad range of African governments, sketching a relatively successful democracy and a failing dictatorship.

South Africa. Just over twenty years ago, South Africa was among the continent's most repressive countries. Today it is heralded as a successful democracy. The strict segregationist system known as apartheid officially began with laws enacted in 1948, though a white minority had led South Africa since its colonial period. Mounting international pressure, economic

Ellen Johnson Sirleaf, president of Liberia, is the first democratically elected female president in Africa. In late 2011, Sirleaf was awarded the Nobel Peace Prize.

sanctions, and the threat of civil war prompted the ending of apartheid between 1989 and 1994. The nation's transition became complete in 1994 when former political prisoner Nelson Mandela was elected president in South Africa's first democratic elections.

Since then, South Africa has become one of the subcontinent's most effective governments and its richest state. Some analysts attribute this success to the nation's "Truth and Reconciliation" process, whereby human rights violations under apartheid have been publicly acknowledged and forgiven.

Zimbabwe. Formerly the British colony of Southern Rhodesia, Zimbabwe gained independence in 1965 under white minority rule. After a civil war, a new constitution was drafted in 1979 establishing an inclusive government. Robert Mugabe, a key agitator in overthrowing white rule, was elected prime minister in 1980 and president in 1987. He has since retained power by changing the constitution and crushing opposition, gaining a reputation as one of the continent's most despotic rulers. Since 2000, Mugabe has led a violent campaign to seize white-owned property in a stated attempt to redistribute land to dispossessed blacks. Commercial farms underpinned Zimbabwe's economy, so land reform and other mismanagement have led the economy to the brink of collapse. In 2008, Mugabe was reelected by a 9–1 margin. However, the election sparked outrage, as many observers charged it was marred by fraud. The aging Mugabe was forced into a power-sharing arrangement with his rival, Morgan Tsvangirai, who became the prime minister in February 2009.

Violence and War

Africa has been marred by civil strife for decades. As of 2012, about a dozen countries are at war or experiencing postwar conflict. Besides civilian and military casualties, there are other costs. Extreme violence causes people to flee their homes and results in food shortages and famine. Money spent on war cannot be invested in businesses or human services. When people wage war, they are not earning income for their families or paying taxes to their government. One terrible reality is that children are often recruited as soldiers in Africa. In addition to large-scale civil wars, terrorism is alarmingly common in Africa. As a rule, the United States has not intervened in African civil wars unless a humanitarian crisis—such as mass starvation or genocide—has occurred. The following examples describe a past U.S. military intervention, a current humanitarian crisis, and a recent U.S. military intervention.

Somalia. When rival clans overthrew Somali dictator Mohamed Siad Barre in 1991, the country plunged into civil war. Militias, led by warlords,

FAMINE IN AFRICA

Famine has long been a problem for African nations. Fortunately, the United States government and the United Nations have partnered to form the Famine Early Warning System (FEWS), which allows aid programs and affected countries to anticipate and better prepare for such emergencies. Satellite systems monitor weather patterns, while the United Nations Food and Agricultural Organization monitors harvests. Consequently, FEWS predicted the 2011 famine in Somalia in August 2010, which gave aid projects time to position food and supplies in the region. Despite the advance warning, hungry people did not get all the food they needed in southern Somalia because militias blocked relief workers' entry. FEWS anticipates that 2012 will likely bring famine to the Sahel region of West Africa, where as many as 8 million people in parts of Niger and Mali are at risk. That area also hosts terrorists, so the challenge—as in Somalia—will be delivering food while providing security for aid workers and migrants.

competed for power and territory. Lawlessness prevailed. In 1992, the United States sent troops into the fray to secure the delivery of food aid to almost a million starving people. A year later, U.S. soldiers attempted to capture warlord Mohamed Aidid, the person blamed for much of the famine. When U.S. troops died in a gun battle, President Bill Clinton withdrew American forces altogether. For more than ten years there was no national government in Somalia. During the Somali anarchy, radical Islamic groups, including al-Qaeda, set up terrorist networks there.

In 1998, al-Qaeda, led by Osama bin Laden, carried out simultaneous car bombings of U.S. embassies in the African cities of Nairobi, Kenya, and Dar es Salaam, Tanzania. Finally, in 2004, Somali politicians agreed to create a transitional parliament, which appointed a president, but the transitional government lost control almost immediately. Warlords, bandits, and rival clans fueled violence and corruption. Islamic militias then overtook much of the country, including the capital Mogadishu. But in 2006, Somali government troops, heavily backed by Ethiopian forces, reclaimed the capital, and the Islamists fled the city.

As of 2012, Somalia's transitional federal government remained ineffectual and had little influence outside Mogadishu. Al-Shabab, a radical Islamic militia, had become the leading rebel faction and controlled large parts of central and southern Somalia. Formally merged with al-Qaeda, Al-Shabab was responsible for terrorist attacks within Somalia as well as in Kenya and Uganda. In recent years, troops from Ethiopia and Kenya have aided Somali government forces and 10,000 African Union soldiers in an effort to win back territory from Al-Shabab.

The lack of government has also caused Somalia to become home to a number in groups practicing piracy in the Indian Ocean and the Gulf of Aden off the Horn of Africa. According to the United Nations, Somali pirates pulled in $170 million from ransoms in 2011, up from about $110 million in 2010.

Sudan. Between 1983 and 2004, Africa's longest civil war raged in Sudan, the continent's largest country. Fighting occurred between Arab Islamic fundamentalists in the north and black Africans who practice Christianity and traditional African religions in the south. The Arab-led Islamic government in the capital of Khartoum described the conflict as a holy war. Rebels in the south refused to live according to Muslim law. Also at stake was the country's oil wealth, 75 percent of which lay in the south. Facing tough international pressure, the two sides finally reached a peace agreement in 2005. The final stage of this pact was fulfilled in January 2011, when voters in the south cast their ballots in favor of independence. The newest African nation, the Republic of South Sudan, was formed in July 2011. However, the two Sudans faced continuing conflict because crude oil from the south must be transported through pipelines into the north to reach refineries and markets. The two sides disagreed over pipeline fees and, because oil revenues are so critical for both nations, the issue threatened their fragile peace.

Moreover, President Omar al-Bashir in Khartoum continued to violently repress rebellions in other regions. In Sudan's western state of Darfur, the government and the tribal militia known as the Janjaweed have been largely responsible for killing and torturing citizens since 2003. Despite the deployment of African Union and UN peacekeepers, violence and disease have reportedly claimed hundreds of thousands of civilians and displaced more than 2 million. In 2010, the International Criminal Court issued a warrant for the arrest of President al-Bashir for genocide in Darfur.

Since South Sudan became independent, President Bashir has sent forces and bombing raids to crush insurrections in other areas—including the disputed southern border region of Abyei, South Kordofan state, and Blue Nile state—where aid workers are routinely banned and human rights abuses have taken place.

On October 23, 2011, a Libyan woman celebrates the end of an eight-month civil war and the ouster of General Moammar Gaddafi.

AP PHOTO/ABDEL MAGID AL-FERGANY

Libya. An Italian colony from 1911 to 1951, Libya was ruled for forty-two years by dictator Moammar Gaddafi. Coming to power in a 1969 coup, Gaddafi had a tense relationship with the United States in the 1980s, due to his support of terrorism. In 1986, in response to Libya's alleged involvement in a European bombing in which three U.S. soldiers were killed, President Ronald Reagan ordered retaliatory strikes on Libyan cities. In December 1988, a bomb planted by two Libyans exploded on Pan Am Flight 103 over Lockerbie, Scotland, killing 270 people. The U.S. government long suspected Gaddafi was behind the attack.

After the September 11, 2001 terrorist attacks, however, Gaddafi pledged to cooperate with the United States and other Western countries in their efforts to fight terrorism. In 2003, Gaddafi finally admitted responsibility for the Pan Am bombing and paid compensation to victims' families. As a result, many Western corporations began to do more oil business with Libya.

Inspired by the prodemocracy movements in Egypt and Tunisia, protesters challenged Gaddafi's rule in early 2011. His forces brutally attacked protesters with gunfire and aircraft, and in response the United Nations Security Council authorized the enforcement of a no-fly zone and NATO air strikes to protect civilians. Civil war ensued, and over the next six months rebels fought Gaddafi forces for territory. Revolutionaries overtook the capital Tripoli in August 2011, and they found and killed Gaddafi in October. A National Transitional Council was formed to manage the transition to democracy, and nations around the world recognized it as the new government of Libya.

Poverty in Africa

When people live amid violence and political upheaval, they cannot thrive. Not surprisingly, many people in Africa, particularly Sub-Saharan Africa, live in extreme poverty. According to the World Bank, about one-half of the region's population live on $1.25 per day. Food shortages have become a chronic problem. Although situations vary, experts cite common reasons for agricultural failure and malnourishment.

During wartime, political instability and violence often cause floods of refugees. Migrating people cannot farm. Also, governmental corruption means that money intended to aid development often does not reach farmers. In some cases, extreme weather, such as droughts and floods, cause famine. For example, the worst drought in sixty years caused famine and a humanitarian crisis in Somalia in 2011.

Despite these depressing facts, some observers note positive economic indicators. Because of increasing urbanization and increasing foreign investment, the Gross Domestic Product of Sub-Saharan Africa grew more than 5 percent in 2011, and it was expected to grow 5.5 percent in 2012.

CURRENT ISSUES

Trade with African Countries. For decades the U.S. government has tried to encourage development in Africa through grants and loans. When foreign aid came under attack, some policymakers argued that African economies need to be better integrated into the global economy through increased trade and investment. In 2000 the African Growth and Opportunity Act (AGOA) went into effect. This law dropped trade restrictions for nations that meet certain requirements—including promoting market economies, protecting workers' rights, implementing poverty-reduction policies, and enforcing the rule of law. As of 2011, 37 Sub-Saharan countries were deemed eligible to export some 6,000 lines of goods to the United States duty-free under this law. A major goal

Ivory Coast is the world's largest producer of cocoa, which is the key ingredient in chocolate. After harvest in the rainforest, cocoa beans dry in the sun (shown here) before they are exported.

of this legislation is to jump-start development and alleviate poverty, which some proponents say could help replace the need for development aid.

Many supporters of AGOA—and African trade and investment in general—argue that such programs reduce poverty more effectively than traditional grants and loans. They cite recent statistics indicating that African economies have grown significantly since AGOA went into effect. By increasing trade and investment in Africa, the United States helps build new industries and improve the overall standard of living there. More money for workers means better health care and education, and, in the end, more people who can consume American products and services—thereby benefitting U.S. companies. American investment, supporters assert, is an important component in influencing democratic reform across the continent. As African citizens become more prosperous and more globally connected, they will demand more transparent and free elections and the ouster of some longtime, corrupt leaders.

Critics of substituting trade for aid point out that some development projects are not profitable and will not be undertaken by corporations— whether local or foreign. One example is clean drinking water, which is a perennial problem in rural areas prone to drought. Others say that basic infrastructure—such as reliable roads, trains, and electricity—is still lacking in many parts of Africa, making it difficult to build factories that can compete in the world market. Still others say that corruption is too prevalent in Sub-Saharan Africa, limiting the amount of money that flows to the neediest people through trade and investment. Furthermore, oil comprises 80 percent of U.S. imports from Africa, a product that benefits multinational corporations and corrupt regimes more so than low-income workers.

Sanctions against Sudan. The U.S. government has imposed sanctions against the government of Sudan since late 1997 as a penalty for its sponsorship of terrorism and its violations of human rights. A trade embargo blocks trade of goods and services in both directions. All Sudanese government assets were frozen. In 2003, when war broke out in Darfur, a further ban on weapons sales was imposed. When the Republic of South Sudan was created in 2011, the status of U.S. sanctions became a matter of debate. Claiming to have given up its terrorist network as well as its most wealthy territory, President Bashir expected the sanctions to be lifted. The new nation of South Sudan, completely reliant on oil revenue, also wanted the

U.S. trade ban eased. In late 2011, the United States decided to renew sanctions against Sudan, but lifted some against South Sudan. In particular, business activities relating to oil in South Sudan are now permitted. However, continuing conflict over oil transport fees in early 2012 meant that oil production ceased, and international mediators were brought in to avert a war.

At about the same time, the human rights group Amnesty International reported that China and Russia have been selling Sudan weapons that Khartoum has used in human rights abuses in Darfur and other repressed areas such as South Kordofan. In these regions, for example, government troops have used foreign-supplied helicopters to destroy homes and churches and kill people. Amnesty International called on the United Nations to extend its existing ban on international weapons sales to the Darfur region to the whole of Sudan.

Supporters of increasing pressure on Sudan, including imposing additional international sanctions, assert that violators of human rights must be held accountable for their actions. They remind skeptics that the International Criminal Court issued a warrant for Bashir's arrest for genocide, the first such warrant ever—testimony to his tyranny. Advocates of sanctions contend that without significant international pressure, his regime will continue to terrorize civilians as he goes to extreme lengths to maintain his control over regions that want to secede. Proponents of sanctions say that tough U.S. embargoes have already been successful in that they helped win the independence of South Sudan. That movement has spawned rebellions in other states that, with continued international pressure, will help unseat one of the most brutal regimes on the subcontinent.

Many experts, while acknowledging Bashir's hardline tactics, argue that the United States needs to be careful in applying a blunt foreign policy tool like sanctions. The peace between Sudan and South Sudan is fragile, and pushing Khartoum to the brink might make the government more desperate and violent. Additional sanctions could inadvertently cause a greater humanitarian crisis or war. Some detractors instead want to see U.S. companies help build oil refineries in South Sudan, so that it can be more economically independent. By supporting the South, rather than increasing penalties for Khartoum, the United States could better maintain a delicate balance. With more subtle diplomacy, Sudan could peacefully elect a new leader who negotiates with the rebellious states. In this manner, Sudan can become more democratic and more responsible.

Fighting Terrorism in Africa. In the last few years, terrorist attacks have been on the rise across Africa. Experts blame three Islamic terrorist networks for most of the violence—the Boko Haram in Nigeria, which detonated a car bomb at the United Nations headquarters in Nigeria's capital in August 2011; al-Qaeda in the Islamic Maghreb (AQIM), located in the Sahara, which kidnaps and sometimes kills Westerners in countries such as Algeria, Mali, and Mauritania; and al-Shabab, the militants based in Somalia that battled the Somali transitional government and sent two suicide bombers to the World Cup final soccer match in Uganda in 2010. These highly publicized events were accompanied by hundreds of less well-known attacks in Kenya, Nigeria, and all across the Sahara.

The top U.S. commander for Africa, General Carter F. Ham, said these three terrorist groups "have very explicitly and publicly voiced an intent to target Westerners, and the U.S. specifically." They pose, General Ham added, a "significant threat not only in the nations in which they primarily operate, but regionally—and I think they present a threat to the United States." Umar Farouk Abdulmutallab, the infamous "underwear bomber," was sentenced to life in prison for attempting to bomb a U.S. airliner on Christmas Day 2009. He is a Nigerian-born al-Qaeda terrorist, a fact that supports the threat posed by African-based terrorist groups.

American policymakers have implemented a broad range of counterterrorism measures in Africa. In some cases, African governments have asked for U.S. military training, particularly in Mali and Mauritania, where soldiers are learning to fight the AQIM. For many years, the U.S. military has helped fight Al-Shabab—except for providing U.S. soldiers. From bases in Ethiopia, it provided drone air strikes against high-level members of the network. The United States also helped fund the African Union peacekeeping forces and the Somali government. For example, it has given Burundi and Uganda, which provided troops to the African Union mission in Somalia, several hundred million dollars in salary, equipment, and training. The U.S. government has also blocked the finances of al-Shabab leaders.

Many critics, however, condemn the current counterterrorism strategy as weak and ineffectual because it relies on relatively poor countries with little expertise. Instead, they argue that the United States should exert

Members of al-Shabab conduct military exercises outside Mogadishu, Somalia. Now officially part of al-Qaeda, al-Shabab has carried out terrorist attacks not only within Somalia, but also in Kenya and Uganda.

its military might to crush these militants before they carry out bombings in the West. Short of invasion, these critics advocate air strikes, special operations forces, and other kinds of military force that would assassinate insurgent leaders, ensure relief supplies are delivered where terrorists block their passage, and free Western hostages held by these groups. Because al-Qaeda already has strong footing in the Horn of Africa and in the Sahara Desert, experts liken those regions to the "new Afghanistan"—the next frontier for training the world's terrorists. The United States cannot afford to take a conservative role in fighting these militants.

Supporters of current measures argue that they are necessary to stem the tide of hatred and violence that feeds such insurgencies. They believe that U.S. leaders have learned much from experiences in Afghanistan and Iraq, allowing African governments and military forces to implement solutions that best suit their circumstances. By acting in a funding and training role, the U.S. government does not dictate solutions with its own weapons and does not risk the lives of its own soldiers. Consequently, local people and militants do not equate Americans with oppressors. Furthermore, U.S. money and expertise equips local forces to fight terrorism, which is crucial for regional stability and American security.

OUTLOOK

Africa has problems, to be sure, and yet it seems better poised than ever to tap its tremendous potential. While terrorism and instability wrack the Horn of Africa, some strongmen in North Africa have been overthrown in dramatic, democratic revolutions. Sudan's human rights abuses continue unabated, but there could be hope for democracy in the newest country, the Republic of South Sudan. Moreover, many African nations seem ready to take advantage of foreign investment and trade in the new era of global competition for energy and resources. The question is, will economic benefits reach the neediest people?

Observers also wonder if longtime African dictators will accede to free and fair elections, ushering in a new generation of democratic leaders.

THE DEBATE: AFRICA

The United States should promote trade with African countries.

PRO: Recent trade policies have promoted economic growth in dozens of African countries that meet tough U.S. standards for workers' rights, market reforms, and rule of law. Increased trade and investment has helped create new industries and jobs for African workers, raising their standard of living more effectively than traditional forms of development grants and loans. Through more U.S. trade and investment, African workers will prosper and demand more transparent, accountable democratic governments.

CON: Emphasizing trade over aid will leave many important infrastructure projects undone and many people impoverished. Some projects are not profitable and will not be undertaken by investors. Corruption is still rampant, even in democratic nations, so profits often do not filter to local schools or other services. Oil is by far the biggest export, a product that helps corrupt strongmen more than it does needy workers. African nations still need U.S. foreign aid.

U.S. policymakers should step up sanctions against Sudan.

PRO: Sudan's President Bashir has committed human rights atrocities in his desperate attempts to retain power. Despite a patchwork of tough U.S. and UN sanctions, Sudan has used weapons from China and Russia to kill civilians and destroy homes and villages in Darfur and other rebellious areas. Such a brutal regime must be held accountable, and stricter international sanctions are the best way to do so.

CON: Sanctions are an inexact tool, and backing Khartoum into a corner could result in more violence and possibly a war. Current U.S. sanctions have already extracted concessions and have helped create the new country of South Sudan. Khartoum is financially troubled from existing policies and needs to work with the international community. More subtle diplomacy behind the scenes will help bring about change in Sudan.

The U.S. government should use military force to fight African terrorist groups.

PRO: The Sahara Desert is set to become the new Afghanistan—the center of world terrorism. The United States must take strong military action to fight those insurgent camps and networks, including bombing missions, aggressive special operations missions with allies, and other strategies short of invasion. The United States should not wait for an attack on Western soil to fight terrorism in Africa. Already the three main terrorist groups in Africa have destabilized their regions.

CON: The U.S. government has pursued behind-the-scenes counterterrorism measures in Africa, without risking U.S. soldiers' lives and without enflaming anti-American sentiments. These strategies allow African governments to learn U.S. military skills yet adapt them to their particular contexts. Afghanistan and Iraq have proven that fighting terrorism is as much a psychological as a military battle. The United States must promote responsible governments and economic opportunities so young men do not join terrorist groups.

ASIA

INTRODUCTION

The largest continent, Asia is home to 60 percent of Earth's population. The region includes the world's most populous nation (China), its largest democracy (India), its most populous Muslim country (Indonesia), its second and third largest economies (China and Japan, respectively), and four of the five remaining communist nations (China, North Korea, Laos, and Vietnam). For these and other reasons, U.S. policymakers consider relations with Asian countries important.

KEY QUESTIONS

- Should the United States pressure China to trade more fairly?

- Should the United States offer incentives to end North Korea's nuclear program?

- Should the United States continue to send civilian aid to Pakistan?

After World War II, the United States sent troops into two Far Eastern conflicts—the Korean War and the Vietnam War—to fight the spread of communism. Since then, U.S. leaders have maintained a strong U.S. military presence in the region to allay security concerns—countering military giants such as China and North Korea, protecting trade routes and allies, and fighting terrorism in Afghanistan and Pakistan. In addition, American policymakers have helped Asian countries prosper, first with postwar aid, but also through trade and investment.

Today, Asia is home to some of America's biggest trading partners. China, Japan, South Korea, and Taiwan are now among the top ten. China and the United States—the world's two largest economies—are deeply enmeshed in trade and finance. Cheap Chinese imports have, for decades, given China a huge trade surplus, and it uses those dollars to loan money to the U.S. government.

The Korean peninsula is another flashpoint. A new leader has American and regional negotiators seeking to disarm the nation peacefully. In short, Asia's arms race and its economic and social development will make headlines for many years to come.

BACKGROUND

Japan

The Japan-U.S. Military Alliance. Japanese and U.S. forces battled against one another in World War II. After U.S. atomic bombs destroyed two Japanese cities in 1945, Japan surrendered, bringing the war to an end. The Japanese adopted a new democratic system of government, and its constitution forbade raising an army. In 1951, Japan signed a peace treaty with the United States, ending nearly seven years of American military occupation. Japanese leaders also signed the Mutual Security Treaty, under which the United States pledged to defend Japan in case of attack. In exchange, the United States maintains military bases there. American military personnel in Japan numbered about 49,000 in 2012.

Japan's Economy. After World War II, Japan rapidly industrialized. Thanks in part to its well-educated workers who were able to adopt, and often improve, foreign technology, Japan's productivity rate eventually exceeded even that

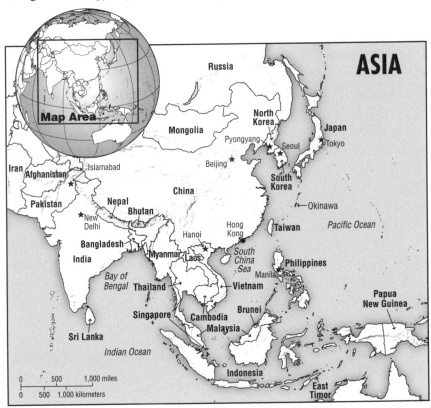

of the United States. Between the 1960s and 1980s, Japan's economy grew faster than those of most other countries in the world. However, during the 1990s, Japan struggled to pull out of a recession. Even with largely stagnant growth for years, the Japanese economy still ranks third-largest in the world, behind the United States and China.

In March 2011, the most powerful earthquake in Japan's history struck the northeast coast of the country, causing a devastating tsunami. In addition to the staggering loss of property and life (about 19,000 people perished), reactors at a nuclear power station melted down and another caught fire, releasing radioactive poison into the environment. A year later, virtually all of Japan's nuclear power plants were idled for inspection, as officials devised reports about how to respond to such disasters and the nation reevaluated its strong reliance on nuclear energy. Policymakers expect that Japan's economy and environment will take years to recover from the triple disaster. Because Japan is the United States's fourth-largest trading partner, economists expect that, as Japan rebuilds, prospects for U.S. trade will likely improve over the long term.

China

U.S.-China Relations. The communist takeover of China in 1949 stunned U.S. leaders, who were dedicated to stopping the spread of communism. At the time, the United States refused to recognize the People's Republic of China (PRC). Instead, American officials maintained diplomatic relations with the PRC's rival, the Republic of China, which had exiled itself to the island of Taiwan. Chinese leaders in the PRC were outspokenly anti-American, and thousands of Chinese soldiers fought against U.S. forces in the Korean War.

By the 1970s, China had become a world power, but its relations with the neighboring Soviet Union were deteriorating. In 1972, President Richard Nixon took advantage of strained ties between the two communist giants and made a state visit to China. Nixon's trip led to improved Chinese-American relations, and President Jimmy Carter established full diplomatic ties with China in 1979.

China's Economic Boom. China was isolated from the rest of the world until communist leader Mao Zedong's death in 1976, when it gradually began to introduce capitalist concepts into its economy. Chinese leaders eventually agreed to share power in the central government and to allow local governments to make more decisions. Furthermore, the government

The Shanghai Tower, expected to be the largest in China upon completion, was under construction in the financial district of Shanghai in 2012. When finished, the Shanghai Tower will rise 128 stories and measure about 632 meters high, making it the second-tallest skyscraper in the world.

has privatized some state-owned enterprises and attracted multinational companies, promoting fast-paced economic development. Between 2000 and 2011, its gross domestic product—the amount of goods and services it produces—grew by an average of almost 10 percent annually. (As of 2010, the state-owned sector of the economy accounted for about 40 percent of China's economic output.) Although Chinese officials have targeted an average growth rate of 7 percent between 2012 and 2015, experts still predict that China will overtake the United States as the world's largest economy sometime between 2020 and 2025.

Strategic Issues. China has enormous territory, 3.7 million square miles, making it a major strategic concern for its neighbors and the United States. Its 2.3 million-strong armed forces constitute the world's largest. In addition, China's economic boom has fueled a military spending spree. In almost every year since 1989, Chinese officials have increased such investment by 10 percent or more. In 2012, they announced China's defense budget will increase 11 percent for a total of $106 billion. Yet American policymakers believe that China's actual military spending is likely more than its leaders admit. These spending increases have been used to develop stealth fighter jets, aircraft carriers, nuclear attack submarines, and other advanced military hardware. Compared with U.S. military spending, however, China's defense budget is far less, whether measured in dollars spent per year, per capita, or as a percentage of its overall economy (gross domestic product).

Human Rights. Another ongoing concern for American leaders has been China's treatment of its people. In 1989, the Chinese military brutally crushed demonstrations in Beijing's Tiananmen Square, where more than 100,000 workers and students were appealing for democratic reform. About 800 people died; thousands more were injured. Although China has gradually allowed some personal liberties, it remains intolerant of political dissent and squelches religious expression.

Trade. In 2001, with strong U.S. support, China was admitted to the World Trade Organization. The United States also established permanent normal trade relations with China by reducing tariffs on Chinese goods and enabling American companies to expand their markets in China. This agreement fostered even greater economic interdependence between the two countries. Americans buy a staggering amount of relatively inexpensive Chinese-made goods. At the same time, U.S. companies continue to invest heavily in businesses in China, and U.S. exports to that country have risen dramatically. Even so, Chinese consumption of U.S. goods has not yet matched trade in the other direction. The U.S. trade deficit with China soared from $10 billion in 1990 to more than $295 billion in 2011. That same year, U.S. exports to China grew by $12 billion, or 13 percent over 2010, making China a fast growing market for U.S. goods.

American businesses and policymakers want to sell even more products and services to the booming country, but several factors make that difficult. The People's Bank of China controls the value of the Chinese currency, and for many years it kept the value of the yuan artificially low against the U.S. dollar, making Chinese imports cheap in the United States. Conversely, the cost of U.S. products in China remained relatively high. For several years the Obama administration has cajoled the Chinese government to increase the value of the yuan against the dollar—to encourage U.S. exports. In 2011 officials in China did allow a modest gain in the yuan's value, though other hurdles to Chinese market access remain.

North Korea

War in Korea. Japan controlled Korea from 1894 until 1945. When Japan surrendered to the United States to end World War II, Korea was partitioned into two sections—the North (allied with the Soviet Union) and the South (allied with the United States). In 1948, both superpowers withdrew their forces, but no agreement was reached on reunification.

In June 1950, communist North Korea invaded South Korea. This military action, supported by the Soviet Union, was an attempt to unify the two Koreas under communist rule. American leaders sent armed forces as part of an allied United Nations "police action" to repel the invasion. The two sides fought to a stalemate and, in July 1953, signed an armistice that suspended combat and established a demilitarized zone between the two Koreas. Today the United States keeps about 28,500 troops on the South Korean side of the demilitarized zone.

North Korea Isolated. North Korea became isolated when its ally, the Soviet Union, abandoned communism and broke apart, and when another important ally, China, established diplomatic relations with South Korea. Through the 1990s, under the hardline socialist dictatorship of Kim Jong Il, the nation experienced economic collapse and widespread famine. Experts believe that more than a million North Koreans died of starvation despite food aid from the United States and international relief agencies. In 2011, the UN World Food Program reported that more than one-quarter of the North Korean population again faced a food crisis. Many policymakers believed that budgetary mismanagement was largely to blame, as food spending was cut 40 percent.

North Korea's Nuclear Ambitions. One of the most heavily militarized nations in the world, North Korea has long pursued conventional and nonconventional weapons, including biological and chemical agents. In 1994, when North Korea threatened to develop nuclear weapons, the nation struck a deal with the Clinton administration. The United States agreed to help build nuclear power plants in North Korea and supply fuel oil, while North Korea agreed to abide by the UN Nuclear Nonproliferation Treaty (NPT), which it had signed. Signatories to the treaty renounce nuclear weapons and allow international inspections of their nuclear sites.

In 2003, North Korea withdrew from the NPT and ordered inspectors to leave the country, beginning several years of talks among the six parties: the two Koreas, China, Japan, Russia, and the United States. Despite agreeing to abandon its nuclear activities in exchange for foreign aid in 2005, North Korea went on to test-fire missiles and detonate a nuclear device. Finally, in 2007, the six countries reached an agreement: North Korea would shut down its main reactor and allow international inspections in exchange for fuel oil, other forms of aid, and the lifting of sanctions.

In 2009, North Korea repeated its pattern of reneging on its agreements. The country tested a second nuclear device, and it again expelled UN nuclear inspectors. In 2010, it launched attacks on South Korea. President Obama announced further economic sanctions against the North, including suspending food aid. In late 2010, North Korea unveiled a facility for enriching uranium, which is used to make nuclear devices. In 2011, facing a food crisis, North Korean leaders sought international help.

A New Dictator. In December 2011, Kim Jong Il died, leaving North Korea in the hands of his youngest son, Kim Jong Un. On February 29, 2012, the twenty-nine-year-old leader and U.S. officials announced a deal much like previous ones. In exchange for food aid, Kim Jong Un agreed to freeze the country's nuclear program and allow inspectors to monitor the main nuclear reactor. After North Korean lanch of a long-range rocket in April, the deal fell apart.

Central and South Asia

Afghanistan and al-Qaeda. Afghanistan has for centuries served as a battleground for competing empires. The Soviet Union invaded the country in 1979 but withdrew ten years later. After a civil war in 1996, a hardline, radical Islamic regime—the Taliban—seized power and provided a haven for terrorists, including Osama bin Laden's al-Qaeda network.

Sanctions imposed by the United Nations in 1999 failed to force the Taliban to hand over bin Laden for trial. After the September 11, 2001, attacks, the United States and Great Britain launched air strikes on Afghanistan in October. That action paved the way for opponents of the Taliban to seize power in the capital, Kabul, within a month.

Foreign peacekeepers arrived in January 2002, enabling the Afghan people to begin building a democracy. Leaders drafted a new constitution and held presidential and parliamentary elections. Meanwhile, U.S. troops—along with allied forces—continued to fight insurgents and hunt down al-Qaeda members.

Osama bin Laden and the Troop Drawdown. Following the strategy used in Iraq, President Obama increased the number of U.S. soldiers in Afghanistan from 38,000, when he first took office, to almost 100,000 in 2010. The goal was to eradicate terrorists and train the Afghan army and police to fight insurgents so that American forces could leave.

In a surprise victory in May 2011, U.S. special forces secretly flew into Pakistan, where they captured and killed Osama bin Laden. With bin Laden gone, policymakers considered ways to end the NATO mission in Afghanistan, which is set to finish at the end of 2014. In February 2012—with about 90,000 U.S. troops in the conflict—copies of the Koran were mistakenly burned in a trash incinerator at a U.S. military base, sparking violence. A few weeks later a U.S. soldier allegedly killed sixteen Afghan villagers, prompting militant reprisals. Such local opposition prompted calls for swift troop withdrawals. Despite these setbacks, military leaders advocated a gradual return, so that Afghans can take over security during a relatively stable transition period.

The Indian Subcontinent. Great Britain granted the Indian subcontinent independence in 1947 and partitioned the territory into two separate countries: the mostly Hindu India and a Muslim homeland in Pakistan. The United States and Pakistan formed an alliance during the Cold War, when Americans sought to limit communist influence. In 1954, Pakistan signed a Mutual Defense Agreement with the

In mid-2011, U.S. military personnel board an aircraft as they leave Afghanistan, beginning the withdrawal of American troops. About 20,000 U.S. soldiers were scheduled to leave Afghanistan in 2012. The NATO mission is due to finish at the end of 2014.

AP PHOTO/MUSADEQ SADEQ

United States. In exchange, U.S. officials granted Pakistan economic and military assistance.

Since the overthrow of the Taliban in Afghanistan, U.S. and Pakistani leaders have renewed their alliance by sharing intelligence and resources in the fight against terrorism. From 2002 until 2011, both the Bush and Obama administrations collaborated closely with Pakistani leaders to rout out terrorists in Pakistan's northwestern tribal areas. As U.S. forces bombed suspected militant safe havens, Islamic extremists launched an increasing number of deadly bombings against civilian and military targets in Pakistan. Intelligence experts believe that the attacks were intended to protest the U.S.-Pakistani alliance.

In May 2011, when American forces secretly raided Osama bin Laden's hideaway in Pakistan—without notifying Pakistani officials—relations between the United States and Pakistan deteriorated. American leaders believed that Pakistani authorities were not doing all they could to fight extremism and terrorism, while leaders in Pakistan decried the breach of their sovereignty.

India, Pakistan's longtime rival and neighbor, is the world's largest democracy with 1.2 billion people. American presidents have increasingly

INDIA: THE OTHER ASIAN GIANT

India's 1.2 billion people make it the second most populous country in the world. But people are only part of the reason for India's growth. In 1991, the socialist government began instituting free-market reforms. Since then its economy has grown tremendously. According to the International Monetary Fund, India has the world's tenth-largest economy and by 2030 could become third-largest behind the United States and China. Many American companies have tried to profit from India's meteoric rise. Because of India's well educated, English-speaking population, some U.S. companies have outsourced call centers and technology help desks there. By the end of 2011, India was already the thirteenth-largest trading partner of the United States. Yet India's future growth depends on it overcoming many obstacles. Even business centers often lack public services and infrastructure such as clean water, sewer systems, reliable power, and police protection. Political corruption and an outdated bureaucracy also hamper efficiency. Many economists think that such dysfunction must be reversed if India's economic dynamism is to continue. One Indian businesswoman said, "In India, it is not because of the government," that things get done. "It is in spite of the government."

engaged leaders in India since 2000. Foremost, U.S. policymakers want to promote peace between India and Pakistan, both of which have nuclear weapons, and encourage them to reduce their stockpiles. To help counterbalance China's military dominance, U.S. armed forces conduct military exercises with their Indian counterparts, and the U.S. government sells arms to India. Furthermore, India, once one of the world's poorest countries, has expanded its economy dramatically since the 1990s, and U.S. trade and investment there have increased.

CURRENT ISSUES

Trading with China. Trade relations with China are complex and frustrating for U.S. policymakers and businesses. In total value of goods and services exchanged, China is our second-largest trading partner. Its economic growth and potential make it a tantalizing market for U.S. companies. Indeed, U.S. exports to China have risen faster than those to any other nation. But because the United States consumes so many more goods from China than it exports there, the trade deficit with China reached an all-time high of more than $295 billion in 2011. Some analysts blame the Chinese government for this imbalance because, as a communist state, it controls virtually all aspects of business, finance, and the economy. It dictates that foreign companies share technology in order to operate there. It then "steals" the advances to make and sell products, giving preferences and subsidies to its domestic industries. In recent years, U.S. policymakers have prodded the Chinese government to increase the value of its currency, which many argue is undervalued by more than 35 percent—a situation that makes Chinese goods inexpensive in the United States and American goods more costly in China. These exchange rates strongly tip the balance of trade in China's favor.

In light of the huge trade gap, some American companies urge the U.S. government to pressure Chinese officials to open their markets more fully and fairly. Many advocates argue that by increasing exports to this rapidly growing country, the United States can create more jobs and prosper economically. One way to do this, many policymakers posit, is to continue pressuring China to raise the value of the yuan against the dollar. Only when American goods are more affordable will U.S. companies make inroads with Chinese consumers. In addition, disputes continue over Chinese pirating of luxury goods, computer software, movies, and other kinds

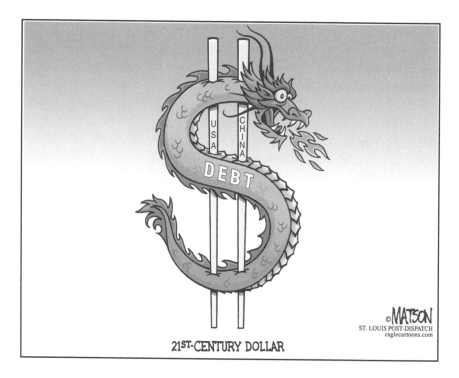

21ST-CENTURY DOLLAR

of intellectual property. Many observers say that if U.S. companies had greater access to Chinese buyers, pirated goods would be less attractive and profitable. Furthermore, supporters characterize the current relationship as unhealthy—China is lending money to the U.S. government so that it can afford to buy more and more Chinese imports. Such over-reliance on China could prove catastrophic to the U.S. economy if China sold off its U.S. government debt holdings, which as of early 2012 totaled $1.16 trillion, or 11 percent of the total U.S. debt. Many policymakers say that increasing exports to China could help balance power between the world's two largest economies.

On the other hand, some analysts, and even some business interests, oppose pressuring the Chinese government too forcefully to open its markets. Companies that hope to profit in China, in particular, fear possible retaliation by Chinese regulators. They note that U.S. exports to China are already increasing more rapidly than those to any other country. Critics of tough pressure on the Chinese point out that multinational companies are dependent on China for profits because its economy continues to grow while Europe and the United States are languishing. Still others point out that China's ownership of U.S. government debt hobbles attempts to hold it accountable for currency manipulation. If the U.S. government angers Chinese officials, they can threaten to sell off U.S. debt, a situation that could throw the U.S. economy into a tailspin.

Negotiating with North Korea. In the 2012 Leap Day agreement, the United States struck a controversial deal with North Korea's Kim Jong Un. In exchange for 240,000 metric tons of food aid, North Korea agreed to suspend testing nuclear devices and long-range missiles. It also pledged to stop enriching uranium and to allow international inspection of its main nuclear reactor. Because its framework was like so many previously scuttled agreements, many observers were doubtful it would work—even with a new regime. Skeptics were not surprised when North Korea launched a rocket supposedly containing a weather satellite in April. American officials condemned North Korea's launch because the rocket technology is the same for launching nuclear warheads. Although the launch ended in failure (the rocket disintegrated over the Yellow Sea), the United States called it a blatantly provocative action and immediately announced it was suspending plans to deliver food aid.

Critics of negotiating with North Korea believe that Kim Jong Un is likely to continue his father's leadership philosophy. In the context of nuclear weapons and diplomacy, one pattern has repeatedly played out: bold provocation and belligerence—either in nuclear tests or military

DEMOCRATIC REFORM IN MYANMAR

From 1962 to 2011, Myanmar was ruled by a brutal military government and was largely isolated from the international community. With the installation of a civilian government led by President Thein Sein, a former military general, in March 2011, a series of democratic reforms ensued. Because of this progress, Secretary of State Hillary Clinton visited Myanmar in December 2011—the first visit by a U.S. secretary of state in fifty years. Clinton said the Obama administration would consider easing sanctions against Myanmar if it continued to see concrete progress toward democratization and human rights. In an April 2012 election, prodemocracy activist Aung San Suu Kyi, who had been under house arrest for nearly twenty years, won a seat in parliament. Her opposition party won a landslide victory, gaining 43 parliamentary seats of the 45 contested. Suu Kyi said, "We hope that this will be the beginning of a new era where there will be more emphasis on the role of the people in the everyday politics in our country."

attacks on South Korea—followed by multilateral negotiations aimed at extracting concessions and aid, then reneging on promises. Opponents of negotiations say that, as long as the North Korean strategy of blackmail works, its leadership will continue to manipulate the international community. Skeptics also deride offering incentives to North Korea because previously delivered food aid was diverted to serve the elites and the military, not starving people. The recent launch also illustrates North Korea's belligerence. Therefore, skeptics advocate that the United States change tack. Instead of focusing solely on nuclear disarmament, diplomats need to reduce tensions on the Korean peninsula generally and make reunification with South Korea the long-range goal.

Proponents of incentives respond that famine was imminent, so engagement was necessary for humanitarian reasons. They claim policymakers have learned from previous rounds that food donations must be monitored and distributed properly. Supporters rationalize that, in helping the citizens of the poverty-stricken North, the United States is positively influencing people who have been cut off from the world. Engaging the "Hermit Kingdom," even on its own terms, is better than no communication at all, they

Ignoring warnings from the United States and its allies, North Korea launched a rocket carrying a weather satellite in April 2012—a move widely suspected to be a test of the nation's long-range weapons capability. The launch ended in failure as the rocket quickly disintegrated. Here, a North Korean soldier stands guard at the launching site.

say. Proponents also fear that, given North Korea's pattern of belligerence, refusing negotiations could risk further attacks on South Korea and imperil innocent lives. Some policymakers take the pragmatic view that diplomacy and incentives are still preferable.

A Tense Relationship with Pakistan. The capture and killing of Osama bin Laden in May 2011 marked a watershed moment in U.S.-Pakistan relations. That the highest Pakistani officials did not know about his hideaway revealed intelligence inadequacy or compromises—facts that undermined U.S. trust. Plus, Pakistan's government was outraged by U.S. forces breaching their sovereignty. Relations ebbed to perhaps their worst in November 2011, when a U.S. air strike inadvertently killed twenty-four Pakistani soldiers near the Afghan border. For several months, the Pakistan border was closed to U.S. and NATO supplies bound for the Afghan War, and Pakistan suspended other military and intelligence cooperation. In early 2012, Pakistan's legislature reviewed new regulations for reopening the Afghan border and renewing some war-related cooperation, but many policymakers believed that U.S.-Pakistan relations were already tracing a new course.

In October 2009, Congress passed the Enhanced Partnership with Pakistan Act, which authorized $1.5 billion in aid over five years from fiscal year 2010 through 2014. When U.S.-Pakistan relations became strained in 2011, many policymakers and U.S. taxpayers called for a halt to U.S. aid. Indeed, $800 million in military aid was suspended that year, though civilian aid continued.

Many observers believe that the civilian aid program should be frozen as well. Opponents of aid argue that until the leadership in Islamabad regains the trust of Washington policymakers, it should not receive billions of dollars in assistance—for any purpose. They propose that civilian aid be made conditional, just like military aid. As long as U.S. officials believe that Pakistani authorities harbor terrorists that threaten U.S. security, American taxpayers should not be funding the Pakistani government—particularly during a period of deep budget deficits. Furthermore, the U.S. government suspects that Pakistan sells nuclear technology to rogue states—yet another reason to withdraw support. Opponents of aid also cite increasing anti-Americanism among the Pakistani public and officials—despite sending them more than $20 billion in aid since 2001. Instead of aid, the United States should encourage trade and investment.

On the other hand, proponents believe civilian aid should continue to flow irrespective of political conditions. Foremost, supporters advocate

In November 2011, students in Peshawar, Pakistan, protested the NATO air strike that mistakenly killed 24 Pakistani soldiers. The placard on the lower right reads, "We want action on the NATO attacks on Pak army."

continuing aid for projects like vocational schools in urban areas, so that the United States can build positive ties with those who are impoverished and young—the very people most likely to be recruited by extremist organizations. Economic opportunity is the best tool to combat terrorism. Moreover, development aid is needed to support small businesses and local government—projects that provide employment and other services while strengthening democracy. By helping in transparent ways that local people can see, U.S. foreign aid can help repair U.S.-Pakistan relations at the grassroots level and thwart terrorism at the same time.

OUTLOOK

The United States faces many obstacles as it continually redefines its relationship with countries in this region of vital economic and strategic interest. Former adversaries, such as China, have become important trading partners, but not without criticism about its unfair trading and finance practices. The U.S.-Pakistan alliance is undergoing dramatic changes, and North Korea's provocations pose a nuclear threat, one that U.S. and regional powers will have to work hard to defuse. Home to some of the world's largest armies and oldest rivalries, Asia will continue to occupy American policymakers for decades to come.

THE DEBATE: ASIA

The United States should pressure China to trade more fairly.

PRO: China has enjoyed a trade surplus with the United States for decades, which has cost American jobs and prosperity. It is high time for U.S. officials to level the playing field. Pressuring China to trade more fairly would increase U.S. exports to this dynamic economy, creating jobs.

CON: The Chinese government controls all aspects of its economy and owns American debt. It will not be bullied by U.S. pressure to trade more fairly. Some U.S. companies operating in China fear retaliation and would rather profit under China's unfair system than be shut out altogether.

The United States should offer incentives to end North Korea's nuclear program.

PRO: New North Korean leaders are unpredictable, so their nuclear program must be stopped. Otherwise, U.S. allies, and eventually the United States itself, will be under threat. The six-party diplomats must develop a better plan to disarm North Korea and maintain peace. Offering food aid and other incentives is a good tool to get the talks underway.

CON: Previous negotiations with North Korea failed to deter its nuclear ambitions. Offering "rewards," even food aid, to the pariah nation says that America can be manipulated by nuclear blackmail. This tactic encourages other nations, such as Iran, to do likewise. To defuse the nuclear threat, the United States should press for Korean reunification.

The United States should continue to send development aid to Pakistan.

PRO: Maintaining aid for civilian projects would prove to Pakistanis that the United States cares about their country. Such programs would support democracy and economic opportunity, thwarting conditions for extremists. Only by helping Pakistan can we ensure that its nuclear weapons are safe from terrorists.

CON: Foreign aid is unlikely to defuse the insurgency in Pakistan or improve governance and the economy. Billions of dollars in aid has so far bought only anti-Americanism. Trade and investment will ensure productivity and self-reliance. Then Pakistanis will fight terrorists and improve their country themselves.

EUROPE AND RUSSIA

INTRODUCTION

After the defeat of Nazi Germany at the end of World War II, a new balance of power emerged in Europe. Europe was divided into two competing camps; Eastern Europe, controlled by the communist Soviet Union, and Western Europe, allied with the United States. Out of this division came the Cold War, which would dominate U.S. foreign policy and relations with Europe for the next forty years.

KEY QUESTIONS

- Are austerity policies in Europe making the debt crisis worse?

- Is NATO still critical to U.S. national security interests?

- Should the United States take a harder line against Russia?

When the Cold War ended and the Soviet Union broke apart in the early 1990s, Eastern European countries moved toward democratic and free-market economic systems. Western Europe—free from the Soviet threat—moved to integrate its already free-market economies into a more "United Europe" as North Atlantic Treaty Organization (NATO) membership began expanding eastward. Meanwhile, the state of Russia took over the former Soviet military arsenal and began modernizing its economy and political system. It also began developing a new, but often still tense, relationship with the West.

Today, Europe remains a key political, economic, and military partner of the United States. This transatlantic partnership means that Europe's ongoing debt crisis—and the debate over austerity versus progrowth solutions—is a serious concern for the United States. NATO has also come under greater scrutiny as it struggled with its mission in Libya and U.S. leaders question the large funding contribution of the United States. Despite some improved relations with Russia after President Barack Obama launched a "reset" in 2009, concern over Russia's autocratic government and differences about missile defense and the conflict in Syria continue to strain the tenuous and complex relationship between the United States and Russia.

BACKGROUND

The Cold War

1945 and the Emergence of the Cold War. In February 1945, before World War II ended, President Franklin Roosevelt, British Prime Minister Winston Churchill, and Soviet General Secretary Joseph Stalin met at Yalta to discuss the rebuilding and division of Europe. World War II had left much of Europe devastated and the economic and political infrastructure in disarray. The three leaders agreed that when the war ended, people freed from Nazi rule in Europe should be allowed to set up their own democratic

and independent governments, and German reparation money should be split up equitably. Both Germany and its capital, Berlin, would be divided into occupation zones. France, Great Britain, and the United States would occupy the western zones of Germany and Berlin, while the Soviet Union would occupy the eastern zones. At the time, Stalin promised Roosevelt and Churchill that free elections would be held in all nations in Europe that his troops liberated from the Nazis.

However, shortly after the war ended, Stalin abandoned his promise and the Soviets established communist governments in Bulgaria, Hungary, Poland, and Romania. Communists also seized power in Yugoslavia and Albania, and Germany was split into two countries. Britain, France, and the United States supported a democracy in West Germany, keeping troops in the western side of Berlin, while the Soviets controlled East Berlin and the government of East Germany. "From Stettin in the Baltic to Trieste in the Adriatic, an iron curtain has descended across the Continent," Churchill famously said in describing the marked divide across Europe. The Cold War began, fought with arms buildups, propaganda, and the use of military and economic aid to win allies throughout the world. For decades this conflict was exemplified by the threat of a nuclear showdown and the policy of Mutually Assured Destruction (MAD). This made tensions high, but prevented direct engagement between the United States and the Soviet Union on the battlefield.

U.S. Policy of Containment. After the Soviets established communism in Eastern Europe, the United States tried to prevent further expansion of communism by working to contain it to areas where it already existed. The strategy of "containment" was carried out through: (1) economic aid to rebuild Western Europe; (2) military assistance to governments challenged by communists; and (3) creation of a military alliance of democratic nations, the North Atlantic Treaty Organization (NATO).

The Marshall Plan. World War II left European economies ruined and its people desperate. U.S. officials believed that a healthy European economy would help prevent a rebirth of fascism or an insurgence of communism in Western Europe. So, the United States set up a foreign aid program called the Marshall Plan (1947-53), which provided $13 billion in U.S. aid, investment, and trade to rebuild Western Europe.

In February 1945, allied leaders Winston Churchill, Franklin Roosevelt, and Joseph Stalin met in Yalta—a Soviet resort town in the Crimea—to set the stage for the post-World War II division of Europe.

NATO. NATO, which originally included ten European countries, the United States, and Canada, was established in 1949 to deter an armed communist attack in Europe and keep the Soviets from America's doorstep. In turn, in 1955, the Soviet Union and its Eastern European allies formed a counterpart to NATO called the Warsaw Pact. At the height of the Cold War, both NATO and the Warsaw Pact countries stationed thousands of troops, tanks, and combat aircraft on European soil and installed nuclear missile sites aimed at each other.

Western Europe Comes Together. After World War II, Western European leaders moved toward developing a framework for economic cooperation that would ensure peace and promote prosperity in Europe. In 1957, they formed the European Economic Community. Member countries planned their economies to complement one another and, by establishing uniform trade rules and policies, worked together to strengthen European competition in the world market.

From the Berlin Wall to Détente. During the 1950s and 1960s, the Cold War dominated foreign affairs, and U.S.-Soviet relations became increasingly tense. In 1961, the Soviet Union built the Berlin Wall, dividing the German capital and closing off all access to West Berlin. This dramatic event solidified Europe's division into competing camps.

RUSSIA'S ENERGY LEVERAGE

One major power player on the European continent sits well underground. That is Russia's sizeable reserves of natural gas. Via a major pipeline through Ukraine, Russia serves as a major energy supplier to many countries in Europe by way of its national energy company, Gazprom. U.S. and European leaders worry that Europe relies too heavily on this source, giving Russia leverage to wreak havoc on their economies by raising prices or cutting off supplies—as it did in a price dispute with Ukraine in the winter of 2009 that left citizens across Europe shivering for weeks. In recent years, nations have been working to diversify their energy sources, including buying liquefied and shale gas from other countries. The European Union is also backing the construction of the Nabucco pipeline, which would transport gas from Central Asia to Europe, bypassing the Russian-Ukrainian pipeline altogether.

In October 1962, the Cold War between the United States and the Soviet Union reached its height, when the Kennedy administration discovered that the Russians had installed nuclear missiles pointed at the United States in Cuba, just 90 miles south of Florida. President Kennedy demanded that the Soviets remove the weapons from Cuba and ordered a U.S. naval blockade of the island. Despite Soviet Premier Nikita Khrushchev's public defiance, the Soviet Union soon removed the missiles. The conflict brought the two sides perilously close to a nuclear showdown. From that point forward, the superpowers saw the need for improved communication between Moscow and Washington in order to avoid a catastrophe. An early result was the first Arms Control Agreement between the United States and the Soviet Union, the Nuclear Test Ban Treaty in 1963.

In the late 1960s, leaders in the United States and Western Europe decided it was more constructive to engage in negotiations with the Soviets—a policy called *détente*. Détente (relaxation of tensions) reflected the belief that, while the division of Europe was unlikely to change, both sides could benefit from increasing cooperation and reducing conflict. During this period, the two superpowers negotiated several treaties, including the first Strategic Arms Limitation Talks Treaty (SALT I) in 1972 which limited antiballistic missile systems designed to intercept and destroy enemy missiles before they reach their targets. The extension of this treaty, SALT II, was negotiated but then withdrawn by President Jimmy Carter in

1979 after the Soviet Union invaded Afghanistan—after which U.S-Soviet relations deteriorated again.

The Gorbachev Era Begins. The first half of the 1980s was a tense period between the two superpowers. When Mikhail Gorbachev became the Soviet leader in 1985, however, he and President Ronald Reagan embarked on a new cooperative phase in U.S.-Soviet relations. Gorbachev slowly introduced the Soviet Union to democratic ideals and economic reforms. His policies of "glasnost" (openness) and "perestroika" (restructuring) moved the Soviet Union away from hard-line communism.

Communism Falls in Eastern Europe. In 1989, communist governments in six Eastern European countries gave up power after thousands of their citizens demonstrated in favor of democracy and free-market economies. Gorbachev refrained from sending in troops to keep the communists in power as past Soviet leaders had done. On November 9, 1989, the Berlin Wall was breached before cheering crowds as the division between East and West Germany began to crumble. In 1990, East and West Germany were reunified under one democratic, free-market system that was part of NATO and the European Economic Community.

The End of the Soviet Union

After communism fell in Eastern Europe, the Soviet economy deteriorated and Gorbachev's popularity and authority suffered. By early 1991, six Soviet republics had declared independence. On December 21, 1991, Boris Yeltsin, the leader of the republic of Russia, and the leaders of Belarus and Ukraine declared the dissolution of the Soviet Union. Gorbachev resigned, and Yeltsin was elected president of Russia. The largest country in the world, Russia assumed the Soviet Union's nuclear arsenal, most of its assets, and its permanent seat on the UN Security Council. All the other former Soviet republics became independent nations.

Russia's Recovery. When the Soviet Union dissolved in 1991, a vacuum existed between the institutions that maintained order under the communist system and the institutions that allow societies to function within a free-market system. The people of Russia were forced to contend with crumbling factories, the loss of raw materials previously supplied by now-independent republics, and a workforce unaccustomed to the wage fluctuations and job insecurity that come with capitalism. These economic conditions led to high unemployment, a devalued Russian currency, and the inability of businesses to pay some of their workers. Despite an ambitious privatization program and international financial support, Russia's economy neared collapse. On December 31, 1999, Yeltsin resigned as president, and was replaced by his prime minister, Vladimir Putin. A few months later, Putin was officially elected president.

The Putin Era. During two terms as president, Putin brought significant changes to Russia that appeared to turn the nation's fortunes around. He revamped the banking and tax system and allowed more land ownership. Steady economic growth fueled by Putin's policies, as well as surging oil prices, increased standards of living, and Putin's firm response to separatist rebels in the republic of Chechnya, boosted his popularity within Russia.

Arguing that Russia lacked the institutions and foundations for full-fledged democracy, Putin implemented "managed democracy." Under this approach, a strong centralized government maintained firm control of the workings of the country. Putin took over the appointment of governors of Russia's regions, clamped down on the media, and marginalized political opposition to ensure favorable outcomes in elections. This brought stability to the political system but raised alarms in the West, which saw it simply as a return to authoritarianism.

In 2008, Putin's handpicked successor Dmitry Medvedev was elected president, and Medvedev named Putin as his prime minister. Although Medvedev distinguished himself by promoting modest democratic and economic reforms, few doubted who ultimately controlled Russia. In 2011, it appeared that the Russian people were beginning to tire of "managed democracy." Opposition parties made gains in the parliamentary elections despite allegations of government fraud. U.S. leaders and other observers criticized the elections and Russian citizens protested in the streets, unsettling Russian leaders. In March 2012, Putin marshaled enough voter support to win the presidency, although international observers and opposition leaders argued that Putin's firm control of the media and government meant the election was unfairly tilted in his favor.

U.S.-Russia Relations. When Putin first came to power, he sought a constructive political, economic, and foreign policy relationship with the United States. After the September 11, 2001, terrorist attacks, Putin supported U.S. military action in Afghanistan. President George W. Bush and Putin also pledged to further reduce their countries' nuclear stockpiles.

However, relations soured as Russia perceived Bush's withdrawal from a missile treaty and launching the war in Iraq as reckless and unilateral and NATO's eastward expansion as a security threat. Relations reached a low point in 2008, when, over Western protests, Russian President Medvedev went to war with neighboring Georgia over the breakaway regions of Abkhazia and South Ossetia.

When President Barack Obama took office in 2009, he attempted to turn relations around with what he called a "reset"—or a new *détente*. This engagement with Russia produced several points of cooperation. The two nations agreed to allow the transit of U.S. military supplies through Russia to Afghanistan, and, in 2010, President Obama and Medvedev signed the new Strategic Arms Reduction Treaty (START). The agreement limits each side to 1,550 strategic nuclear warheads—a roughly 30 percent reduction. On the world stage, the United States supported Russia's long-sought admission to the World Trade Organization (WTO), which became official in 2011, and won Russian support for stronger sanctions against Iran.

However, the reset might have reached its limits. To the dismay of American and many other world officials, Russia has blocked UN resolutions for stronger international intervention in the conflict in Syria.

Russian leaders have responded angrily to American and international criticism of Russia's crackdowns against democracy protests. Further aggravating Russian leaders, members of the U.S. Congress proposed legislation denying travel visas and freezing the foreign assets of Russian officials identified as abusers of human rights.

Missile Defense. One issue, over which tensions remain high, is missile defense. In 2002, President Bush withdrew from the 1972 Antiballistic Missile (ABM) Treaty with Russia. The Treaty banned the two nations from creating nationwide defenses against ballistic missiles. Although Bush asserted the move was necessary so the United States could build defenses against missiles from rogue states like Iran, the Russians feared America sought a strategic advantage that would curb Russia's ability to strike the United States.

To Russian leaders, the United States appeared to be moving further toward that goal with President Bush's 2006 announced intention to deploy a missile defense system in Eastern Europe—including Poland and the Czech Republic. In 2009, President Obama revised the program, delaying installation of sites nearest Russia. But the administration proceeded with the first phase of missile defense deployment in Europe in 2012. Russian leaders threatened to attack the sites, possibly even preemptively.

The European Union

The Road to European Unity. As Russia and former Soviet republics struggled with their transition to democracy and capitalism in the 1990s, their neighbors to the west were continuing the process of building an economic and political partnership. In January 1992, Europe took a major step with the signing of the Maastricht Treaty, which outlined plans for a monetary union, the creation of a single currency, and coordination of foreign and defense policies. On November 1, 1993, the twelve-member European Union (EU) officially went into effect. The entity created a single market where money, people, and goods could cross borders freely. By 2007, the EU counted twenty-seven countries as members, including ten Eastern European nations. Among the EU's newest members are Bulgaria and Romania. Croatia is expected to join in 2013. With more than 500 million citizens, EU countries today form the world's largest and wealthiest free-trade market and generate nearly 30 percent of the world's economy.

The Euro. The EU's goal of a monetary union became a reality on January 1, 1999, when many member countries started replacing their national currencies with the euro. Today seventeen countries use the shared currency, with Great Britain, Europe's second largest economy, being the most notable exception. But the monetary union—the Eurozone—did not include a fiscal union in which a central authority could establish financial rules. This worked fine for the first ten years, when robust growth helped raise the euro's value steadily against the U.S. dollar. However, when the 2009 debt crisis began to emerge, some analysts blamed the lack of central authority for enabling countries to assume large debts and for the difficulties in resolving the crisis.

The EU Constitution. In June 2004, European leaders proposed a constitution for the EU designed to centralize decision-making and unify the various treaties and agreements that had governed the union for two decades. However, voters in France and the Netherlands rejected the constitution on the grounds that it would strip away too much sovereignty from individual countries—an ongoing concern among member nations that has often slowed movement toward greater unity. In the constitution's place, the nations later agreed to the less-comprehensive Treaty of Lisbon, enacted in 2009, which streamlined EU institutions.

BEHIND THE VEIL BAN

Muslim women who want to follow traditional Islamic values and wear a face veil, called a niqab, may no longer do so anywhere in public in France. Starting in April 2011, France became the first country in Europe to publicly ban face coverings of any kind, with a few exceptions like motorcycle helmets. Belgium soon followed suit and other European legislatures are considering similar restrictions. French leaders argued the veil undermines basic standards for living in a shared, secular society and threatens French values of equality for women. An underlying concern among some European leaders is that their Muslim residents, many of them immigrants, purposefully refuse to integrate into European society, creating friction and suspicion. The ban, however, has created more tensions with some of the approximately six million Muslims in France, who feel singled out and discriminated against for their religious practices.

European Debt Crisis. In fall 2009, economic troubles in Europe surfaced in Greece when the government revealed that previous leaders had concealed the size of the country's swollen debt. Since then, the European Union has struggled with an economic crisis over the enormous debts faced by its weakest economies, including Greece, Ireland, Portugal, and more recently and problematically, the larger economies of Italy and Spain.

The EU, the European Central Bank (ECB), and the International Monetary Fund (IMF)—an international lending body created after World War II—put together a $171 billion package of emergency loans to Greece as well as bailouts for Ireland and Portugal that averted immediate bankruptcies. However, the loans required governments to impose fiscal austerity—including slashing social programs and wages and raising retirement ages and taxes, among other measures. These measures sparked massive street protests in Greece that often turned violent.

Ironically, the euro, the common currency that was intended to further unite Europe, is dividing it instead. Stronger economies such as Germany are growing increasingly resentful of having to bail out their economically troubled counterparts that indulged in years of cheap borrowing and unrestrained spending. Meanwhile, weaker economies such as Greece chafe at the limitations placed on them by wealthier countries as a condition of their financial rescue.

To prevent the crisis from worsening, France and Germany led negotiations for a EU-wide fiscal pact, signed by most countries in December 2011. The agreement strictly limits deficits and debts relative to each nation's economy.

Crisis at a Turning Point? Economic growth remained stagnant or even contracted in a number of Eurozone countries through the spring and summer of 2012, and unemployment in Greece and Spain, Europe's fifth largest economy, hovered at more than 20 percent. Voters expressed their anger at the handling of the economy at the polls across Europe, electing representatives from radical parties to parliaments and booting out incumbent leaders, including France's Nicolas Sarkozy. The new French president, Francois Hollande, vowed to renegotiate or append the 2011 fiscal pact to allow for economic stimulus that would spur growth.

Greek citizens, bitterly divided over whether the international emergency loans were worth the strict austerity measures, elected a pro-bailout government in June 2012. However, with Athens far behind on

Protesters clash with police during an anti-austerity protest in Patra, Greece in March 2012.

meeting deficit-cutting targets, it seemed likely that the government would need to renegotiate some bailout terms to remain solvent. If Greece could not pay its bills, it would be forced to abandon the euro and return to using its own currency. Many analysts believe this would lead to the economic collapse of other weak Eurozone countries.

CURRENT ISSUES

Rethinking Austerity. Many analysts worry the debt crisis could spread a crippling recession far beyond Europe's borders, and critics of the harsh austerity measures have urged European leaders to change course. At the May 2012 Group of Eight summit of world economic leaders, progrowth proponents, including President Obama, appeared to make progress in convincing austerity champions like German Chancellor Angela Merkel to consider policies that would postpone budget cutting and allow economic stimulus. Others believe the EU is taking adequate steps to contain the crisis—and ultimately the union will become stronger and more integrated as a result.

Chancellor Merkel has been a forceful advocate for such austerity measures to rein in spending and balance budgets as a way to return economies to sound footing. Two years after these austerity budgets were

German Chancellor Angela Merkel and French President Francois Hollande represent the two biggest economies in the Eurozone as well as differing approaches on how to resolve Europe's debt crisis. Merkel advocates measures to rein in debts, including budget cuts, whereas Hollande proposes measures, including additional government borrowing, to foster economic growth.

implemented, even many supporters would concede that the results have not been what they had hoped. Many European economies have contracted, raising unemployment and poverty levels to new heights—without delivering the expected reduction in debt.

Many economists argue that a debt crisis, somewhat counterintuitively, demands not painful cuts that lead to unemployment and reduced services, but instead greater public spending that will stimulate economic growth. They believe pro-growth economic policies are required to get unemployment down and increase revenues, which will at least help alleviate the debt. Once these nations have achieved a steady level of economic growth, then a fiscal retrenchment can be considered. Critics of austerity also point out that President Obama's economic stimulus package in 2009 helped pull the U.S. economy out of a recession with slow, but fairly steady, growth over the past two years.

Proponents of austerity respond that the debt crisis in Europe is simply too immense to be solved by economic growth alone. Europeans have for years overspent on social programs, health care, early retirement, and lavish worker vacation and pension packages, so the idea of "stimulating" the economies with more public spending is ludicrous, according to many experts and lawmakers. They contend that it is time for nations to do what Germany did ten years ago to make its economy the strongest in Europe — enact painful but critical cuts and focus on economic competitiveness. Austerity advocates also point out that the record of the Obama administration's stimulus policies has been at best a disappointment, delivering only tepid growth, very few jobs, and a larger budget deficit.

The Future of NATO. Besides the EU, the other major institution that supports the transatlantic partnership between the United States and Europe is NATO. When the Soviet Union collapsed in the late 1980s and 1990s, and its military threat was greatly diminished, NATO's purpose began to evolve. NATO sought to stabilize and strengthen former Soviet bloc countries in central and Eastern Europe. NATO has also undertaken new missions, including nation-building in Afghanistan and aiding rebels in the war in Libya. The alliance, now twenty-eight members strong, also cooperates on counter-terrorism and counter-piracy efforts.

NATO's recent missions, however, have drawn attention to its flaws, as well. The alliance has struggled to maintain its commitment to Afghanistan, with some members departing early. And although European NATO leaders took the lead in Libya, problems with supplies and operations quickly necessitated more American support. In 2011, outgoing U.S. Secretary of Defense Robert Gates gave a critical speech to NATO leaders, arguing that the alliance faced "a dim if not dismal future" unless more member nations increased their funding and participation.

Some observers believe NATO has outlived its usefulness and adds little to U.S. security. Although the United States and Europe share democratic values, they disagree over fundamentally important aspects of defense — nuclear weapons, what constitutes external threats, the appropriate use of NATO power, and burden sharing. Europeans count too heavily on the United States for their own security, and even when they take the lead as they did in Libya, they cannot succeed without disproportionate American support. Without more consensus and the ability to act as a unified front, NATO falls short of a proper alliance, say critics. Furthermore, with Americans footing 75 percent of the alliance's bills, NATO is far more trouble and expense than it is worth. The United States must turn its military attention and resources toward countering a possible rising threat from China. America could more cost effectively advance this and other security objectives by building strategic bilateral relationships with individual countries and multi-nation coalitions as needed.

NATO has successfully promoted security in Europe—a strategic U.S. interest—and served as an important partner in U.S. missions in Afghanistan and Iraq as well as the diplomatic and military leader in the ultimately successful mission in Libya, say champions of the alliance. No other region in the world more closely aligns with U.S. values on democracy, human rights, and fighting terrorism. America indeed pays a large share, but also receives a large return. NATO countries serve U.S. interests by providing military bases, flyover rights, and sites for deploying the U.S. missile defense system—which could protect Europeans and Americans from missile strikes from hostile nations like Iran. Having NATO behind U.S. military priorities also gives such missions more legitimacy and support internationally than if the United States acted alone. Alliance leaders recognize problems and are constantly revamping systems to better respond to current and future threats. NATO now serves as a hub for global security—making the world safer for America and Europe.

Eight European countries participated in NATO air strikes on Libya in 2011. After some initial supply problems, the UN-sanctioned mission successfully protected rebels and civilians from attacks by government forces of dictator Moammar Gaddafi.

STEFANOS RAPANIS/EPA/CORBIS

Dealing with Russia. Although Russia is not the foe it once was during the Cold War, the world's largest nation remains heavily armed and sometimes hostile to U.S. interests. Managing this relationship has always been challenging for U.S. leaders. President Obama's reset, hailed by some as heralding more constructive relations with Russia, drew critiques from others who believe the United States must more forcefully confront Russia on a range of issues.

Many experts believe Russia remains a serious threat to the United States and its allies. In the reset, America has compromised its principles and interests to placate Russian leaders and gotten little in return. Muted U.S. criticism of Russia's authoritarian practices has resulted in even harsher crackdowns on the media and peaceful protesters and brazen election fraud that returned Vladimir Putin to power. Critics say President Obama caved to Russian demands on missile defense, only to find the Russians threatening to withdraw from the new START treaty or launch preemptive strikes because of the system's deployment. Furthermore, Russia continues to not only block UN resolutions against government violence in Syria, but also send arms to Syria's dictatorship. Rather than appeasing Russia, the United States needs a show of strength to counter Russian expansionism and hostility.

Opponents of a more hardline approach argue that engaging Russia and seeking points of agreement establishes a more productive relationship. Ratcheting up tensions with Russia only increases the risk of a misunderstanding and makes even basic agreements and progress on human rights unlikely. Furthermore, a confrontational stance simply is not necessary. Russia is no longer America's archenemy—the nations share common interests and have worked together in fighting terrorism, promoting world stability and trade, and reducing nuclear weapons. Engagement works as evidenced by Russian support for the intervention in Libya, sanctions against Iran for its nuclear program, the use of Russian territory for supplying NATO forces in Afghanistan, and the historic START agreement. A more cooperative relationship will also put America in a stronger position to advocate democratic reform.

OUTLOOK

All eyes are on Europe's debt crisis. U.S. policymakers are pushing European leaders to adopt more pro-growth measures because their emphasis on austerity so far seems to be acerbating the region's economic troubles. The stakes are high; economic collapse in Europe would likely also drag down America's fledgling economic recovery and the world economy. In Russia, Vladimir Putin's return to the Russian presidency promises to keep policymakers on their toes. Facing significant calls for democratic change at home, Putin will likely be a weaker leader than he was previously, which will make his actions at home and on the world stage less predictable and possibly more confrontational. This could make it even more challenging for U.S. policymakers to manage relations with Russia.

THE DEBATE: EUROPE AND RUSSIA

Europe should abandon austerity for pro-growth policies.

PRO: Two years of austerity has bought only economic misery and social unrest throughout Europe. The worsening crisis threatens not only EU nations but also the global economy, making it imperative that leaders reverse course and grow their economies through the same stimulus measures that helped pull the U.S. economy out of recession. Once Europe's economy has stabilized, it can and should pursue serious debt reduction.

CON: EU nations irresponsibly ran up huge debts with lavish social programs, and now must make painful adjustments to become more economically competitive like Germany has done. The cuts are unquestionably painful, but to retreat now and indulge in even more public spending, similar to the huge and costly stimulus measures imposed in the United States, will only deepen the crisis. The pay-off of staying the course will be a stronger European economy that is built to last.

NATO is no longer critical to U.S. national security.

PRO: NATO is a Cold War relic that adds little to America's defenses. The Libya mission showed that the alliance continues to rely disproportionately on America's resources. Disagreements about burden sharing render the alliance dysfunctional, ineffective, and wasteful. The United States could get more for its defense investments by instead making bilateral agreements and building coalitions as needed.

CON: There is no better security partner than NATO allies, who share American democratic values, concerns about human rights, and determination to fight terrorism. NATO cooperation gives America critically important access to European military bases, flyover rights, and stations for deploying missile defense. America makes a big investment in NATO but also gets a great return—a world safer for American interests.

The United States should take a harder line with Russia.

PRO: Russia remains hostile to many U.S. interests, as well as democratic reform within its own borders. The reset failed; instead, Russian leaders have blocked UN efforts to curb violence in Syria, made threats against the planned U.S. missile defense system in Europe, and violently cracked down against their own citizens. The United States must confront Russia and stand up for American interests and values.

CON: American interests are best served by engaging Russia and building on common concerns. Engagement has gotten results, among them the historic START agreement, Russia's cooperation on Libya, and the use of Russian territory to resupply U.S. troops in Afghanistan. In a cooperative relationship, U.S. leaders can more successfully press their concerns about Russia's authoritarian practices.

LATIN AMERICA

INTRODUCTION

The United States shares more than a hemisphere with Latin America. Most U.S. communities have residents whose families came from Mexico, Central America, South America, or the Caribbean, and the economies of the United States and Latin America are inextricably linked. As a result, the U.S. government has long recognized the importance of its relationships with the nations in this region.

KEY QUESTIONS

- Should the United States do more to fight drug-related crime in Mexico and Central America?

- Should the United States end the embargo on Cuba?

- Should the United States impose sanctions on Venezuela?

Throughout the 1980s, Latin America endured economic decline, civil war, communist insurgencies, and brutal military regimes. Hoping to deter communism, U.S. leaders gave economic and military aid to many Central American and Caribbean countries. However, in the 1990s, Latin America transformed dramatically. Dictatorships fell, popular elections spread democracy, and free-market economies emerged.

After a rocky period in which some countries endured high inflation and monetary crises, the region has made a remarkable turnaround. Though extreme poverty remains, overall poverty rates have fallen in a number of countries and the economies are expanding despite the world financial crisis. President Barack Obama called the region a model for how to transition from dictatorship to democracy and shared economic growth.

Despite the good news, serious challenges remain for America's policy toward Latin America. Struggling with wars and debts, U.S. policymakers are weighing how to support democracy and economic growth in the region. Lawmakers are also watching the escalating drug-related violence in Mexico and Central America and debating how best to alleviate tensions with Venezuela. And the region's most authoritarian government in Cuba continues to present a conundrum to policymakers torn about whether to abandon the 50-year-old U.S. embargo of the island.

BACKGROUND

Mexico

Geographically, Mexico is part of North America. While it shares a language and culture with its neighbors to the south, Mexico has had close relations with the United States for many years. The two countries share a 2,000-mile border, and Mexico is the United States's third largest trading partner (after Canada and China).

Unlike many countries in Latin America, Mexico has had a relatively stable government. Beginning in 1929, the Institutional Revolution Party (Partido Revolucionario Institucional or PRI) held power for nearly seventy

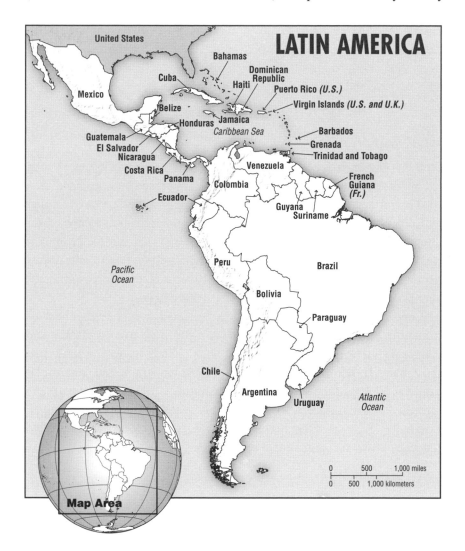

years. However, many historians believe the PRI maintained control through corruption and fraudulent elections.

From 1988 to 1994, Mexico's leaders reformed the economy and helped negotiate the North American Free Trade Agreement (NAFTA). In 1994, the value of Mexico's currency (the peso) plummeted, causing a severe economic crisis. The International Monetary Fund and the United States gave Mexico more than $50 billion in loan guarantees to stabilize the economy. The nation repaid the loans and earned international praise as the Mexican economy grew through the dawn of the 21st century.

In 2000, Mexico held presidential elections, allowing citizens to directly choose their leader for the first time in Mexican history. Voters elected National Action Party (Partido Acción Nacional or PAN) member Vicente Fox Quesada, ending seven decades of one-party domination. In 2006, conservative Felipe Calderón was elected president by a slim margin, prompting angry, and at times violent, protests by left-leaning groups that claimed there had been voter fraud. With Calderón in power, U.S.-Mexico relations have strengthened.

Central America

Central America is a corridor of seven nations located between Mexico and South America. At times, many Central American countries have been ruled by military dictatorships and endured civil war and poverty. During the Cold War, when the United States and the Soviet Union competed for allies around the world, the United States gave financial or military support to nations such as El Salvador and Guatemala to help them fight against communist or leftist guerrillas. Several of these U.S.-backed governments were later accused of committing human rights abuses.

Central American government leaders signed peace treaties with heads of guerilla movements in Nicaragua (1987–88), El Salvador (1992), and Guatemala (1996), ending their civil wars. These leaders promised to implement free-market reforms, become more democratic, and reduce their militaries to lessen the chance of future military rule. For a time, many hoped that Central America would quickly prosper. But in the aftermath of so much civil war, the region has struggled to cope with the growth and violent activities of international drug gangs.

President Barack Obama greets Brazil's president Dilma Rousseff in Brasilia, Brazil, in March 2011. Elected in 2010, Rousseff is the first woman president of Brazil.

South America

South America, the fourth largest of the world's seven continents, is made up of twelve nations and one territory (French Guiana) with great geographic, climatic, and cultural diversity. During the 1990s, democratic movements brought elections and free-market reforms to much of the continent. But after the turn of the century, some South American nations struggled economically. Citizens in several nations — including Argentina, Bolivia, Brazil, Chile, Peru, and Venezuela — have elected socialist-leaning leaders in recent years. Under socialism, government takes partial or full control of key industries such as agriculture and banking and typically implements extensive social programs to improve the standard of living, especially of the poor. Various reforms and improved trade and investment have expanded a number of the region's economies.

Brazil. A Portuguese-speaking nation and the continent's economic giant, Brazil's fortunes have turned dramatically in the last decade. Under the leadership of President Luiz Inácio Lula da Silva from 2002-2010, the world's fifth-largest nation reformed its economy, boosted trade, and lifted more than 20 million people out of poverty. In January 2011, President da Silva was succeeded by Dilma Rousseff, the country's first female president. Brazil became energy self-sufficient with large-scale production of sugar cane ethanol in combination with its oil industry, and became the world's seventh-largest economy. Projecting its new stature on the world stage, Brazil is providing credit and development assistance to nations around the world and seeking a permanent seat on the United Nations Security Council.

However, some actions by Brazil in recent years have irked U.S. leaders. President da Silva helped broker a nuclear fuel-swap deal between Turkey and Iran seen as undermining international efforts to curb Iran's nuclear ambitions and clashed with the United States on issues like Iraq, climate change, and international trade. In 2011, President Rousseff, promised to continue some of these polices but also moved to establish stronger relations with the United States.

Colombia. Colombia is the oldest democracy on the continent, but it has endured violent political and criminal factions for more than forty years. During the 1980s and 1990s, drug cartels—powerful groups that produce and sell illegal drugs—controlled large areas of the country, wielding power through the use of crime and terrorism. In addition, the nation's armed forces have long fought rebel groups such as the FARC (Fuerzas Armadas Revolucionarias de Colombia or Revolutionary Armed Forces of Colombia), who seek to overthrow the government.

The U.S. State Department estimates that between 90-95 percent of all cocaine and much of the heroin brought into the United States originates in Colombia.

SENDING CASH HOME

A significant portion of Latin American nations' income comes from abroad. But rather than hand-outs, it is cash—hard earned by migrants and immigrants working and living in other countries. These cash flows, or remittances, make up between 10 and 20 percent of the gross domestic product of nations in Central America and the Caribbean. Most of the remittances to the region originate in the United States. In 2011, Mexico received the largest amount, roughly $23 billion, making remittances its second largest source of foreign income after oil exports. Many observers believe the remittances—which surpass the amount of direct foreign investments and development assistance combined—play a vital role in Latin America's overall stability and economic growth.

Venezuela. One of the world's top five oil-producing nations, Venezuela is perched on the northern rim of South America. Despite political tensions, the United States remains a top buyer of Venezuelan oil, receiving more than 10 percent of its oil from Venezuela.

Even with Venezuela's oil wealth, the majority of the country's population lives in poverty. Voters elected socialist Hugo Chávez president in 1998, in part because he promised to help the poor. Despite fierce opposition, a recall election in 2004, and a recent battle with cancer, Chávez has maintained his hold on power. During his tenure, Chávez has attempted to address Venezuela's economic problems by pursuing what he describes as a march toward "twenty-first century socialism." He initially enjoyed massive popularity among the country's poor, using money from government oil profits to fund free health clinics and schools.

But Chávez has also steadily increased government control over private businesses and industries. During 2007, he announced plans to nationalize the country's energy and telecommunications sectors, causing panic in the stock market and stirring concerns worldwide. His government also cracked down on independent media. Chávez is a vocal critic of the United States and its policies. He has oil production and shipment deals with Iran, a nation considered a menace to the United States. Analysts suspect Chávez may also be helping Iran elude international sanctions in the regime's pursuit of nuclear weapons. The position of U.S. ambassador to Venezuela has been vacant for several years after previous nominees were rejected publicly by the Chávez administration. Chávez's outspokenness and the slowing of Venezuela's oil-based economy have damaged his popularity at home and in the region. In February 2012, opposing political parties banded together to select one candidate, Henrique Capriles, to face Chávez in a presidential election that will occur in fall 2012.

Peru. In spring 2011, Ollanta Humala, a left-leaning former army officer, won a close election for Peru's presidency. He appealed to the nation's poor who felt largely left behind during the nation's recent economic advances. Retreating from his past leftist platform, however, Humala promised to follow Brazil's market-friendly economic approach for reducing poverty. Since taking office, Humala has taken strong actions to address government corruption, dismissing dozens of police officials suspected of bribery and collusion with drug traffickers. In addition, he has taken a moderate approach to governance, seeking alliances with the United States and

As trade and investment has increased in recent years, many Latin American countries have experienced significant economic growth. Here, container cranes and a container truck sit at the Port of Cartagena in Cartagena, Colombia.

distancing himself from more radical leaders in the region.

The Caribbean: Cuba

The Caribbean Sea holds a group of ethnically and culturally diverse island nations beginning near the southern tip of Florida and stretching to the northern coast of South America. Because of its close proximity, the region has long been of interest to the United States.

The large Caribbean island of Cuba, located just ninety miles from Key West, Florida, has the only remaining military government in Latin America and one of the few remaining communist regimes in the world. In 2006, long-time Cuban leader Fidel Castro, who came to power in a 1959 revolution, handed over provisional control of the government to his brother Raúl. Many Cubans and world leaders hoped the new president would usher in much needed economic reforms. But, so far, the planned proposals, such as limited privatization of small businesses and allowing Cubans to buy and sell houses and cars, have fallen short of expectations.

Thus the United States continues its decades-old embargo on trade with Cuba. The relationship has been sour since the early 1960s, when Castro's belligerent anti-Americanism, human rights violations, and growing ties to the Soviet Union angered U.S. leaders. In 1961, the U.S. government secretly collaborated with a group of Cuban insurgents and engaged in an unsuccessful attempt to overthrow Castro in a disastrous military exercise known as the Bay of Pigs. In 1962, during a tense incident called the Cuban Missile Crisis, U.S. President John F. Kennedy put U.S. military forces on alert until the Soviets agreed to abandon their plan to place nuclear missiles in Cuba. Despite the animosity, the United States maintains a military base (dating back to 1903) at Guantanamo Bay on Cuba's southeastern tip.

After taking office, President Obama eased travel restrictions on Americans with family in Cuba and allowed them to send money. Many of Cuba's citizens, especially younger generations, favor changing the relationship with the United States, but at the diplomatic level relations between the nations remain cool.

U.S. Foreign Policy in Latin America

Early in its history, the United States developed close relations with its neighbors to the south. In 1823, as people in Latin America overthrew European colonial rule, President James Monroe warned European colonial powers against interfering in the affairs of the newly independent states. Ever since, U.S. presidents have cited the Monroe Doctrine as a basis for America's support of—and, when necessary, intervention in—Latin American nations.

Throughout most of the 20th century, U.S. leaders tried to implement policies in Latin America that would contain communism and counteract conditions—such as poverty—that encouraged communist rebellions. As democracy and economic reform spread throughout the region in the 1990s, American officials developed policies to strengthen economic relations between the United States and many Latin American countries. Since the terrorist attacks of 2001, U.S. policy has also stressed security issues, particularly combating terrorists and the illegal drug trade.

Regional Cooperation. The Organization of American States was officially created in 1948. It brings together all 35 independent nations in the Americas, including the United States and Canada, to build regional cooperation on common issues and concerns.

Origins of Economic Aid. In the 1960s, President Kennedy created the Alliance for Progress, an economic aid program that provided government funds for roads, schools, hospitals, and water projects in Latin America. In 1982, Congress passed the Caribbean Basin Initiative, which gave large amounts of economic aid to countries in the Caribbean and Central America, special duty-free status to products made in the Caribbean, and tax incentives to U.S. businesses that invested in the region.

The Reagan Doctrine. When he took office in 1980, President Ronald Reagan began supplying large amounts of economic and military aid to friendly governments in Central America. He believed that communist rebels—supported by the Soviet Union and Cuba—threatened U.S. security. President Reagan also sent U.S. troops to the small Caribbean island nation of Grenada to quell a communist rebellion there in 1983.

During his second term, President Reagan lobbied Congress to support rebels, called Contras, who were trying to unseat the leftist leadership in Nicaragua. Reagan was so committed to the cause that when Congress delayed approval, he circumvented the legislative branch. Reagan authorized secret arms sales to Iran and quietly funneled the proceeds to the rebels (this became known as the Iran-Contra scandal). The unwavering support of anti-communist rebels, from Nicaragua to Afghanistan, became known as the "Reagan Doctrine."

Promoting Free Trade. In the mid- to late-1990s, several Latin American countries underwent democratic reform and economic growth. Economists attributed much of this revival to the promotion of free trade in the region. Several major trade pacts have allowed greater trade between individual countries and the United States.

NAFTA. The North American Free Trade Agreement (NAFTA) went into effect on January 1, 1994, lowering barriers to trade among Canada,

HAITIANS COME TO BRAZIL

Even though several years have passed since Haiti's devastating earthquake in 2010, many Haitians remain homeless and the nation's infrastructure is still struggling to recover. Since then, thousands of Haitians have fled the country in search of work and improved living conditions in Brazil. The Brazilian government has begun issuing temporary work visas to these immigrants who are meeting the demand for manual labor in the jungles of the Amazon and on construction projects related to Brazil's preparations to host the 2014 World Cup and 2016 Olympics.

Mexico, and the United States. Since NAFTA's passage, policymakers have disagreed over its effect on the U.S. economy. After an initial boom in U.S. exports to Mexico, the peso crisis weakened Mexico's buying power and resulted in a large U.S. trade deficit. Although some U.S. corporations moved their operations below the U.S.-Mexico border to take advantage of lower wages, a number of economists think that the overall effect of NAFTA on the U.S. job market has been minimal.

Other Free Trade Agreements. From 2001–09, President George W. Bush promoted free trade throughout Latin America to spur growth in the region and benefit the American economy. Chile signed a free-trade pact with the United States that took effect in January 2004. Since then, U.S. exports to Chile increased 300 percent. President Bush then fought for the passage of the Dominacan Republic–Central America Free Trade Agreement (CAFTA-DR) that includes Costa Rica, El Salvador, Guatemala, Honduras, Nicaragua and the Dominican Republic; it was approved by Congress in 2005.

After the initial success with CAFTA-DR, President Bush supported the Free Trade Area of the Americas Pact, which fell through. His administration then pursued free trade accords with individual countries in the region. In late 2007, the United States inked a trade agreement with Peru and similar deals with Colombia and Panama were eventually approved by Congress in late 2011.

Immigration. An estimated 80 percent of illegal immigrants to the United States come from Latin America. Although in years past many of these immigrants fled political persecution and violence, in recent decades they crossed the U.S. border looking for work. Latin American leaders see immigration reform — particularly legalization of illegal immigrants and safer border crossings — as an important issue.

Fighting Drug Trafficking. The past three decades have seen the rise and spread of organized criminal activity and violence surrounding the illegal drug trade in Latin America. The problem has its roots in the Andean region on the northwest side of South America, particularly in Colombia, where most of the cocaine brought into the United States originates. The United States is a vast marketplace for illegal drugs because of its strong economy and large population of individuals with disposable income.

U.S. leaders have supported a "war on drugs" in Latin America in various forms since the early 1990s when Drug Enforcement Administration agents worked with Colombian police to track and kill the infamous drug lord, Pablo Escobar. The United States has given Colombia billions of dollars in military and police assistance to battle drug organizations that rose to power after Escobar's death.

However, the cartels proved resilient. Between 2004 and 2007, authorities in Mexico—a central transit point for illegal drugs passing into the United States—chronicled an increase in drug gangs basing their operations in that country. The growing violence posed such a threat that Mexico's President Felipe Calderón launched a campaign against the cartels in 2006, deploying thousands of military personnel and police in the effort.

In February 2012, Mexican authorities seized 15 tons of pure powder methamphetamine. The size of the bust alarmed U.S. and international law enforcement agencies and illustrated how the manufacture and sale of meth have grown exponentially in recent years, becoming a rising contributor to the Central American drug trade.

The Central America Regional Security Initiative. As Mexico increased pressure on drug cartels, the production and smuggling operations moved deeper into Central America. Murder rates skyrocketed in Honduras and Guatemala. In 2010, Congress passed a new program aimed specifically at curbing drug trafficking and bolstering security in Central America, allocating $248 million as of 2011.

AP PHOTO/BRUNO GONZÁLEZ

CURRENT ISSUES

The Drug Wars. Despite U.S. financial and technical support, between 2006 and 2011, drug-related violence claimed nearly 40,000 lives in Mexico— nearly 15,000 in 2010 alone. And even with increased border security, the drug trade remains strong, financed by U.S. consumers of illegal drugs and armed by assault rifles (legal in the United States since the ban expired in 2004) and other weapons, many bought and smuggled from the United States. Long a source of cocaine and marijuana, Mexico is now a major source of methamphetamines, inserting another problem into this complex law enforcement challenge. The Obama administration sent unmanned drones into Mexico to help Mexican authorities track and follow traffickers and dedicated $300 million in 2011 to help Central American governments in the fight. But Mexican and Central American leaders stressed that they needed much more support. American lawmakers and citizens debated whether the United States should do more in the fight against drug-related crime.

In support of greater funding and resources, advocates say spending is meager compared with the billions of dollars Colombia needs and compared with the money at the disposal of the cartels. Mexico is losing the battle, and supporters worry that a failed state on the U.S. southern border will result in refugees and the spread of violence within U.S. territory that will be even costlier to contain. Some on this side of the argument go further, demanding that America curb the flow of weapons by strengthening laws and enforcement to prevent criminals or their agents (called straw buyers) from buying guns and smuggling them across the border. Others argue that the United States must crack down on illegal drug use at home, because as long as demand remains high, drug criminals will find ways to supply the goods, regardless of the obstacles.

Others contend most of the violence is between different drug gangs and isolated in certain areas, posing little immediate threat to the United States. They believe existing U.S. laws and assistance efforts are sufficient, especially given the need to reduce federal deficit spending at home. Opponents also believe the Mexican and Central American governments must take responsibility for the conditions that allow violent drug gangs to thrive in the first place—poverty, police and judicial corruption, and lack of good jobs. Some argue that Mexico should invest more in monitoring its border to prevent drug and weapons smuggling. Furthermore, gun rights advocates in particular argue that America's gun laws are adequate, and that the rights of American citizens to buy and sell guns should not be restricted because other nations cannot control their criminals.

The Embargo of Cuba. On February 3, 1962, President John F. Kennedy imposed a total embargo on trade with Cuba citing communist Cuban ties with the Soviet Union. Since then, this embargo has endured through the administrations of ten U.S. presidents, and is now affecting a third generation of Cubans and Americans whose financial, travel, and trade activities have been limited by its restrictions. In 2011, Cuba's long-time leader Fidel Castro formally resigned as head of Cuba's ruling communist party. The move officially ended the dictator's leadership role in Cuban politics. New president Raúl Castro has since taken some modest steps toward economic and political reform, for example, allowing real estate to be bought and sold in an effort to stimulate commerce. Although significant human rights concerns remain, as these reforms take hold and Americans reflect on the embargo's 50th anniversary, some say it is time to revisit the U.S. policy on trade with Cuba.

Critics of the U.S. policy argue that the trade embargo has failed for decades to bring about significant change in Cuba. Rather, the embargo has actually empowered the communist regime because it has been able to blame U.S. policy—not its own failed socialist experiment—for Cuba's poverty. Furthermore, detractors point out that the United States stands alone in its embargo, a fact that alienates America's allies, undermines U.S. influence in Cuba, and leaves American companies on the sidelines as their foreign competitors gradually move in. Engagement with the American people and democracy would accelerate the demand for political and market reforms that would truly benefit the Cuban people.

Supporters of the embargo warn against engaging with tyrants. They argue that Cuba remains hostile to U.S. interests and is the only nation in the Western Hemisphere that appears on the list of countries sponsoring terrorism. Squeezing the dictatorship all these years has worked by preventing it from extending its communist, anti-American agenda throughout the region. To lift the embargo would simply reward the regime's oppression of its people. President Raúl Castro's reforms are only cosmetic; until Cuba's new government demonstrates a genuine shift in policy, the country remains an enemy of the United States.

U.S.-Venezuela Relations. Since Hugo Chávez came to power in 1998, bringing with him a host of socialist policies and a defiant leadership style, relations between Venezuela and the United States have been strained. Chávez's efforts to provide services and jobs to the nation's poor have made him popular domestically, but have required nationalization of private industries, which has angered the international business community. Chávez also has been a relentless critic of the United States and publicly aligned with American adversaries such as Iran, welcoming Iranian President Mahmoud Ahmadinejad on a 2012 visit to Venezuela, even as the United States and other nations were imposing sanctions against Iran for its nuclear weapons program.

In late 2011 and early 2012, Chávez made a number of bold moves that raised concern in the international community, including refusing to participate in a World Bank process designed to settle disputes with foreign companies, threatening to nationalize banks that did not support his national agricultural development projects, and withdrawing Venezuelan gold reserves from foreign banks in an effort to exercise more direct control over national assets. In December 2011, President Obama said he was "concerned about government actions that have restricted the universal rights of the Venezuelan people [and] threatened basic democratic values."

U.S.-Venezuela relations further eroded in January 2012 when a Venezuelan diplomat was expelled from the United States on suspicion of involvement in a plan to initiate "cyberattacks" against U.S. companies.

Despite these tensions, the United States remains an important trading partner with Venezuela. According to the State Department, exports to the United States account for more than 40 percent of Venezuelan trade. In addition, the United States receives more than 10 percent of its foreign oil from Venezuela. This important trade partnership has a strong impact on the relationship between the two governments.

Some foreign policy experts contend that the United States should take a harder stance against Venezuela and align with other nations to force it to improve its human rights record and end close relationships with nations, such as Iran, that pose a potential threat to the United States. These experts see Chávez as a dangerous and unpredictable leader whose access to considerable resources, made possible by the nation's oil riches, make him a dangerous presence in a region that has both strategic and economic importance to the United States. They believe that without significant reforms, the United States should impose economic sanctions on Venezuela or perhaps further curtail diplomatic ties to send a strong message that these actions will not be tolerated.

Other experts believe that Chávez's public snubs of the United States and his cozy relations with U.S. adversaries are just political theater that poses no real threat to U.S. security interests. Opponents of a hardline policy believe that as long as the United States is dependent on foreign oil imports for its economic survival, and Venezuela relies on the U.S. to buy the majority of its oil exports, finding a way to maintain relations with Venezuela will always be a necessity. These experts also warn that imposing economic sanctions on Venezuela to express displeasure with Chávez's tactics may only result in causing hardship for the Venezuelan people.

OUTLOOK

Many policymakers see opportunities in building stronger ties with the region's growing economies, but balancing priorities between Latin America and elsewhere will be an ongoing challenge. Lawmakers will also continue to discuss the strategies on drug violence and Cuba, as well as how to improve relations with important trading partners like Venezuela. With its strong economic growth and cultural ties to the United States, Latin America will be a region to watch in the coming years.

THE DEBATE: LATIN AMERICA

The United States should do more to fight drug-related crime in Mexico and Central America.

PRO: The region is at war and the United States bears some responsibility for it. Unless the United States increases aid and security, unrest could spill across America's borders. Policymakers must also stop the flow of guns and cash to Latin American criminals and find ways to curb America's appetite for illegal drugs.

CON: The violence is mostly isolated between drug gangs and not a severe threat to the United States. The extensive U.S. aid and assistance is sufficient. Rather, the Mexican and Central American governments must take more responsibility to reduce poverty and police and judicial corruption and to prevent gun and drug smuggling across their borders.

The United States should end the embargo on Cuba.

PRO: The trade embargo never worked. Instead, it punished Cuba's people and empowered Fidel Castro by giving him an excuse for failed economic policies. New president Raúl Castro's modest reforms offer the United States a good opportunity to lift the embargo. Greater trade, travel, and political engagement will bring about positive change and benefit both countries.

CON: The embargo remains an essential tool in curbing the repression of Cuba's authoritarian government and preventing it from expanding its anti-American ambition in the region. America should never engage with tyrants. Until the regime demonstrates true economic and democratic change that respects human rights, it remains an enemy of the United States.

The United States should impose sanctions on Venezuela.

PRO: Venezuelan President Hugo Chávez cannot be trusted and the United States should take a harder stance against him. His recent efforts to limit democratic freedoms, disrupt world commerce, and partner with U.S. adversaries show that his government is a danger to U.S. interests. The U.S. reliance on Venezuelan oil imports should not prevent the U.S. government from taking action.

CON: Venezuela and the United States are important trading partners and both countries have a strong economic incentive to continue the flow of oil from Venezuela to the United States. Despite his rhetoric, Hugo Chávez is not a credible threat to U.S. interests and imposing sanctions will only result in harming the Venezuelan people.

THE MIDDLE EAST

INTRODUCTION

Few regions have captivated American attention, imagination, and fear more than the Middle East. A critical area for U.S. foreign policymakers, this complex region is the focus of several major policy initiatives — the Israeli-Palestinian peace effort, weapons proliferation, energy security, the struggle against terrorism, and the promotion of democracy.

KEY QUESTIONS

- Should the U.S. condition aid to Israel on the halting of settlements in the occupied territories?

- Should the U.S. do more to protect Iraq from Iranian influence?

- Should the U.S. actively support democratic movements in the Middle East?

The United States became significantly involved in the Middle East when it struck a security-for-oil agreement with Saudi Arabia in 1945. Since then, America has engaged in several conflicts around the Persian Gulf to ensure the safety of oil supplies, as well as to protect its allies.

Focus on the Middle East intensified after the September 11, 2001 terrorist attacks, committed by 19 members of al-Qaeda. After overthrowing Afghanistan's Taliban government, which harbored the al-Qaeda terrorists responsible for planning and financing the attacks, U.S. leaders turned their attention to other potential threats. President George W. Bush announced new policies designed to confront and defeat terrorists and hostile states before they could attack America, identifying Iran and Iraq as particularly threatening nations.

Although President Barack Obama has continued some of the previous administration's policies, he has also taken a stronger stand in regard to the Israeli-Palestinian standoff. However, his efforts have yet to lead to any major breakthroughs in fostering peace. Indeed, some experts believe that any progress in the peace process is unlikely in 2012. Obama also has shown greater interest in winding down the wars begun by the previous administration, removing all U.S. combat forces from Iraq in December of 2011 and announcing a complete drawdown of American forces in Afghanistan by as early as the summer of 2014.

The U.S. government is also debating how America should respond to Iran's pursuit of nuclear weapons and how the democratic protests and uprisings that gripped the Middle East in 2011 and 2012 will affect U.S. national security interests in the region.

BACKGROUND

A Complex Region

The Middle East is the birthplace of three of the world's major religions and some of the earliest civilizations. Geographically, the Middle East encompasses the area where the eastern tip of Europe, the western edge of Asia, and the northern part of Africa meet. Most people in the Middle East are Arab. Some are Persian. Still, smaller groups represent Jewish, Kurdish, and other cultural and ethnic minorities. The predominant religion is Islam. Many followers of Islam, called Muslims, fall into one of two large and often contentious sects: Sunni and Shiite (or Shia).

Modern Middle Eastern states began to emerge after the breakup of the Ottoman Empire following World War I. The major victors of that war, England and France, quickly set about dividing up the region into colonies. The British Mandate for Palestine (the Palestinian Mandate), established by the League of Nations in 1923, gave Britain control of modern Iraq, Israel, Jordan, the Palestinian Territories, and Saudi Arabia. Before the Mandate, in 1917, the British government issued a statement (the Balfour Declaration) asserting its intention to create a Jewish homeland in Palestine, "it being

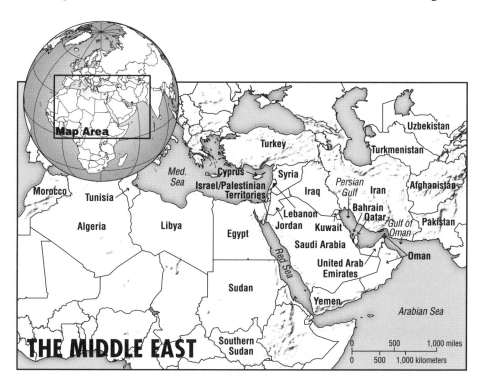

clearly understood that nothing shall be done which may prejudice the civil and religious rights of existing non-Jewish communities" in the area. The French Mandate for Lebanon and Syria gave the French control of the area directly north of the British Mandate including Lebanon, modern day Syria, and part of Turkey.

The Mandate system began to break down during and after World War II, as the United States and the Soviet Union became the dominant powers in the region. During this time, a number of Middle Eastern countries declared independence or had independence restored, including Iran in 1941, Lebanon in 1943, Syria in 1944, and Iraq and Egypt in 1947. When the British Mandate expired in 1948, the State of Israel also declared its independence, precipitating the 1948 Arab-Israeli War in which the armies of the League of Arab States (formed in 1945) unsuccessfully attacked Israel. Initially comprised of six states—Egypt, Iraq, Lebanon, Saudi Arabia, Syria, and Transjordan (renamed Jordan in 1949)—this voluntary association of mainly Arabic-speaking countries (also called the Arab League), was organized as a means of safeguarding their countries' independence and sovereignty and strengthening ties among the member states. A seventh state, Yemen, would join later that year.

While recent Arab Spring uprisings have brought some democratic reforms to a number of nations, including Egypt, Libya, and Tunisia, most Middle Eastern countries remain largely undemocratic, governed by monarchies, dictatorships, or theocracies, and are often wracked by assassinations, rebellions, and coups. And although some of these governments hold elections—some freer than others—many observers claim that the modern Middle East lacks a culture of democracy, at least as defined by the United States and other Western countries.

Oil and Energy Security. The Persian Gulf region—particularly Iran, Iraq, Kuwait, and Saudi Arabia —is home to more than half of the world's proven crude oil reserves. In 1945, Saudi Arabia and the United States established a strategic partnership, whereby the United States provided security and protection for the royal kingdom in exchange for greater access to Saudi oil. Critics contend that this deal has led the United States to ignore Saudi human rights abuses.

Israeli-Palestinian Relations

The Creation of Israel. In the late 1800s, largely in reaction to spreading anti-Semitism in the West, European Jews began to demand a Jewish homeland

The Persian Gulf is home to more than two-thirds of the world's proven oil reserves. A gas flame is seen in the desert at Khurais oil field, about 100 miles from Riyadh, Saudi Arabia.

in Palestine. By the early 1900s, the political class of Western Europe was beginning to take heed. In 1917, the British government issued the Balfour Declaration (named after British Foreign Secretary Arthur James Balfour), which specifically called for a Jewish homeland in Palestine. Tens of thousands of Jews from around the world soon began immigrating to Palestine, joining other Jews who had lived there for centuries. However, the Holocaust—the displacement and extermination of millions of European Jews by the Nazis before and during World War II—led to worldwide sympathy for the Jews and resulted in the rather quick creation of the state of Israel. In 1947, the United Nations adopted a plan to partition Palestine, creating an Arab state and a Jewish state, with the city of Jerusalem remaining under UN control. The plan was accepted by the Jews, but rejected by the Palestinian Arabs as well as by the Arab League.

In 1948, David Ben-Gurion, head of the Jewish Agency and the man who would be Israel's first prime minister, declared Israeli independence; the nation was immediately recognized by both the United States and the Soviet Union, as well as by the United Nations. But a day after Ben-Gurion's declaration, the armies of Egypt, Iraq, Lebanon, Saudi Arabia, Syria, and Transjordan (known today as Jordan) attacked Israel. The Arab armies were ultimately defeated, and by the time a cease fire was declared, Israel included all of the Jewish territory as well as some of the land that had been designated for the Arab state under the 1947 UN partition plan. The remaining Palestinian land ended up being absorbed into other Arab countries, with Egypt holding the Gaza Strip and Jordan holding the West Bank of the Jordan River.

Subsequent conflicts ensued, including the Six-Day War of 1967. Fearing an attack, the Israeli military launched a preemptive strike against Egypt, Jordan and Syria. Israel captured the Sinai Peninsula (which it has since returned) and the Gaza Strip from Egypt, the West Bank and the eastern part of Jerusalem from Jordan, and the Golan Heights from Syria.

Peoples Divided. In 1948, after the fighting began, some Arabs fled or were forced from their homes on land in what is now Israel. The initial conflict created more than 750,000 Arab Palestinian refugees. Today, more than 4 million Palestinians—the original surviving refugees and all their descendents—are registered as refugees with the United Nations. The majority of these refugees live in Jordan, Lebanon, Syria, and in the Gaza Strip and the West Bank—many in squalid camps.

In general, Palestinians demand that Israel withdraw to the pre-1967 boundaries and that a viable Palestinian state be established. They complain that current Israeli fences and roadblocks within Palestinian territory—set

Fearing an attack, Israel launched a preemptive war against Egypt, Jordan, and Syria in June 1967, defeating them decisively in what became known as the Six-Day War. Here, Israeli citizens greet their soldiers as they return from the war.

VITTORIANO RASTELLI/CORBIS

up to deter terrorist attacks on Israel—crush the Palestinian economy. In addition, most Palestinians call for the "right of return" to Israel and want to reclaim land and property now held by Israel and its people. Many Palestinians also call for the destruction of the state of Israel, but most say they would live peacefully alongside Israel if given a Palestinian state.

Most Israelis desire peace, too, but continue to fear Palestinian terrorist attacks on Israeli citizens and worry that Palestinian Authority (PA) security forces might someday turn their weapons on Israel. Many Jewish Israelis believe that the land they currently possess is rightfully theirs and that their claim on the land dates back thousands of years, to biblical times. A politically powerful minority believes Israel must continue to claim additional land for the Jewish state by creating housing "settlements" in disputed areas in the West Bank. These settlements are a major source of contention between the two sides and are seen by the Palestinians as a big impediment to peace.

The United States and the Peace Process. The United States was one of the first nations to officially recognize Israel. U.S. support was an outgrowth of its cultural and religious ties to the Jewish people, and the desire to help Jews establish a homeland after the Holocaust. Since the 1970s, the United States has sought to act as an "honest broker" between the Israelis and Palestinians. Although there have been successes, most notably the 1993 Oslo Peace Accord, American efforts have never produced a lasting peace between the two sides.

In the late 1980s and in response to rising tensions between Israelis and Palestinians in the West Bank and Gaza Strip, the Palestinians launched the "intifada" or uprising, that lasted six years and caused many injuries and deaths on both sides. After the collapse of the Oslo Accords in the 1990s, a second intifada began and lasted until the death of Palestinian leader Yasser Arafat in 2004. In 2005, in their first free and fair democratic elections, the Palestinian people elected as president, Mahmoud Abbas, a moderate from the secular (nonreligious) Fatah party.

Unilateral Disengagement. In 2003, Israeli Prime Minister Ariel Sharon announced a plan to remove Israeli settlers from the Gaza Strip and from several parts of the West Bank. The Israeli withdrawal from these areas was completed in 2005.

The Influence of Hamas. In 2006, the peace process came to an abrupt halt when members of the Hamas political party won the majority of seats in Palestinian Authority parliamentary elections. Hamas, considered a terrorist group by the European Union (EU), Israel, and the United States, rejects Israel's right to exist and sponsors suicide and rocket attacks against Israel. Refusing to deal with Hamas, Israel withheld tax revenues and other aid from the new PA government, and the United States and EU suspended all but humanitarian aid.

In June 2007, despite a power sharing agreement with the PA, Hamas forcibly seized the Gaza Strip from PA governance. President Abbas responded by expelling Hamas leaders from the PA in the West Bank. The Hamas coup divided the Palestinian Territories into two separately governed regions—the PA-governed West Bank and the Hamas-held Gaza Strip. But the fracture among Palestinians also reopened the door to peace talks between Israel and the Palestinian Authority in the West Bank.

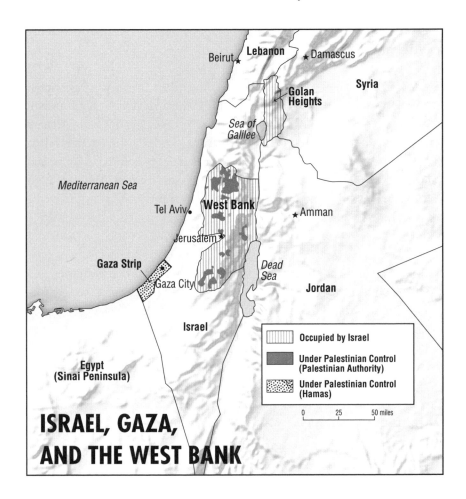

ISRAEL, GAZA, AND THE WEST BANK

Tensions Between Obama and Netanyahu. Israeli Prime Minister Benjamin Netanyahu, leader of the Likud Party, has taken a hardline stance on the Israeli-Palestinian relationship and, particularly, on the issue of settlements. (He quit Ariel Sharon's government in 2005 over the unilateral disengagement plan.) Although President Obama has repeatedly expressed his full support for Israel, the relationship between him and Netanyahu has been shaky. The two men have disagreed on whether Israel should freeze its building of settlements, something Netanyahu has generally been reluctant to do, particularly in East Jerusalem and areas near the city in the West Bank. They have also clashed over whether Israel should agree to set aside the land taken during the 1967 war for a new Palestinian state. Prime Minister Netanyahu has rejected this demand, although he has indicated that Israel might be willing to trade some land for peace.

Meanwhile, Palestinian president, Mahmoud Abbas, has repeatedly rejected an appeal by the European Union, Russia, the United States, and the United Nations, to return to the negotiating table unless there is a freeze on all Israeli settlement construction. Abbas put in a bid for Palestinian statehood at the September 2011 meeting of the United Nations, where support for the Palestinian cause is strong. The United States has indicated it will veto any attempt by the Palestinians for full UN membership, asserting that Palestinian statehood should not be decided by the UN Security Council, but rather by direct negotiations between Israel and the Palestinian Authority.

Iran

A Difficult Relationship. In 1921, Reza Khan overthrew the old and tottering Qajar Dynasty to become the Shah (King) of Iran. He worked to modernize the country's infrastructure while balancing relations with Britain and Russia, both great powers in the region at the time. Since 1913, the British had controlled Iran's oil fields through the Anglo-Iranian Oil Company (now British Petroleum). In 1941, during World War II, Britain and Russia invaded Iran, forcing Reza Khan to abdicate in favor of his son, Mohammad Reza Pahlavi.

While the new Shah proved popular at first, a political post-war crisis led to the appointmentof Dr. Mohammad Mossadegh as prime minister, in 1951. Mossadegh was hugely popular, thanks largely to his progressive social reforms. He established unemployment insurance and forced factory owners to pay compensation to sick and injured workers. But Mossadegh ran into trouble with the West when he nationalized the country's oil fields.

In response, Winston Churchill, Prime Minister of Britain, enlisted U.S. support to topple Mossadegh. In a coup authorized by President Dwight Eisenhower and orchestrated by the Central Intelligence Agency (known as Operation Ajax), the United States overthrew the Mossadegh government, making way for the Shah to reassert his authority.

The Shah's anti-communism and prowestern outlook made him popular with Western, particularly American, policymakers. But over time, his rule became increasingly autocratic. During his years in office, he modernized the country's infrastructure and gave women greater opportunities. But, he also cracked down on civil rights, effectively dismantled the nation's democratic structure, and worked to silence his critics in politics and the press.

In 1979, the Shah, still supported by the United States, was overthrown by Islamic fundamentalist revolutionaries, led by Ayatollah Khomeni, who replaced the monarchy with a theocratic government. Later that year, Iranian students seized the U.S. embassy in Tehran and held 52 U.S. hostages for more than a year—an incident that helped turn Iran into a bitter enemy of the United States and helped lead to the defeat of then-president Jimmy Carter in the 1980 elections.

A Nuclear Iran. In 2003, the International Atomic Energy Agency discovered that Iran was secretly trying to enrich uranium into nuclear fuel, a step on the road to building a nuclear weapon. This clandestine process violated the UN Nuclear Nonproliferation Treaty, which Iran had signed. The treaty grants nations the right to develop nuclear energy, but requires supervision by the International Atomic Energy Agency to ensure that nuclear programs do not ultimately lead to nuclear weapons. When confronted with evidence of its nuclear program, Iran refused to allow international inspectors to see its facilities. The discovery alarmed Western leaders, already deeply worried about Iran's sponsorship of terrorism, its hostility toward Israel, and its alleged role in aiding insurgents in Iraq.

Many believe Iran, led by President Mahmoud Ahmadinejad, seeks a nuclear weapon and that a nuclear-armed Iran would be a major security threat to the region, especially to Western allies and interests. Some analysts worry that a nuclear Iran would ignite an atomic arms race among the nations of the Middle East and would leave U.S. allies, particularly Israel, vulnerable to a devastating nuclear attack. After diplomatic efforts by European nations and the United States failed to persuade Iran to stop enriching uranium, the UN Security Council approved economic sanctions against Iran in 2006 and 2007. In addition, the United States cut off

KEY PLAYERS IN THE MIDDLE EAST

- Israel was formed from the controversial 1948 UN mandate in the land occupied by Palestinians, and its Arab neighbors refused to recognize its right to exist. A series of wars led to Israel's occupation of disputed territories and the displacement of hundreds of thousands of Palestinian Arabs. Israel is a parliamentary democracy. Benjamin Netanyahu serves as prime minister.

- The Palestinians were designated by the 1948 UN mandate to have their own state, but the Arab-Israeli wars and the resulting borders left them without a designated homeland and under Israeli occupation. The current president of the Palestinian Authority (PA) is Mahmoud Abbas of the secular Fatah party. The PA lost control of the Gaza Strip territory to the militant group Hamas in 2007.

- Saudi Arabia has the largest reserves of petroleum in the world and is a longtime U.S. ally and trading partner. It is a monarchy ruled by King Abdullah and it adheres to a strict interpretation of Islamic law. Many Saudi citizens would like to see a move away from monarchy, but dissent is harshly punished by the royal family. Saudi Arabia has seen very little unrest as a result of the Arab Spring.

- Iraq was under the dictatorship of Saddam Hussein from 1968 until the U.S. overthrew him in 2003. American troops withdrew from Iraq at the end of 2011, leaving prime minister Nouri al-Maliki in charge of a fractured state.

- Iran is a fundamentalist Islamic republic with a government ruled by religious and political leaders. The current president is Mahmoud Ahmadinejad although the country's supreme religious leader, Ali Khamenei occupies an even more powerful office. Iran is not an Arab country; most Iranians are descended from Persians. Many young Iranians have called for democratic reforms.

- Egypt is the most populous nation in the Middle East. Concerted youth-driven protests in Egypt's Tahrir Square resulted in the February 2011 resignation of President Hosni Mubarak who had ruled the republic by dictatorship since 1981. Mubarak was sentenced to life in prison and Mohammed Morsi was elected president in June 2012.

- Jordan is a monarchy ruled by King Abdullah II. In 1994, Jordan become the second Arab state to make peace with Israel, and has since tried to further regional peace efforts.

- Syria, like many other Middle Eastern countries, is in revolutionary turmoil, with more than 7,000 protesters killed and thousands more arrested since protests began in 2011. Nineteen of the Arab League's 22 member states have shunned the military regime of President Bashar al-Assad, but the political situation has been complicated by the fact that most of the areas that have fallen under rebel control are Sunni, and many Syrians (particularly Christians and other minorities) fear Sunni control even more than the Assad regime.

- Lebanon has been in a state of turmoil since the assassination of Rafiq Hariri, the popular former prime minister, in 2005. Investigations are still underway to identify the responsible parties, but since the assassination, Lebanon has had three different prime ministers.

- The 42-year rule of Libyan dictator Colonel Moammar Gaddafi came to a bloody end on October 20, 2011, when Gaddafi was killed by Libya's National Transitional Council (NTC). The security situation in Libya remains tenuous, however, and the NTC has been criticized for a lack of transparency. The country, which has no culture of political debate, now faces the daunting task of becoming a democratic state.

- Even Yemen, a poor country with a weak central government, has been changed by the "Arab Spring" movement of 2011-12. President Ali Abdullah Saleh, in power for 33 years, resigned on January 22, 2012, in an agreement brokered by Western diplomats and Gulf leaders which gave him immunity from prosecution in exchange for leaving the country.

international banking funds to Iran and began saying that "all options are on the table," a suggestion that the United States may strike Iran militarily if diplomatic efforts fail.

Early in his term, President Obama reached out to Iranian leaders in an effort to create a better relationship between the two countries. But Obama's overtures produced few, if any, results and by 2010 the president had shifted his strategy, beginning a successful effort to tighten both american and international sanctions against Iran, while still pursuing negotiations. By early 2012, it was clear that the tough new sanctions by the United States and its allies were beginning to bite and that Iran's leadership was becoming increasingly concerned that its already fragile economy would get worse.

The Arab Spring

On December 17, 2010, street vendor Mohamed Bouazizi set himself on fire to protest the Tunisian government's seizure of his goods. His act unleashed the pent up fury and resentment of the Tunisian people toward their government, and particularly their president, Zine El Abidine Ben Ali, who had held power since 1987. For one month, Tunisians of all ages took to the streets, fighting with government security forces, until Ben Ali

THE MIDDLE EAST AND ENERGY SECURITY

Access to affordable energy is a necessity for a modern state, and the United States is the world's largest consumer of energy per capita. Petroleum is an important source of energy, particularly in a country where use of the automobile is so widespread. While a 2007 Consumer Energy Report indicated that the United States imported almost half of the petroleum it consumed—with 20 percent of these imports coming from the Persian Gulf—in just five short years, America's dependence on oil imports has begun to dramatically decline. This decline is due both to a rise in U.S. oil production and a decline in American consumption, bolstered by more fuel-efficient cars and the use of renewable fuels like ethanol. Oil imports are down 15 percent since 2005 and are expected to drop an additional 36 percent by 2035. Many critics of current U.S. policy in the Middle East hope that a decreasing reliance on foreign oil will allow the United States to rethink close ties to Saudi Arabia and other major oil producers in the region. These critics argue that if the United States could dissolve itself of dependence on these dictatorships it could be a more powerful force on civil and human rights abroad.

resigned on January 14. People continued to pour into the streets to demand more responsive government. Following Ben Ali's ouster, elections for a constituent assembly were held on October 23, 2011.

As the situation began to calm in Tunisia following Ben Ali's departure, protests erupted in Egypt. Despite a government crackdown, the largely youth-driven protests in Tahrir Square continued for 18 days straight, putting steady pressure on the government that resulted in President Hosni Mubarak's resignation in February 2011 and a transfer of power to the military. A presidential election scheduled to take place in September 2011 was postponed due to concerns that established parties would have an unfair advantage. Mohammed Morsi was elected president in June 2012, the second election in Egypt's history.

In Libya, a longer and far more bloody uprising ended the 42-year rule of Col. Moammar Gaddafi. Although taken alive in October 2011 by rebels loyal to the uprising's National Transitional Council (NTC), Gaddafi was eventually beaten and killed. Two months earlier, Tripoli had fallen to the NTC, forcing Gaddafi and his family to flee the Libyan capital. NATO's early-stage intervention in the civil war played a decisive role in tipping the balance in favor of the rebels. The NTC now faces the daunting task of organizing the country's first free election in more than four decades, and of reconciling the competing and potentially volatile interests of tribal, regional, and Islamist groups.

The elation following Gaddafi's death lifted hopes that Syria would be next and seemed to revive rebel protests that had begun to stall. But the state security apparatus has responded with brutality to the protests against the government of President Bashar al-Assad. What began in early 2011 as a series of largely peaceful protests against government suppression of political freedoms had, by early 2012, become a widespread armed uprising aimed at removing the current regime. To date, more than 7,000 have been killed and thousands more arrested with no end in sight. Because Assad's military is not large enough to occupy the entire country, government forces often have singled out certain cities, villages, or even urban districts for punishment, often using tanks and artillery to shell residential areas.

By spring 2012, the United States and other Western nations have been unwilling to intervene militarily in Syria, as they did in Libya. However, Western countries, joined by Turkey and most Arab states, have increasingly been putting economic and diplomatic pressure on the Assad regime, openly calling for his removal and a peaceful transition to democracy. These efforts suffered a blow in early February 2012, when China and Russia vetoed a UN Security Council resolution backing an Arab League plan calling on Assad to step down. Assad also has received support from allies such as Iran, which is alleged to be supplying the Syrian government with weapons.

In Yemen, as in Syria, the uprising began as simple protests against some government policies, but as demands went unmet, the protests grew into a full-scale mobilization. For a time, President Ali Abdullah Saleh clung to power; his loyalist troops fought not only student protesters but also tribal bands and defecting soldiers. But, on January 22, 2012, Saleh ended his 33-year rule as president, boarding a plane to Oman. His exile opened the way for what was hoped would be a peaceful transition of power.

In addition to these uprisings, protests emerged in Bahrain, Iraq, Jordan, Morocco, the Palestinian Territories, and Saudi Arabia. The common thread in all of these events has been an Arab desire for self-determination and an expansion of civil and economic rights. And in some places, notably Morocco, the government has initiated political reforms in response to these protests.

CURRENT ISSUES

An End to Settlements? One of the most divisive issues in the Israeli-Palestinian conflict is the Israeli practice of building settlements in Palestinian occupied territory. Israel has for decades built settlements in land that it captured and has occupied since the 1967 Six-Day War. While the United Nations has called on Israel to return the land, Israel has used the settlements to create a buffer between itself and hostile Arab territories. Israel abandoned its settlements in Sinai as part of the Camp David Accords (1979) when Egypt formally recognized Israel; in 2005, Israel unilaterally abandoned settlements in the Gaza Strip. But Israel has settlements in the West Bank, East Jerusalem, and the Golan Heights. As of 2009, 305,000 had settled in the West Bank, 192,000 in East Jerusalem, and 20,000 in the Golan Heights. Many U.S. officials, namely President Obama, are urging Israel to stop building new settlements.

Supporters of the administration's efforts to deter Israeli settlements believe that it is difficult to expect the Palestinians to negotiate with the Israelis while Israel continues to build settlements in Palestinian territory. They also point out that the United Nations has, on numerous occasions,

Palestinian President Mahmoud Abbas delivers a speech to the UN General Assembly in New York on September 23, 2011, asking the UN to recognize a state for his people.

called Israel to abandon its settlements and return to its pre-1967 borders. Opponents of these settlements also claim that Israeli settlements further impoverish Palestinians, creating crowded living conditions, destroying farmland, and establishing perfect conditions for terrorist rhetoric to take hold. Lastly, critics argue that the idea of "natural growth," asserted by the Israelis as a reason for expansion, is invalid. They point out that no other country on Earth can demand territory from its neighbor to accommodate natural growth and, even if allowable, the population growth rate of the Palestinians is far larger than that of the Israelis.

Those who support the building of Israeli settlements argue that they are an Israeli concern only, and it is not the place of the United States to dictate security issues to another sovereign nation. Secondly, they point out that there is much lawlessness in the Palestinian territories, which are often used as staging grounds for rocket attacks on Israel. Therefore, Israel has a right to take land into its possession to create a buffer zone. Furthermore, they argue that many new settlers are simply moving into neighborhoods that are already heavily Jewish. Lastly, as Prime Minister Netanyahu has asserted, Israel has a right to naturally grow to fill out neighborhoods where it already has settlements. They argue that cutting off natural growth will strangle the towns, many of them literally suburbs of Jerusalem, on the border between Israel and the Palestinian territories.

Iraq, the United States, and Iran. United States officials believe Iran is the single greatest threat to American interests in the Middle East. Not only is Iran likely pursuing nuclear weapons development, it is also supporting the terrorist groups Hezbollah and Hamas and taking a hostile stance toward Israel. Finally, Iran is meddling politically and militarily in Iraq, potentially contributing to the undoing of everything that has been achieved since the 2008 surge of American forces. This dramatically reduced Iraq's sectarian fighting and restored some measure of order and peace to the country. Now American combat forces are gone, leaving Iraq to defend itself against forces inside the country as well as external threats.

Those who advocate for a greater role for the United States in Iraq say that the United States should reverse course and bring some combat forces back into the country. They argue that U.S. troops are needed to help prevent sectarian violence, which has increased dramatically since the last American combat forces left the country in December 2011. American forces would be a stabilizing presence, just as they were in the three years after the surge. In addition, U.S. troops will help keep Iranian influence in check. With three times Iraq's population, Iran is attempting to become a kingmaker in Iraq, much the way Syria has been in Lebanon. The current Iraqi Prime Minister, Nouri al-Maliki, has close ties to Iran and there are fears in the United States that he could position his country as the junior partner in an Iran-Iraq alliance. The presence of American combat forces will give the United States the leverage it needs to ensure that does not happen.

But others contend that reinserting American forces would make matters worse and certainly not serve Iraq's long-term interests. To begin with, they say, the continued presence of American troops would be divisive, particularly if there was no timetable for them to depart. In addition, it is unlikely that 30,000 or even 50,000 American troops could or would prevent sectarian violence. Finally, advocates of withdrawal say that American forces are not needed to prevent Iranian domination. Iraqis—from common people to political leaders—have repeatedly said that they have no desire to be Iranian puppets. Furthermore, Iran is not really in any position to dominate Iraq. The Iranian regime has its own deep difficulties to contend with, ranging from a growing opposition movement to international sanctions that are crippling its economy.

Supporting Democratic Movements. One of the key policy decisions facing the United States is how to engage, if at all, with the Arab Spring

The peaceful protests that began in 2011 in Syria against President Bashar al-Assad's government turned violent in 2012. Assad's security forces launched a brutal crackdown on the demonstrations and killed more than 7,000 people by April 2012.

revolutions and protests. Many policymakers and commentators urge the United States to take a more active role in supporting the uprisings while others urge caution and even detachment.

Those who favor American support for pro-democracy movements argue that the United States now has an opportunity to unequivocally do the right thing in the Middle East and to make a gesture of support for true self-rule in a region where the United States has often backed dictators in order to maintain stability. Specifically, the United States can provide technical assistance as these countries struggle to form new constitutions and forms of government. At times, some argue, the United States should also provide military support, as it and its allies did in Libya in 2011, an action that saved the lives of thousands and led to the end of more than four decades of dictatorship. Indeed, if U.S. leaders merely stand by and watch citizens struggle for democracy against despotic dictators, the United States does not deserve to consider itself a leader among democracies.

Critics of a more active U.S. role argue that the United States should learn from its mistakes. Its efforts at nation-building in Afghanistan and Iraq have cost billions of dollars and created widespread resentment throughout the Arab world. Even in Libya, initial military successes have been marred by chaos and violence. Indeed, the United States cannot be sure whom they are dealing with in these uprisings. While many of the protesters are ordinary citizens with deep concerns about the direction their country is headed, others may be criminals, would-be dictatorial thugs who are looking to grab power, looters, anarchists or, worse, terrorists who have a vested interest in creating instability. Even efforts by the United States to provide moral support to opposition movements should not be assumed to be without risk. In the past, these actions often have been viewed as meddlesome and have ended up discrediting the very actors American policymakers were hoping to promote.

OUTLOOK

The Middle East will continue to demand a significant amount of American resources, effort, and time. Fears over Iran's nuclear ambitions and its designs on Iraq, chaos and sectarian violence in a host of other countries (including Iraq) and the ever present Israeli-Palestinian conflict will likely preoccupy American policymakers in the near future and possibly for years to come. Even the Arab Spring movements of 2011 and 2012 present American policymakers with as many potential problems as opportunities. Indeed, hopes that democracy and self-determination will take root in Middle Eastern countries such as Egypt and Libya, have already been tempered by legitimate fears of continued violence as well as the prospect of military dictatorship or even Islamist theocracy.